# I AM MY BRAND

# I AM MY BRAND

*How to build your brand
without apology*

KUBI SPRINGER

BLOOMSBURY BUSINESS
LONDON • NEW YORK • OXFORD • NEW DELHI • SYDNEY

BLOOMSBURY BUSINESS
Bloomsbury Publishing Plc
50 Bedford Square, London, WC1B 3DP, UK
1385 Broadway, New York, NY 10018, USA

BLOOMSBURY, BLOOMSBURY BUSINESS and the Diana logo are trademarks of
Bloomsbury Publishing Plc

First published in Great Britain 2020

A catalogue record for this book is available from the British Library.

A catalog record for this book is available from the Library of Congress.

ISBN:  HB:    978-1-6355-7996-3
       ePDF:  978-1-4729-7188-3
       eBook: 978-1-4729-7189-0

Typeset by RefineCatch Limited, Bungay, Suffolk
Printed and bound in the United States of America

To find out more about our authors and books visit www.bloomsbury.com
and sign up for our newsletters.

# CONTENTS

# ACKNOWLEDGEMENTS

To all the people who have helped me to get to this point in my career, I want to take the time to thank you for your words of encouragement, your mentorship and your endless support.

I particularly want to thank the following people:

My daughter, Angel-Natalia – your smile kept me going during the highs and lows of writing this book. You are the reason I do what I do. Mommy loves you, baby girl. Thank you, Michael Owusu, for the last eight years and for helping me with our amazing daughter.

My parents, Dee Springer and Clive Sinclair, brothers Kwame, Kas, Azana, and Aunty Janet – thank you for stretching me, pushing me to be better, and reminding me always to deliver from a place of excellence. To my extended family (the Springers, Johnsons, Francis, Phillips and Goodings), to my BFFs Sophie Medd, Heidi Harrison and all my friends, you know who you are – thank you for the cuddles during the tough times and the laughs that kept me going. I adore you all.

To Kanya King from the MOBO Awards, Rebekah Roy, Eryca Freemantle, Eleanor Richards and Portia Saw from POP PR – thank you for mentoring me during my career; you exemplify the true meaning of boss ladies and have inspired me no end.

To the ladies who gave up their time to contribute to this book – your words of wisdom and experiences are priceless. Thank you for your knowledge, dedication and willingness to be part of I AM MY BRAND.

To my agent, Kizzy Thomson – we did it, babe!

To Haddy Folivi, Calvin Da-Silva, Zoe Chan and all the team at SheBuildsBrands (past and present), photographer Kosher Osei-Yaw, and everyone at Bloomsbury Publishing who worked on this book – a big thank you for making this happen and believing in my dream.

To all my clients – the last 23 years have been phenomenal and I can't wait to serve you more and take your brands to even greater heights.

To my granny, Stella Springer – you always told me 'reach for the stars, and you might just get the moon'. Granny, you were right. RIP. Love you now and always.

# INTRODUCTION

Dear Reader

Thank you for taking the time to explore this book. Whether you bought it, were given it as a gift, found it at a friend's house and 'borrowed' it, or stumbled upon it, I am pleased *I AM MY BRAND* found its way to you.

I can honestly say that despite working with some of the world's biggest brands from Nike, to L'Oréal, MTV to Aston Martin, writing *I AM MY BRAND* has by far been the hardest thing I've ever had to do.

When I started the process I thought I was ready to write a traditional brand marketing book, full of methodologies, strategies and tactics, and whilst this book contains all of that, it is so much more. As I began to write I very quickly realized that I couldn't produce a book about personal branding unless I was willing to address the *person* first. There are so many of us who are creating brands that we think the world wants to see, rather than creating brands that are a true personification of who we are. As such, I had to peel back the curtain on my own career journey to address the real issues at hand – who are we, and how do we market the most authentic version of ourselves?

To do this, I needed to not only write the book, but also partake in each and every one of the exercises that I put in here. I had to do the very work that I'm asking you to do, and in doing so I found myself being forced to write from a place of vulnerability. As hard and painful as it was, I became open and often raw about the highs and lows of my own personal brand journey, in order to give you permission to own your truth. Only once we're willing to be honest with ourselves can we find ourselves, and then, and only then, can we market ourselves with any level of real sustainable success and happiness.

This ideology wasn't something I always subscribed to.

When I started my career in 1996, as a bright-eyed 18-year-old intern, I believed that you should 'fake it 'til you make it'. At the time this was such a populist thought and I bought into it lock-stock-and-barrel. However, over the course of the first decade of my career, life and all its complexities taught me that people can see through the BS, so you had better show up as you! In 2009, when I taught my first *I AM MY BRAND* masterclass, I was reminded, after delivering a very poorly received class, that faking it was never going to work. I have spent the last twelve years researching, studying and discovering the tools needed to build an effective personal brand. I have worked with countless clients both in the UK and around the world, famous and on the rise, helping them to hone their personal brand for commercial success, and I have done this as the backdrop of the business landscape has dramatically changed. When I started, Facebook wasn't even launched, and the idea that a young black girl from South East London could build a global freelance career was a complete novelty. But I have done just that over the last five years. I have taught brand marketing all over the world, from Malaysia to Dubai, Ghana to Jamaica, Spain to New York City. And I am not alone. The opportunity to build a successful freelance career is growing. Today there are 53 million freelancers in the United States and 1.6 million in the UK. Freelance numbers have increased by 45 per cent in the EU, making them the fastest growing group in the EU labour market; and by 2020 half of US workers will be registered as freelance. But whilst the notion of freelancing as a career choice has increased, the idea of a job for life has diminished. According to the UK Bureau of Labour, the median number of years that wage and salary workers have worked for their current employer has decreased from 4.6 years in January 2014 to 4.2 years in January 2016. What's more, this average is proving to be lower amongst younger people, with the median tenure for workers aged 25 to 34 being 3.2 years. This evolving workforce creates an opportunity for individuals to not only recognize the importance of being a personal brand, but to also acquire the practical tools to effectively create it.

However, whilst some things have changed, the disparity between men and women in the workplace is still an ongoing issue. According to the Women's Equality Party (2015), in the UK, for every hour worked, women still earn just 81 pence of every pound earned by men, and in total, women earn just 52 per cent of what men do every year. This isn't just because of the gender pay gap, but because they end up sacrificing their career to bring up children. But yet, the OECD (2012) has shown that if we unleashed the true potential of women, the UK economy could grow by an extra 10 per cent by 2030 – adding an extra £180 billion to growth. According to the World Economic Forum (2019), only 6 out of the 187 countries measured on gender discriminations give women equal legal work rights as men. From receiving a pension to freedom of movement, such factors influence the economic decisions women make during their careers.

All of this knowledge, experience and frustration, has led me to write this book.

I AM MY BRAND has been designed to give people like me – and you – the tools to build our personal brands, despite the imposed limitations. I wanted to create a hands-on, practical book that goes beyond the usual 'bumper sticker' quotes often seen on social media, and instead provide realistic, implementable techniques. I AM MY BRAND is therefore not telling you what to do; it is teaching you *how* to do it, and pushing you, without excuses, to get up and deliver on the work needed to make it happen. This is not a passive read, but rather an experiential activity, with every chapter giving you 'homework' to implement what you have learnt straight away. As such I encourage you to write all over the book and make it your personal brand guide that you can return to time and time again. Whether you're just starting your career or you're a seasoned professional, I'm gifting you everything I have had to do in my career, and continue to do today. No holds barred!

To help me along the way I turned to some amazing women whom I've met in my career to distill their knowledge and expertise into this book. I am so grateful to feature the following powerful women, established female brand builders from around the world, all of whom have come together to support you on your journey to personal brand success:

- Alex Agboke, Founder, Style Peg

- Datuk Dr Hafsah Hashim, Chairman, Serunai Commerce Malaysia

- Emma Liddiard, Area Business Director, Global Media

- Erinn Collier, Co-Founder and Chief Revenue Officer for technology firm Just3Things

- Idara Otu, Vice President US Rates Sales, Barclays PLC

- Jaz Rabadia, Senior Manager of Energy and Sustainability at Starbucks

- Lydia Slater, Deputy Editor of *Harper's Bazaar* and *Town & Country* magazines

- Luiza Gibb, Managing Director, Curator, and Founder of Flat Space Art

- Maria Purcell, Leading Commercial Partnerships EMEA at Workplace by Facebook

- Marisa Peer, Founder, Marisa Peer Method

- Narjice Basaran, Digital Marketing Consultant, eSecta and Pure Modus

With their help, *I AM MY BRAND* explores the techniques used by women from across different sectors to build a personal brand. With a focus on the skills needed to succeed, their stories and advice, coupled with my own experience and expertise, have enabled me to create the '8 Pillars of Personal Branding'.

Decision. Vision. Clarity. Strategy. Tactics. Metrics.
Ownership. Be Unapologetic

These eight pillars to personal brand success are the premise of this book. Here is an overview:

1 *Decision* – The first pillar outlines the need to make a conscious decision about your personal brand's direction. Too many ignore the basic principle that success is a choice, not a given. You have to choose to make the decision to win, despite the fear, anxiety, worry and nervousness. Irrespective of your limiting self beliefs, you have to *decide* to win. This decision is not a one-time event, but a daily practice that requires you to show up. To not waver at the first or second hurdle, but to stay focused on the decision at hand. Once you are clear on where you're taking your brand, then you need to ask yourself – what am I prepared to struggle through, to get what I want? In this first pillar we explore your 'Success Tool Box', your 'Personal Brand Journey', your 'Brand Mission' and your 'Brand Promise'. We will review these in depth later, but for now just hold onto the premise that your decision is less about you, and more about those you serve. Your abilities and dreams, talents and desires haven't been given to you, for you. They have been given to you for the impact that you will bring to someone else.

2 *Vision* – The second pillar focuses on your vision. Your vision is the ability to think about or plan the future with your imagination. Your vision is the thing that you can see when your eyes are closed, with full understanding of where you want to go and *who you need to get you there*. In this section we uncover Your Tribe: the people who sit in your brand's ecosystem. Beyond your customers, or your co-workers, who else sits within your personal brand stakeholder group? Who are the gatekeepers, influencers and power brokers that you need by your side to make your personal brand a success? Who needs to buy into you to make your dream a reality? Who do you not have rooting for you, and how do you go out and get them?

3   *Clarity* – Being clear about what your brand represents is extremely important to your success; after all, 80 per cent of communication is nonverbal. Whether you like it or not, you are making a statement, before you have even opened your mouth! Therefore the third pillar is about gaining clarity on your brand messaging. Be clear on your Brand Archetype, Brand Colours, Brand Story, Brand Signature, Brand Promise, Brand History, Brand Packaging and Style. All of these come together to send out a very clear statement about who you are and what you stand for. I often tell my clients – define your brand, or the world will define it for you! So become clear on how you want the world to see you. When you do, you will use your uniqueness to make a statement, knowing that your difference really is your strength.

4   *Strategy* – The fourth pillar is about your brand strategy. Not having a strategy when building your personal brand is like driving a car without knowing how to reach your destination, refusing to use a SatNav and hoping you'll find your way without directions! Being clear on the strategic steps to move from point A to point B is a necessity. 'I want to make more money' is not a strategy, it's not a target, it's not a vision or even a decision. It's an odd statement made by too many, and means absolutely nothing. How much money? By when? Is that profit or revenue? There are endless variables with statements like these, making them a non-starter. Whereas your strategy has a clear GO-AA-TA (goals, objectives, awareness, approach, targets and applications), which needs to be concise and measurable. In this section, we will explore your GO-AA-TA and give you the tools to create your personal brand strategy.

5   *Tactics* – When attempting to build a personal brand, most people jump straight to this point. They skip steps 1–4 and go straight to tactics: registering a Facebook page, posting on Instagram, attending a

networking event, writing a blog. These are all tactics. But when you start using tactics without knowing the strategy, or being clear on your brand messaging, promise and 'why', you are literally stabbing in the dark, with nothing more than a hope and prayer. Therefore this fifth pillar ties your strategy in with your tactics. It explores how your tactics strategically hit your targets, and ultimately makes your personal brand vision a reality. We examine how to deliver a social media campaign, how to promote your brand and how to develop your brand story. Whilst tactics are fun, I would encourage you *not* to jump to this section of the book without first doing the work needed beforehand. Trust me when I say I have seen it again and again, people doing tactical work with zero results. This is simply because they failed to do the groundwork first, and then they're left wondering why their 'Likes' never turn into 'Liquid Cash'!

6   *Metrics* – The sixth pillar outlines which methodologies can be used to measure the success of your personal brand marketing. For example, how will you measure the success of your PR campaign? How will you measure the success of your advertising campaign? How will you measure the success of your social media campaign? How will you measure the success of the networking events you attended? What have been the results of all the tactical work you've done? The data should be driving the decisions you make, which means that you need to review the data and analyse the results. Metrics are the backbone to your personal brand success; they should always inform the decisions you make. Subsequently, we will explore which tools are on the market that can help you along the way. Enabling you to stop making decisions based on what you feel like or want to do, but rather ones that are informed by market demands, industry trends and career opportunities.

7   *Ownership* – The seventh pillar focuses on how to promote your true
    worth, demand your value, and add tax on it multiple times! The reality
    is, when you've put in the work and developed your brand excellence,
    you will feel much more confident in owning your brilliance. In turn,
    when you really own your brand, it changes how you ask for a raise,
    negotiate a deal and secure that promotion. When you own your brand
    you can walk away from companies and projects that are not serving
    you, and you can turn down clients and investments that do not align
    with your brand values. Owning your brilliance is like an anchor
    during the turbulent winds of business, it keeps you rooted to your
    truth when everything else around you is in chaos. This section will
    explore the 'Three Tiers of Networking' providing the tools needed to
    pitch, secure the deal and gain real power and influence.

8   *Be Unapologetic* – Your brand is not meant for everyone, it is meant for
    those who need it the most! Your brand will not be liked, admired,
    adored or respected by everyone. There will be times when your
    personal brand might not gain the validation that you think it
    deserves; the Likes, the Followers, the Engagement, the company that
    said yes, the sponsor that believed in you, the promotion that was due
    to you. There will be times when you feel like the only person that
    understands your brand is you. Then what do you do? In those
    moments of uncertainty, how will you show up? In those moments
    when life seems like it's not on your side and business is dwindling,
    who do you become? The reality is, personal branding starts with the
    person, the true you: your 'I AM'. *But what is your 'I AM?'* Often, we
    don't even know what this is until life gives us an unexpected blow,
    then who shows up? Oh, it's easy to say, 'I am fabulous', 'I am strong',
    'I am resourceful'. But are you? Does a strong, fabulous, resourceful
    woman show up when all hell is breaking loose? This last pillar is
    birthed out of my own pain. When life forced me to rediscover my

'I AM', it wasn't something I wanted to share, but rather I felt that the only way I could finish this book was to share it. I really didn't want to bare my soul in the pages of this book, but I made a promise to myself to give you my truth, and so my truth has been given. I hope that, in sharing my story, it encourages you to discover or rediscover your 'I AM'. Because when you truly know your 'I AM' you can own it and show up to the world, unapologetically you!

So, if you're ready to own your greatness. Then this book is for you.

If you are ready to give yourself permission to step into your spotlight and own your brilliance, then *I AM MY BRAND* is for you. If you're ready to uncover your mastery, package your abilities and promote your unique voice, then *I AM MY BRAND* is for you. If you want to be a different sound amongst the noise and uncover your defining point of view, then *I AM MY BRAND* is for you. If you're ready to show the world that you're worth investing in, that you're a bankable entity who has something different to offer, then *I AM MY BRAND* is for you. If all of what I have written petrifies you, then *I AM MY BRAND* is for you!

Welcome to the BossSquad – a tribe of visionaries who refuse to give up on themselves. A group of leaders and big dreamers who know that despite what anyone has ever told them, or what society may or may not expect from them, they are more.

Together, let's be unafraid of our dreams, let's challenge the status quo, let's own our true worth, demand respect, and build our brands without apology.

Enjoy the read.

Kubi x

# References

OECD (2012). 'Closing the gender gap: act now'. OECD Publishing. http://www.oecd.org/gender/closingthegap.htm

Women's Equality Party (2015). https://www.womensequality.org.uk/

World Economic Forum (2019). '7 surprising and outrageous stats about gender inequality' by Kate Whiting, 8 March 2019. https://www.weforum.org/agenda/2019/03/surprising-stats-about-gender-inequality/

# 1

# Own Your Truth

If you think you are beaten, you are;
If you think you dare not, you don't;
If you'd like to win, but think you can't,
It's almost a cinch you won't.

If you think you'll lose, you've lost,
For out in the world we find
Success begins with a fellow's will,
It's all in the state of mind.

If you think you're outclassed, you are;
You've got to think high to rise.
You've got to be sure of yourself before
You can ever win a prize.

Life's battles don't always go
To the stronger or faster man;

But sooner or later the man who wins

Is the man who thinks he can.

WALTER D. WINTLE

This is by far one of my favourite poems as it cuts to the core of effective personal branding: a willingness to allow yourself to think . . . that you can win. For the woman that believes she can, and the woman that believes she can't, they are both right. So if you believe you can win, then you can win!

## *. . . here come the gremlins*

Now don't get me wrong, you won't win just by thinking it; Lord knows there are ample techniques and tools needed to cross the finishing line. But having the tools given to you, whilst you still think you can't win, is like having a brand new car handed to someone who can't drive; both of you will end up going nowhere fast.

Over the years I have often said that if I could just teach people the practical tools of personal brand building, they would get it, own it, and make it happen for themselves. But the actuality is that it doesn't pan out that way. I see people who follow me on social media and watch my daily Lives, attend my webinars, buy all the books and e-courses, but then a year later they are still where they were, but this time much more exhausted!

So what's going on? Why is it that some can take the information and run with it, whilst others will simply freeze, make up all sorts of excuses, or worse still – just start running on the spot?

The answer is . . . they don't think *they* can win.

They believe it for others, but they don't believe it for themselves. Oh, they may appear like they think they can win; they say all the right things, utter their daily mantras and post the motivational quotes on social media. But deep down, when they are alone and dealing with themselves . . . they question, second guess, constantly ponder on the options – because they don't really think *they* can win.

I know this because I was once that person. I thought if I could just be exposed to the right people, have the right amount of money, be in the right place (sound familiar?), then I would win. So I started my Masters, moved to America and borrowed endless amounts of money, leaving myself in debt, with an outwardly appearing successful career, but an internal doubt that just wouldn't go away. That doubt is what I like to call 'the gremlins' – the feelings of doubt, fear, uncertainty, inadequacy, rejection, being misunderstood, feeling like an imposter: they are all 'the gremlins'.

Imagine for a minute having these tiny little people that sit on your shoulders, one on the right and one on the left. They are like twins: they are dressed the same, speak the same and they are always there. Every time you think you want to do something new and exciting, they pop up on your shoulders and start talking to you. They are small, but extremely impactful. They jump up and down rapidly from your shoulders to your ears, whispering and sometimes even shouting negativity to you, constantly. 'You're not good enough' is what they say, 'Who do you think you are?' These become their repeated mantras: 'You're way too fat, too tall, too black, too white, too poor, too dumb . . . they don't want you', their voices echo. They are there, day and night, week after week, year after year, annoyingly on your shoulders.

Imagine them for a minute; close your eyes and see them.


In my case, those gremlins were holding me back from doing what my heart really wanted to do: write this book and spend my time travelling all over the world teaching people like you how to build their brands. Teach hundreds of thousands of people via TV, radio and the stage! Instead of doing what my heart screamed for me to do, I listened to my gremlins and I found myself running a brand marketing agency. On the outside it looked amazing. It was super cool to say I ran an agency with clients that included Rolls Royce,

Aston Martin, and the London and New York Fashion Weeks. At times it was even fun. But it wasn't what my heart was craving and as such it was completely unfulfilling.

> The gremlins that were screaming at me were my limiting self-beliefs.

For some it's the fear of failure, but for many, including me, those little gremlins come about through fear of success. When I was a child I used to dance and I remember my school mates saying things like 'You think you're too nice.' Every single time they saw me on stage or heard about an achievement I had with my dance career, they would tease me at school with these same five words: 'You. Think. You're. Too. Nice.' For a 12-year-old who really wanted to fit in, those words cut like a knife and stayed with me forever. Success equals loneliness was what I soon told myself. So, despite my yearning for more, the 12-year-old in me warned me to stay 'normal'. Stay where you are, don't shine too brightly, shine a little, but not too much. So for years, I ran an agency and kept myself in an acceptable box, trying not to dream too big.

Nelson Mandela famously said:

> Our deepest fear is not that we are inadequate. Our deepest fear is that we are powerful beyond measure. It is our light, not our darkness that most frightens us. We ask ourselves, Who am I to be brilliant, gorgeous, talented, fabulous? Actually, who are you not to be? You are a child of God. Your playing small does not serve the world. There is nothing enlightened about shrinking so that other people won't feel insecure around you.

The fear of success is as real as the fear of failure, but neither is ok.

So eventually I decided to write this book, not because I had suddenly overcome the fear, somehow defeated my gremlins and shut my 12-year-old self up. On the contrary, I decided to write this book *despite* the fear. In fact, as

I write, sitting here in my home office, I have fear. I am terrified at the thought of not getting this right. My 12-year-old self is screaming at me 'Don't do it. You can't do it!' But despite the fear, I write anyway.

In my opinion, our gremlins, our limiting self-beliefs, are not here to be conquered as some personal development books might tell you. I do not think it is our job to focus on getting rid of them; to meditate them away, or chant them into non-existence. I also do not think it's our job to pontificate on why they are here. Or to spend years in therapy analysing what foundations brought them to us. Whilst I think therapy is important and has its place in the journey of self-discovery, I also think it's imperative to remember that what you focus on gives it life – at some point you need to say, 'I get it, my past gave me a raw deal, but now what do I want to do?'

I would even go a step further and say that I actually think these gremlins are somewhat healthy, because they remind us that we are human. It's normal to feel fearful, anxious and nervous. It's ok to try something new and doubt whether you're good enough. It's completely understandable to feel rejected if someone says no to you because, guess what? They did just reject you. But so what? In fact, a more important question is: *now* what?

Those who have built a successful personal brand don't stop having those feelings. They don't stop having rough starts or bad times. They, like you and I, have their own fair share of gremlins. But they have done something that is so simplistic, most don't believe it's effective.

They make up their mind . . . to win.

That's it.

They decide to win.

Irrespective of the feeling attached to the thought, irrespective of the gremlins and their constant annoying banter, irrespective of terrible pasts and trauma.

They choose to win.

For success is a choice, not a given.

Personal brand success is based on you making the decision to win.

The truth is that the right people to help you are everywhere; the right money opportunities are in abundance; and the right place is within your reach. But you can only see it when your eyes are open to the idea that *you deserve it*. Winning won't make you lonely. Winning won't make you better than anyone else. Winning won't make you less attractive to romantic partners. Winning is your birthright. You deserve to win. When you make up your mind, despite how you may feel, that the win is for you, and you continue to choose the win each and every day, what happens next is amazing. Your thoughts inform your actions, your actions create your habits, and your habits give you your results.

Once you have made up your mind that you want to win, what I teach you in this book will be of relevance. This book is designed to give you the tools needed for personal brand success. But it doesn't matter how many strategies I give you, or how many tips I provide; if I teach you how to create a brand promise, or detail the importance of your PESTLE, show you how to be effective across social media, create a brilliant brand story, network and gain influence, or secure coverage in the media. None of that matters if you have not decided to win. *Irrespective of how you feel.*

But here is a word of caution: if you are not going to do the homework set out in this book or partake in the exercises, then you won't get the most from this book, because when you don't put in the work all you're doing is pretending that you want success when actually you don't. And that's ok too. Just stop complaining about not winning and start enjoying your life! Not everyone is meant to rule the world. But if you do want to rule *your* world; if you do want to impact the world; if you do want to shine brighter and get more than what you have right now, then be honest with yourself and know that:

**Success is a choice, it is not a given.**

Let's look at a scenario to explain this further.

*You want to get a promotion, but as soon as you say it, your gremlins pop up. They are delighted to hear that you want to do something amazing, because now is their chance to tell you that you can't. Off they go:*

*'You're not clever enough to get that promotion,' is what they whisper the very moment you start to think about it.*

*'This tech company is only interested in men at the top, look at it, it's like an old boys' network around here . . . they'll never accept you.'*

. . . and on and on go the gremlins.

Now in that moment you have two choices: you can agree with the gremlins, bow your head with defeat before you have even started and continue to wish and daydream about a promotion. Or you can tell the gremlins to back off and inform them: 'I am going to get that promotion; one way or another, I'm going to sit at the table!'

Once you have made that decision, your job is to focus, and *stay focused*, on all the actions needed to make that decision come to fruition. Your job is not to get mad when it doesn't happen in the timeframe that you want it to. Or to retreat at the first sign of the 'old boys' network' playing out. No. Your job is to stay focused on the choice that you made – to get a seat at the table.

Once you have made a choice, that's when the marketing tools, insights and techniques in this book start to work. But if you have the tools, without making a decision to win, you will never win. Once you say 'I am going to get a promotion', your thinking should be directing your actions to do one single thing, which is to get that promotion.

If you are resolved, that's when your personal brand marketing kicks in: *you read around your subject area and prepare for the team meetings, so that you have something of real value to add to the discussions and show them your clear brand differentiation. You network with other employees outside of your department to create internal alliances and increase your social capacity. You start blogging on LinkedIn to demonstrate your knowledge and enthusiasm of the subject area, whilst creating an effective digital footprint. You study your company's business objectives, to ensure that your skills and capabilities offer something fresh to help them achieve those objectives.*

But winning takes time, and as such I can assure you that your gremlins will show up and try to convince you that it's never going to happen. But because you have made a decision, because you have made up your mind, your actions are not in vain. The anxiety of not being noticed and valued might still be there but nevertheless the very next day you get right back up and keep acting as a person who deserves a promotion. These actions over time become your habits and your habits of adding value to the company at hand will be noticed. And if your current company fails to notice them, you need to leave and go to a company that *will* notice them and give you the promotion you deserve. Either way, you win. You get the promotion because your focus isn't on the company, or the boss who is a tyrant. Your focus isn't on the old boys' network. Your focus is on getting your promotion. Your job is to push your personal brand and concentrate on the win.

Now, because personal branding doesn't happen overnight, you can easily lose focus. But that is when you need to accept the idea that a choice to win is not a one-time action. It is a weekly, often daily, decision to stay focused and win. Without excuses! Just because it's snowing outside, you can't refuse to go to the trade exhibition because it's too cold. Or if your friends decide to go on holiday, you can't now take a vacation when you have your business plan to finish. Or, if you do, you need to complete the plan whilst on holiday. Or someone once said you weren't any good, so now you're too scared to get on stage. Or your boss shouted at you in front of your co-workers, so now you're nervous about speaking in the meeting. Or you have tried ten times and lost money, and so now you refuse to really try again. Those things are all a big ... SO WHAT?

So what if you feel scared? So what if you feel anxious? So what if you feel undervalued? So what? The question isn't *how do you feel*, the question is:

*What are you prepared to struggle through to get what you want?*

Acquiring the win is less about feeling that you can win and more about focusing your thoughts to the win, whatever that 'win' is for you. Your feelings will come and go, so focus on what you want, not how you feel. The key is not to wait until you believe you can win, but instead to *make up your mind to win*. To say – irrespective of the emotion – I am here to win. When the gremlins show up, you can acknowledge the feeling, maybe even take a minute to talk to the twins, letting them know that they are welcome – after all, the gremlins are showing you that you are human. But then you have to work on the actions required to win and to do so despite the gremlins on your shoulders. To get up and move: prepare the to-do list, attend the event, speak at the conference, make the sales call, sit with the accountant. Do it all, with the gremlins shouting at you and jumping up and down like raging spoilt children. Let your gremlins have a tantrum, whilst you focus on the actions. After a while those gremlins will get bored that you are still doing it despite their negative words. They'll get tired of you not stopping. The more you do, the more your actions and results will start to quieten down the gremlins, and as the negative thoughts quieten down, that feeling of having self-belief will start to rise.

## LET'S DO THE WORK

*What are your gremlins?*

_____

_____

_____

_____

_____

_____

# The dog or the wolf?

There is an ancient and very powerful Latin American story that I once heard being told by Professor Srikumar Rao. I don't remember every single detail of the story but the overarching message really resonated with me.

There was once a young man who was about to turn into an adult. As part of the local tradition he went to the medicine man before he became an adult in the tribe. When he went there, the medicine man told him:

*'Here is this dog, it represents love, joy, positivity, happiness, kindness and faith. Here is this wolf, it represents hate, pain, negativity, cruelty and fear. Both the dog and the wolf live inside of you and they are fighting.'*

The young man looked amazed and said:

'Who is going to win?'

The medicine man took his hands and said:

'Whichever one you choose to feed.'

In all of us, every single day, we have the capability of feeding our dog; we can be kind and hopeful, we can be happy, joyous and positive. But we can also, and too often, spend too much time feeding our wolf.

As an example, when you join in with your co-workers at the water cooler and gossip about your boss, you are feeding your wolf. When you tell yourself that it's impossible to raise the money for your business, you are feeding your wolf. When you scroll on social media and find yourself jealous of someone else's success, you are feeding your wolf.

Every day, you have a choice: who are you going to feed today?

Who will you allow to win, your dog or your wolf?

The more you feed the wolf – listening to negativity, having friends who constantly doubt your dreams, telling yourself that you can't do this or can't do that – the more you say it, the more you focus on it, and the more you focus on it, the more you are thinking about it. The more you think about it, the more your actions align with your thinking. The more your actions align with this negative thinking, the more your results will give you what you thought about.

> Remember: your thinking determines your actions, your actions repeated enough times become your habits, and your habits determine your results.

Let me explain this another way. I was recently sitting in the hairdressers and for two hours the lady who ran the shop, who also happened to be doing my hair, spent the entire time moaning and moaning about the bills she had to pay. She went on and on about how much of a burden the shop was and how difficult it had been for her to run her business. She literally spent two hours breaking down every single struggle she had had to go through in order to get to where she is. She then went on to tell me, repeatedly, about every struggle she has in order to stay where she is, and every struggle she thinks she is going to need to overcome to take her shop further. (She was feeding her wolf on overdrive!)

Then, at the end of the two hours she turned to me and said: 'It's so frustrating but I can't find any good staff to help me in the business.'

Are you surprised? Why would anybody want to come and work for this organization when the founder hasn't created an atmosphere of thriving? When you walk into the establishment it feels heavy because all she does is moan about the things that are going wrong. I asked her if I could be honest with her, and she said yes, I assume thinking she was going to get some free brand marketing advice. So I said:

How can you possibly expect to attract the right staff when you are not acting right? How can you attract the right strategic partners to help take the salon to new heights, when you're not enthusiastic and happy and appearing to be a good person to do business with?

While I appreciate the need to vent every now and then to offload some stress, the lady had forgotten branding 101: you, the founder, the personal brand, need to start thinking positively to attract the positive things for your brand to thrive.

Too many people fail to stop and listen to how they talk – to themselves and when others are around. Going on and on about all the things that are difficult, rather than showing a real sense of gratitude and an enthusiasm for life, is only going to breed negative habits, and negative results. You can't wait for life to be perfect before you talk about how perfect it is.

**Like attracts like, because energy is contagious.**

I am a strong believer that the universe is like a big genie in a bottle and every single day the universe is saying, 'Your wish is my command.' If you turn round and say 'I want to build my personal brand,' then the universe will respond: 'Your wish is my command.'

The universe doesn't know anything different, other than what you said.

'I *want* to build my personal brand' means you are not doing it, it's something you're hoping for in the future, and so every day that you say 'I *want* to build my personal brand' you're putting the success of building your personal brand in the future because the universe is saying 'Your wish is my command.'

The key here is to remember that where your focus goes, your energy flows. Whatever you are focusing on and talking about, and constantly repeating like a mantra on replay, is exactly what you are going to get. So why not try focusing on something else? Why not try saying something that actually helps you get to where you want to be?

How about you try this: 'I am so happy I am building my personal brand' or 'I am so excited that money and deals have landed in my account.'

Say those things out loud. Or replace them with what you want and what you need. Does it sound corny or odd? If it does it's because you're so used to feeding your wolf that it sounds silly to feed your dog. Think about that for a minute. It means, to you, that it sounds silly for you to be positive!

But if you keep doing it, keep thinking it, even if you start off by doing it for yourself only, then over time it will start to feel natural. Remember, the more you speak about a thing, the more it comes true, because you make it true. You say it, the universe agrees with you and your thoughts determine your actions, your actions when repeated give you your habits, and your habits give you the results. Now don't get me wrong, of course things will go awry, and I am not telling you to ignore the negativity that's happening in your life. I am just reminding you to not *focus* on it. Do not focus on the size of the problem, but the scale of your achievements. Do not feed the wolf, even in the most desperate of moments, even when the gremlins start screaming at you; acknowledge whatever bad thing has happened and then focus on feeding the dog.

Neuroscience has proven this theory, explaining that cognitive ease or fluency is the measure of how easy it is for our brains to process information. The cognitive ease associated with something will alter how we feel about it and whether we are motivated to invest our time and effort in it. Nobel prize-winning economist Daniel Kahneman explains that our brains have two modes of thinking: the first that operates automatically and quickly, with little or no effort and no sense of voluntary control, and a second system that pays more conscious attention to information presented, especially in the case of that which demands more cerebral effort such as complex calculations, for example.

When cognitive ease diminishes, because the mental effort required is too much or too complex, we engage this second system of 'effortful mental activity' and switch to a state of cognitive strain. The cognitive ease principle reveals that when people have to switch to the second system of thinking, causing cognitive strain, they become more vigilant and suspicious. It results in a decrease in confidence, trust and pleasure involved in completing the mental action. In other words, people are happier and more receptive towards familiar and easily understandable situations in which they feel safer, more confident and at ease.

As a result, if you repeat or expose information to yourself frequently you're more likely to feel that it is true because things that feel true relate to a cognition of ease; they feel good/familiar/effortless and as such cognitive ease can be artificially created. Therefore your job is to pay attention to what is coming as an 'easy thought'. What words are you extremely comfortable saying about you and your brand? When you study your truth you will identify if you are feeding your dog or your wolf.

---

## LET'S DO THE WORK

*How have you been feeding your wolf? How better could you feed your dog?*

_____

_____

_____

_____

_____

_____

---

# Stopping is not an option

My best friend once asked me: 'Kubi, how is it that when life kicks you, you somehow always bounce back? You have the best bounce-back of anyone I know.' I laughed, and at first I really didn't know how to answer that. I had to think for a moment – how do I bounce back? If I am honest, it goes back to the principle of the wolf vs. dog. Here are some key things I do:

1   *Don't dwell on the negative* – When things happen, I allow myself
    time to feel it and acknowledge the pain associated with it. I see the
    gremlins for what they are and recognize that the emotion is real and
    the negative thing is also real. But I do not dwell. I don't call up every
    girlfriend and tell them what's happened. I don't spend days writing
    about it in my journal. I don't allow myself to spend weeks in bed
    crying over it. I refuse to sit in the negativity. I choose to acknowledge
    it and then quickly turn to finding a way to resolve it.

2   *Focus on the solution, not the problem* – I remind myself of what I want
    and why it's important. I go back to the vision at hand and remember
    that there are many routes that can be taken to get to any destination. So
    I focus on the new route. What's the solution that will get me from where
    I am, to where I actually want to be? I get hit, I cry and feel down, but
    then I go straight to the solutions; I do everything in my power to feed
    my dog. Feeding my dog in the midst of a crisis is the most important
    thing for me. As an example, I was once launching a fashion brand from
    the Middle East*, they had a sizable budget for me to play with, and my
    team and I had secured some phenomenal brand partnership for their
    campaigns. The entire project was due to last for six months, and
    included me travelling to and from their country to get them ready for
    London Fashion Week. It was one of those dream contracts. However, as
    we drew near to the end of the project it became apparent that they
    didn't have all the money they claimed they had; or if they did, they were
    trying not to spend it. Despite the contracts, NDAs and legal paperwork
    in place, they ended up finishing the project with money outstanding.
    They went back to the Middle East and left me in the UK with a
    tremendous bill for third-party suppliers. Now in that moment I could
    have got mad. I could have tried suing them, but, honestly, the cost of

\* for client confidentiality I won't go into detail on who they were or what part of the Middle East they
come from, but I will say this: the campaign I was doing with them was epic!

legal fees and international travel to recoup the money would have ended up being more than what they owed. So suing them was not an option. What did I do? Did I dwell on the negativity? Did I spend months complaining how bad it was? Did I stop running my agency and never work with another international designer again? No. I focused all my energy on finding the solution. Got the suppliers paid. Picked myself back up. Learned from the lessons. Tightened my legal and payment frameworks and kept it moving! To dwell would have been a pointless emotional exercise. The key to personal brand success is to find the solution, and find it fast.

3   *Get help* – I find people, whether they are my family, friends, mentors or associates, who can help me find the solution. If I don't have anyone around me to instil the wisdom I need, I turn to my friend 'Dr Google' and search for an answer. I watch YouTube videos, and listen to podcasts, indulge in 'expert' material to find the solution. I hate problems, so I spend hours and hours focused on how to solve them. 'What is the solution?' is on repeat in my brain and 'Who can help me get there?'

4   *Sleep* – Arianna Huffington's book *The Sleep Revolution* talks about how lack of sleep led to her collapsing with exhaustion. She details how she tried to run her business on the notion of 'I will sleep when I am dead', and she nearly died! Since then she has been dedicated to re-educating entrepreneurs and professionals on the importance of sleep as we embark on our journey to success. For me, it's imperative. When life kicks me, I often start my recovery journey by pulling the covers over my head and forcing myself to sleep. If I am exhausted, I can't think straight, so I give myself permission to go to bed early so that the next day I am fresh to find the solution.

5   *Get off social media* – I put my phone on 'do not disturb' and I stay off Instagram. The last thing I need when I am down is to try to post

something inspiring and educational. When I have nothing to give, I stop trying to be superwoman, take off my superhero cape and stop giving. I don't scroll through other people's pages because I don't want to be influenced. I force myself to come off it as I definitely do not want to treat social media like a therapy room! Social media is the last place to journal your pain, as it will negatively impact your personal brand. So I stay away.

6  *Put on comedy* – When I am down, I try to change my mood by listening to things that will make me laugh. So I watch standup routines by my favourite comedians, or indulge in their movies and TV shows. I force my mood to change through laughter.

7  *Turn to your happy box* – I have a virtual box of things that make me happy. Again it's one of those silly little things I like to do, but it works. In my happy box are a list of things that make me feel joyful when life is kicking me. On my list are:

- Go to the theatre and lose myself in the magic of a musical.

- Get all glammed up and watch a ballet at the Opera House.

- Go swimming and block out the world under water.

- Go to the spa and get pampered for the day.

- Listen to gospel music; I always end up crying, praying and then feeling 1,000 times better once I am done.

8  *Move your body* – A study by the Mental Health Foundation discovered that, of '[p]eople with severe symptoms of mental health problems, 37.6% of them also have a long-term physical condition. This compares with 25.3% of people with no or few symptoms of a mental health problem'. This study reinforces the importance of making sure you move your body when you're feeling like you can't win. When life kicks me, I get up and move. Sometimes I might just go

for a walk. Other times I will go to the gym or hit a dance class. If I'm exhausted I will do some light yoga to try to stretch the problems away and get re-energized via breathing exercises.

Choosing to develop your personal brand and win is just the start. Staying focused on winning, and getting through the hard times, is the key. The ones who become successful are the ones who refuse to stay down. They, like everyone else, get knocked down, but they refuse to stay down. As such you have to have a routine, a go-to list of people and things that help you through those moments. When life has kicked me, I don't dwell, I turn to things that help me bounce back, quickly. I take the time out that's needed and recharge. I watch what comes out of my mouth: who I speak with and what I speak about. I monitor what I allow myself to consume: from the news to music, anything that doesn't feed the dog doesn't get consumed. A friend of mine described it like this: when there is something wrong with your car, you take it to the garage. At the garage they have a toolbox of things that will fix the car. But what is in your toolbox when *you* need to be fixed? It's so very important to recharge your spirit and feed your soul, so that you have the energy to go again. I allow myself to pause, for a minute, and then keep going – stopping is never, ever, an option.

## LET'S DO THE WORK

Write down five things that could be in your happy box.

---

---

---

---

---

Write down five things that you could do, or do already, when life gives you a kick.

_____

_____

_____

_____

_____

## What's your decision?

A lot of people are not successful because they lack the discipline required for success. They are like a Jekyll and Hyde in their brain; they say they want to be successful but then they complain the minute they have to put in the extra work. They say they want to be successful, but then they are not honest about what success looks like for them. To build your personal brand you need to appreciate that you might not always feel like you want to do the things that need to be done, but you need to get them done anyway. Building your personal brand will take time; it is fun, but it's also a lot of long hours, dedication, focus and smart work. So, if the answer is 'I am already happy where I am' or 'I am not too happy but I don't want to put in the work to go further,' I applaud you for speaking your truth. It's better to be honest with yourself now rather than going down the road and feeling the pain of 'failure' and spending the rest of your life complaining that you 'failed' when really you just didn't try hard enough! If it's not for you, it's not for you.

If however your answer is yes, I want you to take it up a gear and be ready for whatever it takes. If it excites you and scares you all at the same time, you are ready. If it makes you happy and petrified simultaneously, your heart has already made the decision for you. Ignore your head, follow your heart.

Let's continue.

Now that you have made the decision to win, the next question is, what does 'winning' look like for you? For some it might mean that they are running a

Fortune 500 company; they see themselves as the CEO of a large corporation or sitting at boardroom level. For another it might be that they are a famous photographer, shooting all the A List celebrities in the world. For someone else it might be that they run a small but profitable business that allows them the freedom to spend time with their children. For another it might be travelling the world to consult on projects globally; they don't have a big team, but they make a big impact.

What does it look like for you? What does winning look like?

Take a minute to close your eyes and feel it. Even if you don't know what the job title is or the exact company. Just close your eyes and feel the feeling of winning. Imagine what it looks and feels like. Now take a minute to describe that feeling.

---

## LET'S DO THE WORK

Answer these questions before we move on:

Where are you? Is it hot or cold? Is the place large or small? Are there lots of people in the team or are you working solo? Are you behind the camera as a back office person, or in front of it leading the business and being the face of the brand? Do you work with your hands or use your intellectual capabilities? What impact is your work having on those around you? What work are you doing? How does it feel to be doing it?

_____

_____

_____

_____

_____

_____

# It's bigger than you

The vision and the dream aren't just for you. The desire to win might be for yourself but the result of winning – the manifestation of your business, your talent, your skills being put to use – is going to impact a much wider audience than the audience of one. It is for this reason that you need to 'feel the fear and do it anyway'. Your abilities and dreams haven't been given to you for you. They have been given to you for the impact that you will bring to someone else; for the lives you will touch and the people who will be impacted by the work you have done. This is irrespective of your industry, whether you're an architect with a gift of designing buildings that generations to come will discover; a construction worker with the ability to build roads that will help people drive to new destinations; a banker who is brilliant with numbers and whose capabilities will create new processes for how banks function, which in turn will support how customers are treated and give them a little bit more financial stability. Every gift, every skill, every talent that we have … they are not designed for us. They are designed to be used for a much broader audience. So your journey – your decision to win, your choosing to step out, your tenacity to step into your light – the journey will bring out the best in you, but the win will bring out the best in others.

Focus on the want being attached to something outside yourself, something that has a much higher purpose than your own personal win. Maybe what you want is connected to supporting your family, training for a new career or even leaving a significant legacy, such as curing cancer or eradicating modern-day slavery. Attach your want to a wider need, as it will help you when you are feeling as if you're not able to win. It is said that as humans we perform better when we are trying to achieve something that goes beyond our individual needs and desires, which is a beautiful thing. As you undertake the journey to personal brand success, it's good to have something bigger than you. That way, when you're trying to secure sponsorship for an event, for example, the feeling of rejection if potential sponsors say no will mean nothing when the focus is on how the event can help others in a meaningful way. In this example what you want isn't really sponsorship: the sponsorship is just a vehicle to achieve the higher goal, which means that when people say no you either a) don't take it personally (after all, this event isn't about you and your needs) or b) you find alternative ways to secure money to make the event work or c) you end up scrapping the event and finding an alternative way to achieve the bigger goal. Attaching your personal brand to a higher purpose adds new meaning and motivation when the gremlins come out to play.

To get started, why not go a few layers deeper than where you are. If I were to ask you why you want to develop your personal brand and you say 'to increase my income', I would ask you to go deeper. Why do you want to increase your income? Other than financial security for you, why else? When you dig deeper it might be because you want to be in a position to support your extended family or send money back to loved ones in other parts of the world. That has so much more meat on it than just 'I want to make more money!' So now when you're having an off-day, you can acknowledge the gremlins and keep it moving, knowing there are others depending on you.

Or, maybe if I were to ask you, you might say that you want to develop your personal brand to help propel your business and gain financial freedom. But why do you want financial freedom? When you dig deeper, maybe it's because you want the extra time and resources to travel the world volunteering to help a charitable cause. The business therefore becomes a vehicle to give back; it's no longer just about profits, but rather profits that allow you to do more with your time. This change in perspective means if the first business fails, you can start another; you are no longer attached to the business, but instead it's about what the business can do for you and those around you.

When you attach your personal brand success to a higher purpose – an outcome that is greater than yourself – it becomes easier to ride the waves of uncertainty. When you know that your children are relying on you to win, or your friends are looking for you to be the only example they have ever seen, or your local community is impacted by the wins you get, or your industry has potential for growth based on the wins you and your team make, or your world has a new example of excellence by the wins you secure … when you attach your win to something else, it adds pressure to your desire, but it also adds fuel to your engine.

Try to see your personal brand success as a contribution to making others happy. Or try to see how what you do adds value to someone or something else. We are all put here for a reason, and it's not just to make money, or have a nice house, or pay our bills on time, or create extreme wealth. Yes, those things are lovely and, in some cases, very necessary, but we are here for so much more than that. Your talents, gifts, character, personality, abilities and knowledge are in you for more than just you. Believe it or not, you have been uniquely designed to help solve a unique problem in this world. You haven't been created just for you, you have been created for others to enjoy what you bring. It might sound super corny, but the world actually needs what you have. Your world and those in your world, really *really* need what you have, to show up, without apology. The darkness all around us needs your unique light. When you switch on your torch, your light creates a way for others to see. Yes, it might well be scary knowing that there are others who are dependent on your win, but it's also very rewarding when it happens. What's more, in the dead of the night when you are feeling like you can't, it's good to know that others are hoping you can.

So don't just try to win for you, try to win for them. Take the 'I' out of your journey to personal brand success and create a 'we'. *I AM MY BRAND* starts with you, but it shouldn't end with you.

The totality of Nelson Mandela's speech went like this:

*Our deepest fear is not that we are inadequate.*
*Our deepest fear is that we are powerful beyond measure.*
*It is our light, not our darkness that most frightens us.*

*We ask ourselves,*

*Who am I to be brilliant, gorgeous, talented, fabulous?*

*Actually, who are you not to be?*

*You are a child of God. Your playing small does not serve the world.*

*There is nothing enlightened about shrinking so that other people won't feel insecure around you.*

*We are all meant to shine, as children do.*

*We were born to make manifest the glory of God that is within us.*

*It's not just in some of us; it's in everyone.*

*And as we let our own light shine, we unconsciously give other people permission to do the same.*

*As we are liberated from our own fear, our presence automatically liberates others.*

# 2

# Let's Start at the Beginning

When I was 18 years old I dreamt of working for the biggest celebrity brands in the world. On my university dorm walls I had a vision board with Destiny's Child, P. Diddy and Will Smith as dream clients. During my second year I found myself writing a university report on the founder of the MOBO Awards, Ms Kanya King, on how she built her brand and the MOBO empire, and as a youngster I dreamt of working in this arena. Fast forward 23 years and, with lots of sweat and tears, I had worked with all of the brands on my wall; minus Will Smith . . . I am still working on that one! But instead of him I managed to add Justin Timberlake, Mariah Carey and Eminem to my roster of celebrity brand marketing activities. By the age of 40, I had officially ticked off my bucket list of personal branding clients, from Rio Ferdinand to Beyoncé, coupled with a portfolio that included corporate brands such as Nike, L'Oréal, Facebook, Rolls Royce and Aston Martin; my CV was certainly impressive. But beyond bragging rights, what exactly had I learnt from these experiences? What single most important thing had I taken away from it all? What lessons have I derived from my 20-plus years of branding?

> Brand marketing is a formula.

Beyond the creativity, there is a strategic science that, when combined with innovative ideas and brilliant content, connects with audiences and creates magic.

It is this knowledge that has led me to write this book. Having witnessed the truth behind the curtain, I want to unpack the mystery to help you, the reader. I am writing this book not only because I want you to know what your personal brand is, but to be able to package your brand, market your brand and ultimately make money from your brand. Irrespective of what sector you are in – media, music, the arts, fashion, health care, technology, science, finance, insurance, law – I want you to be unafraid of your unique voice. To be proud of your specific gifts and to capture all of the opportunities that your career or business ventures give you to become a success. Over the last decade, I have taught over 500 classes and during each class students have asked very similar questions: How do you create your personal brand? How do you communicate your brand? How do you make your brand make you money? I will seek to answer all of these in this book.

But in order to create this magic, you need to be clear on what a brand is and what it is not. Irrespective of what area of branding I am teaching, I always start every masterclass in the same way. I ask this simple, but seemingly complex, question: 'What is a brand?' Most people tell me they want to build a brand, they want to promote their brand, they want to take their brand to an 'international' level, but most don't actually know the answer. Stop for a moment, pause from reading the next paragraph, while you ask yourself: 'What is a brand?' What answers do you come up with? Write them down.

_____

_____

_____

_____

Usually when I pose this question there is silence in the room; blank faces stare back at me before someone plucks up the courage to answer. 'A brand is a logo' is the usual reply, or 'a reputation', 'a business', 'an image' are some of the other usual responses, but none of them are right. A brand is not a logo or a strapline, nor is it a design feature, and it definitely is not a business. Neither is branding the same as marketing; they are completely different things. A brand is not a set of colours, or a reputation, nor is it a personality, a signature, a set of values, a theme song or even a promise. Whilst all of those things are important, they, in and of themselves, are not a brand.

So, what *is* a brand?

**A brand is an emotional connection with its target audience.**

From Nike to Coca-Cola, Disney to McDonalds, Donald Trump to Barack Obama, Oprah Winfrey to Richard Branson, all established brands, both personal and business, are designed to connect emotionally with their target audience.

Take a minute to think about a brand that you like. What do you *feel* when you think about that brand? What do you *feel* when you buy from that brand? What do you *feel* when you experience that brand? What do you *feel* when you tell your friends that you have that brand? Is it joy or happiness? Do you feel at peace or relaxed? When you think about purchasing a product from that brand do you feel powerful or cool? Established or distinguished? Do you feel responsible or adventurous? Do you feel sexy or inspired?

When you really think about the brands you love, you don't think at all; you *feel* something. There is an emotion attached to all great brands.

As an example, Disney wants its target audience to feel Magic, Nike wants its target audience to feel Powerful, Oprah wants her target audience to feel Inspired and Coca-Cola wants its target audience to feel Happy. All great brands conjure up an emotion in their target audience. The things that people normally mention when I ask the question 'What is a brand?' are merely the tools we marketers use to connect emotionally with the desired audience. All of the elements that are presented as a brand – the logos, straplines, colours, recognition signs, etc – are not a brand, they are the assets used to create the brand. To reiterate, a brand, by definition, is an emotional connection with its target audience.

Let's review this in more detail. The assets we marketers use to create the emotion are as follows.

# The Brand Promise

The Brand Promise is an idea that articulates what all of your stakeholders will experience when doing business with you. When done well it engages the buy-in from all facets of the organization: from staff to suppliers, customers to investors, as it aligns your values, your vision and your Brand Mission. It goes beyond the benefits of the product or service as it represents so much more. It's the heartland that runs through the entire brand experience. As a personal brand, you too have a Brand Promise, but first let's review a business's Brand Promise.

If we take Nike as our first example, Nike's Brand Promise is 'to bring inspiration and innovation to every athlete in the world'. Its co-founder, the legendary University of Oregon track and field coach, Bill Bowerman, said, 'If you have a body, you are an athlete' (Nike, 2019). As a teacher, Bowerman wanted to teach athletes the secrets to achievement. Nike's promise therefore is not about its products, but about how the products will make you feel, and what the products will enable you to do and achieve. Nike wants its desired audience to feel powerful.

This Brand Promise, when communicated consistently, builds trust and ultimately changes consumer behaviour, which is why every time I claim I want to lose weight, I join the gym and head straight to the Nike store! And I am not alone. According to *Business Insider*, Nike is positioned as the biggest player in the athletic apparel market, with US$34.35 billion global revenue and 1,142 retail stores worldwide – and not all of those can be professional athletes (2017; DMR Business Statistics, 2019).

This idea of a Brand Promise is not restricted to business brands; personal brands also have Brand Promises. As an example, Barack Obama, in the 2008 presidential election, gave us the Brand Promise of 'Hope and Change'. Through his multichannel approach, his speeches, TV appearances, rallies and social media engagements, he promised his 'target audience' a new day and a new way. Even as he left the White House in January 2017, during his Presidential Farewell Address in his hometown of Chicago, Illinois, his message and Brand Promise was still communicating 'hope'. Whether or not, over the eight years in office, that promise realized itself is a topic for political discussion, but the consistency of the Brand Promise is what (in part) won him two terms as President of the United States. The consistency of the promise helps to drive the emotion, and the emotion is what helps the brand's target audience to say yes.

So how can you start to create your Brand Promise? Think about how you want your desired audience to feel when they buy from or buy into your brand. How do you want your co-workers to feel when they work with you? What words will they use to describe you when you leave the room? How do you want your customers to feel when they engage with your brand; how will they describe you? Not the product or service itself, but *you*, the brand founder, the face of the company, the personal brand?

## LET'S DO THE WORK

1. Write down five descriptive words to describe your brand. Make sure these words are emotive.

_____

_____

_____

2. Choose one out of these five words that is most authentic to your Personal Brand.

_____

_____

_____

3. Complete this sentence: When you think of my brand, you will feel…

_____

_____

_____

# The logo

The logo is the creative expression of the Brand Promise. It brings your brand alive. The use of fonts, symbols, choice of colours and logo design all work together to enable the logo to become a visual assertion of the Brand Promise. By doing so the logo creates interest and intrigue, it creates loyalty and recognition, it distinguishes you from the competition and reveals your identity.

Continuing with Nike as our example, in 1971, Carolyn Davidson, who was a graphic design student, created the design of the Nike Swoosh for Phil Knight who co-founded Nike with Bowerman. The logo was created as a check mark shape that is fluid and indicates movement and speed. Davidson, in an article with OregonLive.com, said that it was 'a challenge to come up with a logo that conveyed motion, that looked good on a shoe, and that Mr. Knight and the rest of the team would like' (MailOnline, 2011). She thereby designed the logo with the name in mind ('Nike' is named after the ancient Greek Goddess of victory; Greek folklore has it that the Goddess Nike influenced countless brave warriors to win battles of their motherland), creating a logo to resemble the wing of the Nike Goddess to indicate speed, and motion.

Since Nike wants us to feel powerful, and they promise inspiration, innovation and achievement, the logo is a perfect illustration of all of this. The Swoosh (which looks like a tick) reinforces that Brand Promise. Think of it like this: what do you do once you have achieved something? You tick it off your list. Furthermore, the sound of a Swoosh is something that moves quickly. All of these elements – movement, speed, motion and power – help to reinforce Nike's Brand Promise.

But, once again, this idea isn't restricted to business brands. Referencing back to Barack Obama, this is a brilliant example of how a logo can be a creative expression of a personal Brand Promise. As outlined previously, Obama promised 'Hope and Change', which is why in 2008 Chicago-based design firm Sender LLC created a logo that utilized the 'O' from his last name to produce a sun rising over the horizon. The illustration of the sun and the rising was created to demonstrate the idea of a new day and a new way. Sol Sender, Principal at Sender LCC, in an interview with *Crain's Chicago Business*, said 'Obama has developed a brand and that's new [as a Presidential Candidate]. There are logo types, which is taking the typography of the candidate name and trying to develop new elements around it, but in terms of a mark that can truly stand alone, that is not something we have seen.' He goes on to reiterate that 'the Obama work was influenced by corporate branding ... the logo itself is not that complicated', but it's what it stands for: 'it's the 'O' and the rising of a new era in American politics' (YouTube, 2011).

While on the surface this may all appear to be common sense, and of course brands need logos that reinforce their Brand Promise, the reality is that a large percentage of brands fail because of the lack of consistency in the development of the brand. As an example:

- *London Olympics 2012 logo* – Although a vague 2012, the shapes were irregular and had no meaningful relation with London or its landmarks. Comments by industry insiders said it looked like a passing resemblance to a distorted swastika. The result was embarrassment on its unveiling.

- *Hillary Clinton campaign 2015* – Her logo has been likened to a hospital sign. Many people said that its big red arrow symbolized a shift to the right. Many rejected the simple design because it looked too amateurish. As a result it did not reflect the feel of the Clinton campaign.

- *American Airlines – Business Insider* (Weller, 2016) commented that 'There was absolutely no need to change it [the logo] . . . this redesign is a soulless shell of its former self.' As such the development of the new logo broke rule #1 in design: *If it ain't broke, don't fix it.*

While not all personal brands need a logo, it is worth having a font type that is associated with your brand, which you can then use across your CV, your personal brand website, your blogs and personal brand emails. By doing so you start to create a uniformity to your brand.

## LET'S DO THE WORK

What fonts or typography represent your brand?

_____

_____

_____

_____

_____

# The brand's strapline

The strapline is the three–five words that encapsulate the Brand Promise. Since brand marketing is about concise communication, the best straplines are simple, easy to remember and convey not only your Brand Promise, but also your brand story (or at least part of it). This is why Nike tell us to 'Just Do It'. There is urgency in these words, a push for you to move forward to something great. These words inspire us, they move us, and they motivate us. Imagine if Nike's strapline were 'Maybe You Can Do It'... would it have the same effect?

But Nike is not the only brand to have an emotive strapline. The drinks giant Carlsberg says 'Probably the best ...' which has a tongue-in-cheek meaning as 'almost certainly the best'. Carlsberg are proud of their heritage, not boastful and have for many years adopted a playful humour in their marketing campaigns. The Brand Promise is to simply deliver the best to its consumers *but* it is for you, the consumer, to decide if you like it or not. To better understand this we need to look at the founder, J.C. Jacobsen, a pioneer with a purpose. When he founded Carlsberg in 1847, his vision was to do much more than brew great beer. He wanted a beer to stand the test of time. Almost two centuries on, his legacy is extraordinary, with brewing virtually unchanged and humour at the centre of it.

L'Oréal – 'Because You're Worth It'. As a cosmetics brand making women feel fabulous, L'Oréal has used the 'Because You're Worth It' campaign for many years. It works by telling women that they deserve to treat themselves and make the best of themselves. Recently, adverts have expanded on the company's strapline with the marketing slogan 'Because We're Worth It', designed to help women feel the same as the celebrities endorsing the products. Ultimately, L'Oréal wants its consumers to feel they are worth something special, knowing that a lot of women do not always feel like they are worth anything.

Kit Kat – 'Have a Break, Have a Kit Kat'. A lunch box favourite, the iconic Kit Kat strapline is one that has stood the test of time. But what is Nestlé really saying? They are giving a promise of a relaxing break moment that can be shared and as such the strapline encapsulates this idea.

To start to develop your own brand strapline you should think about three to five words that encapsulate what you are promising your end users. Now don't get me wrong, I am not expecting you to start every meeting with 'Hi my name is … and my strapline is …'; that would be very odd indeed. But understanding your key words can allow you to utilize them as part of your brand marketing messages. In pitching presentations or on social media, knowing your keywords means that you can slice them into conversations as part of reinforcing what your brand stands for and why someone should do business with you.

## LET'S DO THE WORK

Write down five to ten words that could be used in your brand strapline.

Don't try to make them make sense at this stage, just simply write them down as individual words. We will create the strapline later. For now, just be clear on some key words.

_____

_____

_____

_____

_____

# The brand colours

Similar to the use of the logo and the strapline, the choice of colours is also a tool used by marketers to reinforce the Brand Promise. Swiss psychiatrist Carl Jung (1875–1961) was famously quoted as saying: 'colours are the mother tongue of the subconscious'. As such, colours are used every day to help connect the brand emotionally and subconsciously with its desired audience. In a recent study entitled 'The psychology of colour in marketing and branding'

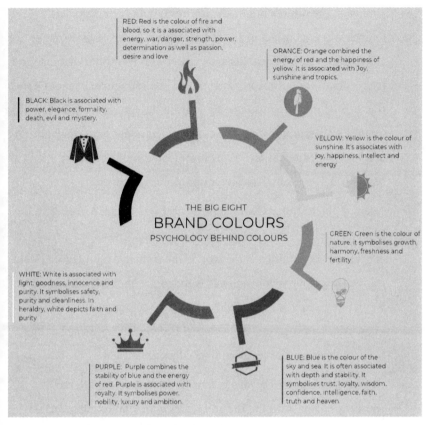

RED: Red is the colour of fire and blood, so it is a associated with energy, war, danger, strength, power, determination as well as passion, desire and love

ORANGE: Orange combined the energy of red and the happiness of yellow. It is associated with Joy, sunshine and tropics.

BLACK: Black is associated with power, elegance, formality, death, evil and mystery.

YELLOW: Yellow is the colour of sunshine. It's associates with joy, happiness, intellect and energy

THE BIG EIGHT
BRAND COLOURS
PSYCHOLOGY BEHIND COLOURS

GREEN: Green is the colour of nature, it symbolises growth, harmony, freshness and fertility

WHITE: White is associated with light, goodness, innocence and purity. It symbolises safety, purity and cleanliness. In heraldry, white depicts faith and purity

PURPLE: Purple combines the stability of blue and the energy of red. Purple is associated with royalty. It symbolises power, nobility, luxury and ambition.

BLUE: Blue is the colour of the sky and sea. It is often associated with depth and stability. It symbolises trust, loyalty, wisdom, confidence, intelligence, faith, truth and heaven.

FIGURE 2.1 *The big eight brand colours.*

(*Entrepreneur*, 2016), researchers found 90 per cent of snap judgments made about products can be based on colour alone.

So what are the meanings of colours and how do they impact your brand colour choices?

- *Red* – Coca-Cola. The famous Coca-Cola bottle got its colour right before 1900. Tax officials used to check the contents of their trucks whilst they were distributing the soft drink. To make it easier for them to distinguish alcohol from Coca-Cola, the soft drink bottles were branded a striking red colour. Today the red is seen as vibrant, effervescent and energized ... all the elements that Coca-Cola promises us about their brand.

- *Orange* – 'The future's bright, the future's Orange' (2008 slogan). Orange was established in 1994 by Hutchison Telecom. The orange colour was selected due to its association with Feng Shui elements and it also stands for optimism, warmth and joy. The square logo of Orange was created to distinguish the brand from the spherical citrus fruit. The Orange logo communicates the company's message very efficiently and it is widely credited as one of the most iconic and instantly recognizable logos in the telecommunications industry.

- *Yellow* – The National Geographic Society was founded in 1888 in the United States. It is now one of the largest nonprofit scientific and educational institutions in the world. The rectangle represents a photo frame. The colour yellow represents the sun, without which our planet would not be as it is today. Yellow is also the colour associated with knowledge and wisdom. The *National Geographic* magazine has had a trademark yellow border around its edges since 1888.

- *Green* – Land Rover. The logo is an all vivid green oval with the company's name in white. The green stands for vitality and reflects the spirit of the brand; wandering far away from grey roads, closer to nature, which reinforces Land Rover's Brand Promise of its off-road capabilities.

- *Blue* – Boeing. The use of the bright blue colour in the Boeing logo embodies the sky as well as the supremacy, strength and excellence of the company.

- *Purple* – Cadbury. The chocolatier started swathing its chocolate bars in royal purple wrappers over 100 years ago to honour Queen Victoria, associating the brand with nobility and luxury.

- *Black and white* – Chanel. Designed by Coco Chanel herself in 1925, the black in the logo represents elegance, elitism and wealth. The white symbolizes purity. Additionally black accentuates the essential. For Coco it reminded her of the monastic rigour of the uniforms of the

Aubazine orphanage. Black evolved from garments of servants and those in mourning to become, since 1926, the colour of elegance epitomized by Chanel's little black dress. White was important because in the beginning Coco said it reminded her of the cornets of the nuns from her childhood and of the communion dress given to her by her father. 'Women think of all colours except the absence of colour. I have said that black has it all. White too. Their beauty is absolute. It is the perfect harmony' (Coco Chanel).

The importance of colour in creating the brand is not limited to business brands alone. When used well, colour can reinforce the Brand Promise of personal brands too, and create stunning brand identities. For example, American music artist Janelle Monáe started her career wearing pant suits and tuxedos in only black and white. Her reasoning was to pay homage to her grandparents' humble beginnings as uniform workers and to remind herself to remain grounded. Then there is fashion designer Karl Lagerfeld, who dressed in high collars, last worn by late nineteenth-century aldermen, fingerless gloves and sunglasses, worn day and night, indoors and out. Plus he had the infamous ice-white pony tail, so reminiscent of a Georgian periwig, which turned out to need regular dusting with white powder as it was not naturally quite as snowy as it looked.

Developing a strategy for how you'll employ colour as a personal branding tool is imperative. To do this, first identify the colour that best exudes your brand. That doesn't mean you should choose your favourite colour, it means you should select the one that conveys your authentic and differentiating brand attributes. It should be noted that in the psychology of colours, black and white are not defined as colours as they do not have a specific wavelength. Often in branding, people use black and white with an accent colour. The next step is to infuse that colour into all of your brand touch points. We discuss this further in Chapter 5, 'Your Difference Is Your Strength', but for now let's note that the choice of colour is just as important as the choice of design in the logo and words in the strapline, which all work together to reinforce the Brand Promise and create the emotional connection to the brand. Go to SheBuildsBrands.com for more about the psychology of colours.

---

## LET'S DO THE WORK

Use the colour chart to establish your colour(s).

_____

_____

_____

_____

_____

_____

---

# The brand signature

Finally, the brand signature is the last element needed to create your brand. The signature is important as it creates a distinction for the brand, usually tied into a colour or design feature that further reinforces the Brand Promise. Some examples follow.

## Christian Louboutin created the red-soled shoe

In 1993 Christian Louboutin had thought of making a shoe inspired by Andy Warhol's 'Flowers'.

> The prototype, a pink stacked heel with a cartoonish cloth blossom, had arrived from Italy. 'I was very happy, because it was similar to the drawing,' Louboutin

recalled, 'but the drawing still was stronger and I could not understand why.' Louboutin continued, 'There was this big black sole, and then, thank God, there was this girl painting her nails at the time.' Louboutin grabbed the nail polish – it was red – from the assistant and slathered it on the sole of the prototype. 'Then it popped,' he recalled, 'and I thought, this is the drawing!'

Interview with *New Yorker Magazine*, quoted in Glamour.com, 2011

Christian Louboutin wants his shoes to say one simple word: sex. 'Everything about them – from their disco styles to the aggressive thrust of the shoe's curvature, to the almost-pornographic red sole, flashing observers from behind as the lady walks away – shouts sex' (*Sydney Morning Herald*, 2010). As a result of this effective emotional connection, Louboutin has over 135 stores in 44 countries and 'the accounts [filed in September 2017] showed UK sales surged to £52.5 million from £44.2 million, in the year to 31 August, 2016' (*Evening Standard*, 2017).

## Taking a bite out of the Apple logo

1 April, 1976. The name Apple, apart from being simple, was chosen because it stood for fun, making computers look less intimidating and friendlier to ordinary people, not just corporates. On the naming of Apple, Walter Isaacson, in his biography on Steve Jobs, quotes Jobs as saying that he was 'on one of my fruitarian diets'. He said he had just come back from an apple farm, and thought the name sounded 'fun, spirited and not intimidating'. With regards to the small bite: Rob Janoff, who created the logo, says 'the single bite out of the Apple logo originally served a very practical purpose: scale. The size of the bite showed that the shape was an apple, not a cherry or any other vaguely round fruit' (Conradt, 2015). As a result, this world-renowned brand has helped the company to become one of the most commercially successful technology firms in the world.

There is a key difference between the development of personal brand and business brand signatures. Generally, I find that personal brand signatures tend to be associated with things that we as human beings don't like about ourselves, such as a distinguishing feature on our body, or in our personality, that is so different from others' that we hate it in ourselves.

I remember years ago I had a PR agent who asked me why I always look so moody in my press pictures. She said that in person I am really joyful to be around, but in my pictures I never smile. I realized that because I have a gap in my teeth, which at the time I hated, I would take pictures without a full smile to try to hide the very thing that made my brand distinguished, and thus was my signature. Now that I know the power of my gap, you can't stop me from smiling!

---

## LET'S DO THE WORK

*What distinguishing feature or personality trait do you possess that is your brand signature?*

 

 

 

 

 

 

---

As we've explored in this chapter, all of the above – the Brand Promise, logo, strapline and signature – are used as tools to create an emotional connection with the desired audience. But they are only the beginning of the resources we marketers make use of to build a brand. Additional tools include the brand history, the brand values, the brand culture and the brand personality. As this book progresses we will uncover these in-depth, and review not only what brands, both personal and business, have been doing, but what you can do to adapt their techniques to your own personal brand. As we take this journey together we will reveal tools that will enable your personal brand to have a clear brand differentiation and identity. We will unpick ways that your brand marketing can enable you to connect with your desired audiences and stand out from the competition. Ultimately, we will help you to drive connections, network more effectively and achieve better results in your career or business.

However, you are not a manufactured product with a brand attached. You are not a Nike trainer or a Coca-Cola drink, because you are a human being with feelings, history, emotions and beliefs that will impact your personal brand development. Before we can focus on your brand, we first need to focus on you. I often tell my clients: once we have taken a minute to build you, we can then build the brand that will truly represent you.

A personal brand is the authentic expression of the individual. It is a personification of who they really are. Therefore before you can connect emotionally with others, you first need to emotionally connect with yourself. You need to study and analyse you, and learn your truth to be able to market it. You simply can't skip to brand marketing without first creating the brand, and you can't create a personal brand without first dealing with the person.

Are you ready to uncover your truth?

Let's go!

# References

Apple (February 2018). https://www.apple.com/uk/newsroom/2018/02/apple-reports-first-quarter-results/

Conradt, S. (2015). Did Alan Turing inspire the Apple logo? Mentalfloss.com, 1 June 2015. http://mentalfloss.com/article/64049/did-alan-turing-inspire-apple-logo

DMR Business Statistics (2019). '35 amazing Nike facts and statistics 2019' by Craig Smith. https://expandedramblings.com/index.php/nike-statistics/

Entrepreneur (2016). The psychology of colour in marketing and branding, 13 April 2016. https://www.entrepreneur.com/article/233843

Evening Standard (2017). 'Christian Louboutin steps up UK revenues but warns on rates and rents' by Joanna Bourke, 15 September, 2017. https://www.standard.co.uk/business/christian-louboutin-steps-up-uk-revenues-but-warns-on-rates-and-rents-a3635891.html

Glamour.com (2011). 'The true story of how Christian Louboutin shoes got those trademark red soles', by T. Lomrantz Lester, 21 March 2011. Glamour.com https://www.glamour.com/story/the-true-story-of-how-christia

MailOnline (2011). '"I never get tired of looking at it": Woman who designed Nike's swoosh explains how chance encounter with Phil Knight led to its inception 40 YEARS ago' by B. Clark Howard. MailOnline 16 June 2011. http://www.dailymail.co.uk/news/article-2004273/Woman-designed-Nike-swoosh-explains-story-inception-40-years-ago.html#ixzz5BdOUb0H9

Nike (2019). Nike promise: https://help-en-us.nike.com/app/answer/a_id/113 https://www.quora.com/Why-did-Steve-Jobs-name-the-brand-Apple-and-create-its-logo-the-way-it-is

Sydney Morning Herald (2010). 'Christian Louboutin and the shoes that shout sex', by H. Freeman. Sydney Morning Herald 2 April, 2010. https://www.smh.com.au/lifestyle/fashion/christian-louboutin-and-the-shoes-that-shout-sex-20100331-rebk.html

Weller, C. (2016). 'The 14 worst logos of all time, according to artists and designers'. Business Insider 13 June 2016. https://www.businessinsider.com/the-worst-logos-of-all-time-2016-6?r=US&IR=T

YouTube (2011). 'Inside Brand Obama'. Crain's Chicago Business, 8 July 2011. https://www.youtube.com/watch?v=diJKZImjbWU

# Websites

American Airlines – https://www.aa.com/newamerican

Apple – https://www.quora.com/Why-did-Steve-Jobs-name-the-brand-Apple-and-create-its-logo-the-way-it-is

Apple – www.macworld.co.uk

Carlsberg – a legacy: https://carlsberggroup.com/who-we-are/about-the-carlsberg-group/our-rich-heritage/

KitKat – http://mentalfloss.com/article/69593/12-snappy-facts-about-kit-kat

KitKat – https://www.scribd.com/document/279250250/Kit-Kat-Brand-Analysis

L'Oréal – https://www.lorealparisusa.com/about-loreal-paris/because-youre-worth-it.aspx

# 3

# Time to Look in the Mirror

Decision. **VISION**. Clarity. Strategy. Tactics. Metrics.
Ownership. Be Unapologetic

Earlier this year I was at a Wellness Conference in Mauritius speaking on the Power of Personal Branding. I was asked to deliver a presentation to an audience of wellness specialists: coaches, fitness instructors, yoga teachers, product manufacturers, hotels and spas. During my 45-minute talk, I could see a very pretty lady looking at me intensely throughout. As the presentation progressed, she appeared to become more and more frustrated. Unlike the rest of the audience who were writing notes and taking in the information, she wasn't writing at all; instead she continued to stare at me, rolling her eyes and appearing to be annoyed with my delivery. At the end I opened the floor for my usual Q&A and welcomed a question from her (after all I was curious as to what could be making her so mad!).

'I don't agree with you,' she blurted out. 'I have tried every marketing trick in the book. I have hired great PR agencies and graphic designers; I spent a fortune on my website and still no results. As far as I am concerned it's bullshit and it doesn't work!'

The crowd was shocked by her bluntness and turned to me immediately to see what my reaction would be. I took a deep breath and replied: 'So you have tried every marketing trick in the book, you say?'

'Yes,' she said, with a snarling tone.

I continued: 'Well, maybe brand marketing is not what you need right now. Perhaps what you need is a Brand Audit.'

I paused to give her time to respond; she didn't, so I went on. 'Far too often I see brands spending lots and lots of time, money and resources pushing out brand marketing messages, before they've even created their brand. Yes – they may have a logo, or a strapline but they don't have a brand . . .'

The lady cleared her throat and interrupted me: 'But I *do* have a brand. I have been in this industry for years and people know my brand. I just need more people to know about it and this marketing you are talking about, well, I have tried but it just doesn't work. It's all a con so that we can pay people like you more money.'

Once again the audience members turned back to me in unison to see what I would say.

'Whilst I appreciate your experience,' I said in a slow yet warm tone, 'I would ask you to maybe think about this in another way. If your brand marketing isn't working, maybe it's not the marketing that's the problem, maybe it's the brand. Often I work with clients who, like you, are finding that the marketing is not connecting, so I suggest they do a Brand Audit. A Brand Audit is like a health check for your brand. It's a brilliant way to put a mirror up to the brand to ascertain what about the brand is working and what is not working. During a Brand Audit you review the internal brand. Are the values aligned? Is the mission clear? Is the company culture embedded effectively? The Brand Audit also looks at your external brand assets. Is the logo working? Are the advertising messages clear, and digital channels correct? As a personal brand, is your styling and the clothes you wear giving off the right messages? Once you have done that, then you review the customer experience. Are your marketing activities supporting your sales processes? Is the customer journey any good – and sealing the deal once the marketing has generated the leads? Or are there bad reviews online that are conflicting and stopping customers from believing your marketing messages?'

There was a silence in the room and I could see tears in her eyes.

'So it's not them, it's me, that's the problem?' she said, almost to herself.

'Maybe it is them, maybe you did hire a PR agency, graphic design team and web developer who weren't good at their jobs. But chances are it's more than that; the chances are that there is something not connecting with your brand,' I said.

Her demeanour changed and she softened, taking out her phone and writing something down, so I turned to the audience at large: 'A Brand Audit is so important, especially if you've been going for a while. Maybe you started off on your journey getting clients with ease and now you're finding it's a struggle. Or maybe you are trying to get a promotion and something is blocking it. Once you do a Brand Audit and put that mirror up to what is happening, you can amend it, and then allow marketing to do its job of working for you, and not against you.'

That day I walked away with a new client. It wasn't the pretty lady – she quietly disappeared, not saying much after our exchange – but I did get a celebrity fitness instructor signing up for an eight-week audit, with the brief for me to review why her longstanding brand was now not making an impact. What I did with her to get the answers is what I am going to suggest to you now. The process of a Brand Audit is important as it allows you to identify whether what you envision for your brand is aligning to what is actually happening with your brand. To achieve this, there are key questions that you need to ask yourself and answer from a place of truth. So here we go, it's time to put up a mirror to your brand and start your Brand Audit.

# What problem are you solving?

When reviewing your brand, you need to ask: What is the real problem that you are solving and is that problem relevant? Is there still a need for the solutions that your brand brings to the table?

As an example, whenever I go into new client meetings I always ask them this question: 'What is your brand challenge?' I do this because I am keen to ascertain if my brand can actually deliver what they really need. As with all of us, I need to know what problems I am solving; I can't make assumptions. I have to be clear on the problem and how my varied skillsets, experiences and expertise, help them. I therefore ask the question 'What is your brand challenge?' so that I am clear as a brand expert, how my brand delivers a solution to their specific problem. If I went into a pitch meeting not knowing what problem I was solving, I would probably end up pitching something they simply don't need. Or it might be that they do need it, but I communicate my ability to deliver the solution in the completely wrong way, using language and examples that are not relevant to them.

Imagine you are trying to get a promotion in your job. You know you have the skills and knowledge, and so you think you should be in the running for this promotion: after all, you work hard, get to work before everyone else and deliver great results. But without speaking with your boss and identifying the problems facing the company, the department and your direct boss, you won't know how you, and your unique skillset, can help be part of the solution. How much more powerful would you be if you could go into your review meeting saying: 'I know the company is trying to digitalize all of its processes, and I recognize that in our department we particularly need to achieve this in the next six months; as a result, I want to work with you, as my direct boss, to bring my knowledge around digital transformations and cultural behaviour to the organization.' How much more of a specific and powerful position would that put you in? Versus: 'I believe I should get a promotion because of my work ethic!' Don't be a generalist; identify the specific problem and position yourself as the solution.

Sometimes we start off with real clarity on the problem and thus know the solution; we do this for a while, but then we find that something has shifted and our brand is no longer connecting. This is because we have failed to recognize that, as times change, problems change with them. As an example, at a recent masterclass an attendee who has a CV-writing business was feeling confused as to why her clientele of young graduates was diminishing. For me it was obvious: the problem (I don't know how to write a CV) was being answered by cheaper and, in some cases, free solutions. As a result, her business and Brand Solution were becoming obsolete. I informed her that, while that might have been a great business when she started, young graduates seeking to enter the workforce today are able to Google how to write a great CV; they can watch YouTube videos on it; and recruitment firms have whole departments, tips and blogs helping them to do it for free. What she didn't realize is that as time goes on and consumer needs change, along with technological advancements, the problem you are solving today may no longer be relevant tomorrow. This is why you do an annual Brand Audit to make sure there is still enough of a demand for the solutions that your brand presents.

Whilst your Brand Promise will never change, your Brand Solutions (and thus your products and service offerings) will need to change to adapt to the new problems at hand. Let's look at a high-profile brand as an example.

Coca Cola started on 29 January 1892 in Atlanta, USA. The Brand Promise for Coke has always been to conjure up a feeling of 'happiness'; when you look at all the advertising slogans over the years, they all pull consumers into the notion of feeling happy:

- 1922 – 'Thirst Knows No Season'
- 1948 – 'Where There's Coke There's Hospitality'

- 1956 – 'Coca-Cola . . . Makes Good Things Taste Better'

- 1971 – 'I'd Like to Buy the World a Coke'

- 1979 – 'Have a Coke and a Smile'

- 1987 – 'When Coca-Cola is a Part of Your Life, You Can't Beat the Feeling'

- 1990 – 'You Can't Beat the Real Thing'

- 2001 – 'Life Tastes Good'

- 2009 – 'Open Happiness'

Over the years their advertising messages have reflected the Brand's Promise: drink Coke and you will feel happy. But as consumer consumption trends, such as greater health consciousness and lifestyle, have changed, Coke has introduced new products to be solutions to these new problems. Whilst they still want you to feel happy (the Brand Promise), now you can feel happy with Diet Coke and Coke Zero (the Brand Solution), which is reflected in their advertising campaign's messages. Go to SheBuildsBrands.com for more information on this.

In the same way that for over 200 years Coke has promised the same feeling of Happiness, you too need to ensure that your Brand Promise never changes. The feeling that people will get when they work with you, and the promise you give them, should never change, but the way you solve their problems should and must change.

Going back to the celebrity fitness instructor, whom I met at the Wellness Conference, I quickly established that, whilst her Brand Promise of 'Transformation and Freedom' was still relevant to her clients, her delivery to that solution was no longer working. When she started in the early 1990s she would hire a private studio in LA and her then up-and-coming celebrity clients would come to her. As they grew in status, she would do 1-2-1 classes at their houses. But with the advent of Instagram and Facebook, her clients became afraid that people would put their fitness journeys on social media: paparazzi might see her coming to their house or other celebrities might see them at her classes and Tweet about it. Whilst they loved the transformation she gave their bodies and the feeling of freedom they felt when they lost the weight (hence they still believed in her Brand Promise), they hated her Brand Solutions. After doing her Brand Audit, we came up with the idea of an app that her clients could use, with private tailored fitness programmes that they could take when they travelled and 1-2-1 digital classes that she could do with them over video conferencing. These new solutions eradicated any ways in which people could see her coming to them or them leaving and joining her classes, which increased the level of privacy they needed. After 12 months she found that her existing clients not only stayed but they introduced her to their friends, increasing her new business by 22 per cent. By asking the question 'what problem am I really solving and is it still needed?' she was able not only to save her business, but grow her brand and increase her market share.

## LET'S DO THE WORK

*What problem are you solving?*

_____

_____

_____

_____

_____

Is it still needed?

_____

_____

_____

_____

## Where's the evidence?

Once you have identified what problem your brand is solving, you then need to take a long look at yourself and ask the hard question: where's the evidence that I am the one to solve this problem?

I have found that too many people are seeking to promote their proposed differentiation with zero evidence to back up their claims. They spend a lot of time and money promoting their services and products but do not spend enough time and money collating evidence to prove they are the real deal. Considering we live in a time when people are becoming increasingly distrustful, the need for you to show proof is even greater. According to behiring.com, the average hiring manager receives 250 CVs per job post and spends just six seconds reviewing each CV before moving on to the next one. As such, your CV needs to be reflecting more than just work experience and skills; it needs to be evidence based. As an example, when writing down all the areas you worked on, always outline the results you created. It is the results of the work you did that provide the evidence that your great skills, hard work and brilliant mind can add real value to the company you are looking to work for. In today's competitive workforce, I would go further and state that you should create a CV website, one that adds even more evidence to the CV you have presented. As an example, if you say you succeeded on X project, bringing in X results, your CV website would then show the results in picture or video form, with testimonies from previous bosses and work colleagues.

If you are a freelancer or a budding entrepreneur promoting your brand, where is the evidence that you are any good at what you claim to be good at?

Do you have case studies on your website with the brief you were given, the process you used and the results you generated? This is a good way of getting potential clients to see how you work. It allows them to get a window into your critical thinking, creative approach, systematic processes and, most importantly, your ability to deliver on the brief at hand. It is not good enough to simply promote that you are good; you need the evidence to support this claim, especially as there are so many other people also competing for the same work and client briefs. If you already have case studies on your website, here are other ways to show evidence to substantiate your brilliance:

- *Written testimonies* – These are good because you can pull out bite-size information to use across your social media and print materials as well as the full testimony for your website.

- *Video testimonies* – It has been proven that video converts potential clients 80 per cent more than written words, so a video testimony gives you greater leverage to showcase how brilliant you are.

- *Behind-the-scenes videos* – Doing these allows prospects to see you in action. Without saying you are doing it, it shows you doing it and presents the evidence of the success of your work.

- *Industry reviews* – It might be useful to undertake industry reviews in the form of a blog post that gives your thoughts on how you would use your skills, contacts and abilities to do something better within your industry. I once used this technique when I heard that a particular brand had an advertising backlash from one of their promotional videos. I wrote an industry review, outlined how I would have done it differently and sent it to the company at hand. I posted it on LinkedIn and tagged them in the post. The result was a meeting with their head of marketing to discuss my thoughts and a three-month contract!

- *Lives* – Using Instagram, YouTube and Facebook Lives to answer potential client questions is another way of showcasing evidence that you are the expert in your field. It allows real-time engagement with prospects and gives them an insight into your methodologies and approach. It also connects them with the personality of your brand, which builds relationships and trust. I personally have found that my #AskKubi Lives have generated enormous amounts of new business leads. I have even had corporate clients say that watching my Lives helped solidify their decision to get me in!

When undertaking your Brand Audit you want to identify the path of least resistance; in other words, you want to find the methods that easily work for you. If you don't like being on video then use written testimonies and industry reviews. If, like me, you enjoy engagement, use Lives and Behind-the-Scenes videos. The key is to use methods that work for you and to use them to show that you are more than just your claims. You are the one to work with because you have evidence that you can deliver.

---

## LET'S DO THE WORK

### Where is the evidence?

Write down a list of things you could use to gather evidence for your personal brand. If you are already doing them, great. What else could you be doing? Or how much more consistent do you need to be with evidence gathering?

_____

_____

_____

_____

_____

_____

# Who is already doing it?

'Who is already doing it?' is a key question to ask. The reason is because success leaves a footprint and there are people out there who are already doing what you want to do and doing it well. It's your job to review: whose footprint can I study to help me grow my brand?

In the first instance you should identify who is already doing what you want to do; these people are your *aspirational* competitors. If you want to be the VP of Sales, who is already at that level and what have they done to achieve that level of success? What associations are they part of? Which members' clubs do they go to? What degrees did they study? Identify who is in the marketplace doing what you want to do. This will give you an idea of some of the things you can implement to make your brand a success. I remember when I was 18 years old, starting out in 1996, I wanted to be a cross between Oprah (as a media personality) and Jameel Spencer (one of the best marketing gurus in the world). I studied them both, analysing their career paths – and took two key things from them: 1. Oprah became rich by owning her own media content (today I own all of my own TV and radio shows) and; 2. Spencer associated himself with the most high-profile brands in his industry (so I went about my career seeking out Nike, L'Oréal, Aston Martin and the like). As you do your Brand Audit each year, ask yourself 'Who is already doing it at a higher level than me? What footprints have they left that I can learn from?' Even today, with 20-plus years in the game, I am still asking that question. It doesn't matter how 'big you get', there are always people doing it bigger than you, so look to them for inspiration.

The second part of the question is to ascertain who your *direct* competitors are; meaning who is already doing it at your level? Who are the people offering the same products or services as you at the same or similar price points, targeting the same or similar customer or client group? For me, when I started, Oprah and Spencer were not direct competitors; other graduates with big dreams and broke pockets were! So it was good for me to study my peers, to ascertain what routes they were taking and to keep an eye on them as they progressed. In a similar way to those who are more advanced in their brand building than I am, my direct competitors also leave a footprint of success. Their actions and results teach me something about what is happening in the market and how my brand can benefit or grow from this. Often my direct competitors' failures were just as good a teacher as their successes.

The third part of this question is who are my *non-direct* competitors? Companies or individuals whose products or services are not the same as yours, but they could satisfy the same consumer needs. Your non-direct competitors help you spot industry and market trends, and they are often perfect fits with which to establish potential partnerships and strategic alliances to connect better with your clients. As an example: you might be a freelance makeup artist; you are the business and your brand is you. As such, your aspirational competitor might be Pat McGrath (the highest paid makeup artist with a net worth of US $1 Billion), so you study McGrath's journey to success and identify key stepping stones that resonate and might work for you. Your direct competitors may be other makeup artists who, like you, have 10,000 Instagram followers, and your non-direct competitors may be makeup product manufacturers and brands. You should be looking to collaborate with these non-direct competitors to promote their products as an affiliate or ambassador, with the view of eventually creating your own makeup line with them. Identifying who is already doing it enables you to expand your knowledge, establish effective stepping stones and make relevant contacts.

Another reason to understand who is doing it is to be able to position yourself correctly in the marketplace. Often I work with startups who ask me the question 'how much should I charge?' They know they are just starting out and are unsure of how to position themselves. I tell them to study who is already doing it and how much they charge. Often, if you study your aspirational competitor and charge close to their price point, you will out-charge yourself. Not because you can't necessarily do the job at hand, but because you don't have the same level of evidence that you can deliver to that standard. When people won't pay you what you have priced yourself at it's not because they can't find the money, it's whether or not they think your brand can solve the problem to the same degree as the competitor you have positioned yourself next to.

For example, if I wanted to charge £40k for one of my masterclasses, it wouldn't happen, but if Oprah came in and asked for that, plenty of companies would find the money! It's not that my masterclasses are not as good as Oprah's (I know they are), it's that my brand doesn't have the Oprah appeal, the evidence of greatness that she has. Now I can be salty about it, or I can go about gathering the evidence to be able to charge Oprah prices . . . what do you think I will do?

Reviewing who's doing it allows you to see where you sit in the marketplace and identify how much perceived value you bring to the market. It tells you what you need to do to get your desired audience to believe your brand solves the problem to the value that you are charging. If you are struggling to get people to pay you it means that your brand is not being positioned in the way that communicates that your business can solve the problem. It doesn't necessarily mean that your audience does not have the money. It means they are not sure *you* can solve their pain-points and give them solutions to the value of what you have charged. So they don't have the money for *you*. It's important to charge your products and services at a price point that matches the degree of the solution you are giving your target audience. You can only do this when you analyse who else is doing it, how they are evidencing their success and expertise, who they are connected to and what level of knowledge they bring to solve the problem at hand. Once you identify these things, you can communicate *why You*, in a much better way – and trust me, when people believe you are the solution, they will find the money.

## LET'S DO THE WORK

*Who else is doing it?*

*List your aspiring competitors:* _____

*List your direct competitors:* _____

*List your non-direct competitors:* _____

# What is your PESTLE?

A PESTLE analysis is a look at the Political, Economical, Sociological, Technological, Legal, Environmental trends in your market. It enables you to identify what is going on in the marketplace, and how what is happening is impacting the success of your brand.

Recently I was delivering a Keynote at a conference in London and I asked the question 'who watches the news?' Only a few people put up their hands. Most of the people in the room told me they didn't watch it as they felt it was sad and depressing. But you should be watching the news (both business and trade news) to understand where you sit in an ecosystem that is rapidly changing. When I told them the news tells us what's going on, someone shouted 'sort of'. I smiled and said 'No, not sort of. You need to analyse it to identify the truth from the illusion. You need to analyse it, but you have to watch it to analyse it. You can't play ignorant when in business.' The key is to study and analyse what's happening to identify where the opportunities lie. What new problems are occurring as a result of technological changes, global warming and globalization? Be aware of what's happening in your sector, read your industry trade publications and the wider business news so that you can not only be aware of the shifting trends, but also understand these trends and position your business to provide solutions to new industry or consumer needs.

I tend to take half a day a week to review the news. I watch Bloomberg, CNN and CNBC. I read *Business Week, Harvard Business Review, Marketing Week* and *PR Week*. I indulge in *Business of Fashion, The Dots* and *Brand Republic*. I skim read the articles to keep abreast of what's happening so that I can add greater value to my clients. Reading around my sector gives me that competitive advantage. Remember, you have to be in it to see the opportunities. If you don't know what's happening in your sector, how can you know what problems you are solving?

As an example, in 2012 I reviewed what was happening economically in the global market and I started to feel that working in the UK seemed like working in a saturated market (a saturated market is one in which there are lots of competitors and not enough demand). For me, I began to see a shift; whereas in 1996, when I started, the term 'brand' was very new; by 2012 it appeared as if everyone and their mamma wanted to be a Brand Consultant! All going after the same or similar client group. At the same time I noticed a real shift in the so-called 'emerging markets' and really felt that with my skills and portfolio I could add extra value. I began to recognize that these markets would become a hungry market for someone like me (a hungry market is one in which there is lots of demand and few direct competitors). It was as a result of this PESTLE in 2012 that I took my career to South East Asia, and over the last six years it has led me to work in Malaysia, Indonesia, Dubai, Ghana, Jamaica, Barbados, Turkey, Morocco and Mauritius, working as a Brand Consultant. What's more, as I continue to study the global shifts and continue to undertake my PESTLE analysis, I am seeing that the Latin American market is opening up. With more multi-millionaires than Dubai, the Latin American market has a growing entrepreneurial hub of activities with companies needing my level of insights and expertise. The PESTLE analysis continues to provide me with these insights, which are continuing to open up new opportunities for my brand. If I had not done my PESTLE in 2012, this would not have happened for me.

Here are some examples of the how PESTLE trends are impacting high-profile brands:

**P** – Political – Facebook has had to review its data protection and data sharing because of political pressure from the UK and the United States.

**E** – Economical – Apple manufacturing costs will increase if China increases its labour costs, whilst simultaneously the possible decline in the middle class in Europe and the United States will impact the cost of its products' affordability.

**S** – Sociological – Starbucks has had to think about the 'green' and 'ethical chic' consumers who care about the use of plastic and waste when it comes to how they package their food and beverages.

**T** – Technological – Uber took advantage of the rise in app downloads and the ease of their use as part of the core offering of its brand and business.

**L** – Legal – Nike has to constantly consider the copyrights and patents of its products to avoid illegal counterfeits.

**E** – Environmental – Coca Cola has to make sure it operates in countries around the world where there is no shortage of water to be able to continue its global production of soft drinks.

When you study the PESTLE in your sector you can see both potential opportunities but also potential pitfalls. However, I see people stuck in their businesses and careers, not sure why their brand is not making the mark and wondering what is going on. The answer is they are not studying the market and as such they keep doing the same thing they have always done. (There is a saying: doing the same thing over and over again and expecting a different result is insanity – surely you see yourself as a sane person!)

The sad thing is that both small and large brands find themselves in this rut. When what they are doing stops working they start to think it's them that is not working. They begin to internalize it: 'maybe it's me that's no good', 'maybe my products are rubbish'; when in fact it's the market that has changed, consumer needs have shifted and new trends have impacted market demands and thus the way their brand is being responded to.

I was recently doing some work in the UK with a lovely lady who produced African-inspired headwraps that were not selling. I explained to her that her price was not the issue (consumer analysis showed that her consumers could afford her prices, which were in line with those of her direct competitors). Her designs were beautiful and clearly not the issue; for her, having not done a PESTLE was the issue. She didn't realize that actually what was happening was that she was in a heavily saturated market. She needed to change the distribution and marketing of her products from just the UK to Europe (particularly France, Italy and Germany) where there are many black women who want African-inspired headwraps but where there are fewer brands producing them. I also said she should review the Middle East where wearing headwraps is part of the cultural norm and where there are also growing African populations in places like Dubai.

It's important to know what's going on in the marketplace and to position yourself correctly. You need to stop promoting your brand and start researching your market. Stop posting cute pictures on Instagram and take time to really review what changes are happening in your sector. In doing so you will realize that you are in fact fabulous, it's just that you need to take your fabulousness somewhere else or promote it in a completely different way.

## LET'S DO THE WORK

*What's your PESTLE?*

_____

_____

_____

_____

_____

_____

_____

# What *really* is your brand perception?

So you have a vision for your brand. An idea of how everyone sees it. But the question is, do they really see it the way you want them to?

When a consumer sees or hears a brand name, and is aware of that brand, something unique and psychological happens. Whether the consumer is aware of it or not, an initial reaction that entails their thoughts and feelings towards the brand almost always takes place. This mental reflection is a result of what we marketers translate into brand perception. Brand perception is a special result of a consumer's experiences with a brand. It's highly pivotal to a marketing strategy as it's often what elevates a simple product or individual into a brand.

When undertaking your Brand Audit you need to make sure your vision of how you want to be perceived is lining up with what is really happening. Here are a few ways to do this:

- *Social listening* – Use social media to review what people are saying about your brand. Review their comments and analyse the words they use when they describe your brand. Now don't get me wrong, there are always going to be trolls and negative people on social media, but if

there is a pattern that is coming through, chances are there is a
perception in there. Whether good or bad, it's your job to be aware of it
and change it if you deem necessary.

- *Ask your stakeholders* – Those who have been working with you for a
while will be able to give you some solid feedback. Whether that's
long-term customers or colleagues who have been working with you
daily. Speak to them, asking such questions as: Why do you keep
buying X from my brand? What benefit does it give you? What five
words would you use to sum up my brand and working patterns? If
you could change anything about my personal brand and how I work
in this team, what do you think could be changed? How would you
describe my brand to your friends if I wasn't in the room? Don't be
afraid of the answers, knowing gives you an opportunity to correct it
or enhance it.

- *Net promoter score* – You can test how willing your customers, boss or
colleagues are to recommend you to others by the Net Promoter Score.
Ask them to score from 1–10 (1 being the least likely and 10 being the
most likely) if they would recommend you. The resulting percentage
can quickly illustrate how much brand loyalty you really have.

- *Ask new customers* – When someone is new to your brand they bring a
unique set of perspectives; maybe your brand promotions made an
impact, or they liked your sales offering, or your competitors had let
them down so now they are looking for something new. Ask them
questions like: What made you buy for the first time? Why have you
not tried out my freelance services before? What stood out for you in
my recent interview? What did you not like about the other
candidates? Use an appropriate time to get these answers, but ensure
you take the time to know.

- *Ask lost or non-customers* – You can learn a lot from those who choose not to work with you. If you have recently lost customers ask them: Why did you choose to leave? What could I do to get you back? Or if you didn't get that job, follow up with an email asking for feedback: How could I have improved my interview? What things did you like about the person you chose to hire? Those who don't work with you give you valuable insights into how you are currently being received and what you need to do to improve.

## How can you strengthen your strengths?

I have a saying, one that I have taken from someone along the way, but one that I live by: if you are going to do it, do it, and do it well!

If you produce digital content, you should be able to tell me something new that I can't easily Google – you need to be striving to be an expert, the master in your field. If you do clothing, make sure the quality is fantastic and the designs are both original but also wearable. If you do makeup, have a creative flair that sets you apart from everyone else. If you are a wellness instructor bring new techniques to the market that rubber-stamp you in the marketplace. If you are in banking security, be seen as the most qualified with original thought and critical thinking.

You have to identify your strengths and really, really play to them. You have to take your strengths and ramp them up! Show me something I haven't seen, tell me something I don't already know. But to do that, you need to study for success. You need to master your gifts. You need to represent excellence so that when you start to create and promote your brand, people will keep coming back because you are the best at what you do. Once you take the time to be excellent, you will find that your customers will be your ambassadors and your brand awareness will grow quickly.

Don't worry about your weaknesses. I have dyslexia, so when I write a book or a report, I hire a really good proofreader and PA to review my work. Having someone protect my weaknesses allows me to really enjoy and strengthen my strengths, to the point where I become the absolute best at what I say to the world I work in. You too need to take the time to build your expertise and strategically partner with others to help to further strengthen what you have to offer. I recently had a client who ran a very successful e-commerce business, which she started whilst at university with her co-founder. The two of them loved fashion; one wanted to be a stylist and designer, while the other was a business student who simply loved all things fashion. They realized that if they partnered their individual strengths they would counteract the other's weaknesses; the designer now had someone to focus on the business and the business person now had someone who understood fashion trends. As a result they have grown the company in the last five years to over £1,000,000 turnover and have nearly 1,000,000 followers on Instagram!

I recently sat down with Erinn Collier – CEO of technology firm Just3Things. During our discussion we talked about how so many women fail to master their strengths or even begin to acknowledge them. Here is what Erinn and I talked about:

**Erinn** *Once you start to see your strengths and weaknesses, you realize that all the other people who are in the meeting room with you have shortcomings as well. They are good at some things, but not so great at others! The first time I was asked to build a team that would be working for me, I started to approach it very much as if I had four hires or six hires. Instead of hiring people who are like a carbon copy of each other just to maximize productivity, I started to ask – how do I make sure that I am getting the most out of each of those people? When you start to think about hiring people or promoting people into roles in that way, it really helps you reflect on who you are. I am like this too; here is* *my strength, but here are my shortcomings and this is what I need in the team. So much of being a manager is being able to recognize both your superpower and those shortcomings, and then implementing that skill on finding the right people to work for you, and then building a unit amongst all of those people to help you all reach your objective.*

**Kubi** *When you are hiring, or trying to get hired, it is like trying to put a jigsaw puzzle together – how are you part of that jigsaw puzzle, and who else do you need in that jigsaw to make the puzzle complete?*

**Erinn** *A hundred per cent. Obviously our unconscious bias means we are drawn to like people who are similar to us. I love having a good chat with someone in an interview, but you really need to discipline yourself because I need to sit back in the meeting and not jump in right away with a suggestion because that person may be going through different thought processes than I have. The fact that they are thinking differently is really valuable to me, but that involves me letting go of ego and assumptions, which are typically driven by insecurities.*

**Kubi** *And then going into negotiations, promotions or even presenting the organization – all of them require you to recognize where you fit into the jigsaw puzzle and then telling them the reason why they should hire you.*

**Erinn** *Absolutely! Also, people may offer you jobs that might not be the best fit for you, and it's equally important to know when to just say thank you very much, but no thanks. I used to work at Salesforce and they're good at career progression, with a wide range of opportunities. However, you might come to the end of a year and decide that you want to do something different, and they might give you three options to explore, all of which will look good on paper, all of them will pay well, but you've got to know which one is really going to complement your skillset and play to your strengths, interests and passions. I am not going to go and work in a financial services sector, for example; I am* *not the best person for that, they don't really want to be talked to by a little petite American who doesn't have a CFA licence and that is ok, because I don't really want to be talking about financial products either, but you have got to be explicit with yourself and be honest.*

This requirement to be brutally honest is why the Brand Audit has been created. It is designed to ensure that the vision you have is actually being communicated and created. If it is not, you then have a chance to change it. As such, your Brand Audit is the most important aspect of building your personal brand. It should be done yearly, as it forces you to answer the following questions: What problem are you solving? Where is the evidence you are the right person to solve that problem? Who is already doing it? What is your PESTLE? What *really* is the perception of your brand? How can you strengthen your strengths and find your superpower?

## LET'S DO THE WORK

*How can you strengthen your strengths?*

_____

_____

_____

_____

_____

_____

_____

To help you further, I want to give you an insight into a conversation I had with an amazing friend of mine. Her name is Idara Otu and she is a Vice

President of Interest Rate Sales at Barclays PLC in New York. She is also a track and field Olympian, having run in the 2012 Olympics whilst working at a senior level in banking. Here's a little sneak peek at what she does when it comes to her Brand Audit. Hopefully it will inspire you to do yours. I started by asking Idara what her annual Brand Audit consists of and here is what she had to say:

**Idara** *There's a class I took in college for my master's degree called GEM, Global Entrepreneur Marketing, and in our term paper our project was 'Tell me where you're going to be in ten years? Create this fictitious "I'm going to be married, I'm going to work here, I'm going to live here, etc." and then tell me how you get there.'*

*That exercise was very tough because you really have to think about it, you can't just say I want to be a doctor because you have to factor in med school, then there's residency, there's fellowship, there's deciding when that will all happen. So I ask myself where do I want to be in ten years and is what am I doing now putting me on that path?*

*Because of my clarity of direction I've made some radical decisions in my career . . . For example I left Goldman Sachs after a year of being there, which was the best thing on the street when I first started, and I lost a lot of contacts as a result of me leaving early. Some of my biggest sponsors essentially deserted me because they were not happy with my choice. But it ended up being the best decision for me, if I hadn't left Goldman at that time I would never have become an Olympian. I took the unpopular route and I moved from New York to Houston to trade power and natural gas. At that point the goal was to trade; anything else that was not part of the goal or part of the plan was irrelevant, so staying in New York would have been great but moving to Houston was the fastest way to hit that goal.*

**Kubi** *Before we move on to the journey of becoming an Olympian, I just want to go back a little step. How did you get the courage to say 'I'm going to*

*go against the tide, I'm going to leave New York, I'm going to go to Houston?'*
*What did you have to do to just trust this was the right thing?*

**Idara**  *One thing that I also do is I bet on myself and I stubbornly stick to my*
*goal, so whatever that is, I stick to it.*

*When I was interning at Goldman it was for two summers; my second*
*summer there I knew I wanted to be a trader, that was the career goal at that*
*point.*

*I came out of school in 2009, we should have gotten our offers by October*
*2008, but that was when Lehman Brothers crashed [that was the start of the 2008*
*world financial crisis], so because of that everything got pushed back. That entire*
*summer I over-networked and I was expecting an offer in the trading side, which*
*was not where I had interned. I didn't get it and they told me to 'be grateful that*
*research wanted me', which is where I interned that summer. So I took the role,*
*but at the end of the day the focus was to be a trader and I was just following that*
*to the T. Whilst I was grateful, grateful I had the job especially at that time in the*
*market, a lot of my friends who had Lehman offers were unemployed. I took the*
*job but I was still networking, I still wanted to be a trader and based on everything*
*that I knew at the time, the longer it took me to get into trading the harder it*
*would be to realize that goal. Time was running out, so again I was networking,*
*I was doing my thing, and then I had the opportunity to leave Goldman, which*
*was number one back at the time and go to JP Morgan. Not that I was going to*
*an unknown entity . . . JP Morgan is a strong tower as well, but for trading and*
*what I was working at in Goldman, it would have been seen as a step down. But*
*at the end of the day, for me, I had the opportunity to trade, and that's what I*
*wanted to do. I would rather take a chance and do what I wanted to do, rather*
*than just be unhappy knowing that I wanted to be somewhere else.*

**Kubi**  *I get that.*

**Idara**  *All these people who were my sponsors weren't helping me, they didn't*
*come home with me at night, right, they didn't fund my life. As much as you*

*want to please the people who support you, they are not you. If I'm miserable going to work every day because of the environment and I don't want to do it, it doesn't make sense; I might as well go and at least get a chance at the one thing I at least know for sure what I want to do. So I had to bet on me.*

**Kubi** *I totally understand that. So how did that move help you to become an Olympian and how do you think that has helped shape your brand?*

**Idara** *Oh, in so many different ways! I raised my hand when an opportunity came up in Houston and whilst I thought it through, I didn't really think it through. I didn't have any friends down there, I didn't have family down there, I was literally 'chasing it by any means necessary'.*

*So now that I'm in Houston things are good; I'm in the job that I wanted, life's a little bit slower, life is good, I have my car, my place, I'm adulting at this point. But about six months into it, I realized that I should have thought it through before I got down there. Although I am working I'm like 'well, work isn't really my identity, right?' It's something I do and I do it well, but then I realized I don't have any friends, and I don't know anybody. So that's when I guess I'm 'putting the mirror up' and now that I've actually slowed down, I've met this part of the goal, now I'm assessing where I am in this goal. Up until this point my goal was to be a trader, but now that I am a trader, now what?*

*So I have to set a new goal: either a momentary goal, a personal goal or a life goal. I decided to shift my focus to life, because I can't just work, money's not everything for me. When I started taking inventory, I asked myself 'who are my closest friends?' and all my closest friends were generally people I was on teams with when I was doing track and field back in college. My best friend from college is a track girl, most of my closest friends from college are people who are athletes or were on track with me. One of my old training partners from college was based in Houston, and I knew she was in a training group, so I reached out to her and I joined her training group. Literally my main goal was just to make friends. My goal wasn't to be an Olympian; my goal was to make friends. As* basic as it sounds, that's it; the goal to be in the Olympics was gone, that was a childhood dream, 'you just don't do that anymore' is what I told myself. So my focus was, I want to have friends to go out with on Friday night.

I was probably training with the group for a month before there's a little bit of drama. We trained in Rice University in Houston. There were two groups that trained there: Camp A, which was my first camp, and then Camp B. Camp B was run by a physiotherapist. I was starting to have knee issues and so everyone said to go to Camp B, and it was definitely the higher calibre group. Higher calibre athletes . . . like they were serious, they were former Olympians and brilliant. But that wasn't my focus so I was cool with Camp A. I just wanted to not have pain in my knee, so I went over for treatment and Camp B essentially recruited me. The founder was telling me 'you know you have a great frame to be a great 400m runner, you're really weak right now, you should come train with my girls' . . . I told him I would think about it because the ones that I started training with were now becoming my friends.

Even though I told him I would think about it, he actually went behind my back and told my coach in Camp A that I was changing training groups. So then my coach essentially kicked me off his group, he was like 'oh yeah, I heard, see yah!' I didn't want to give it up, because I was just trying to make friends and he essentially cut off the five friends I was starting to make, to put me in this other group, which I never said I wanted to be in. I didn't want the drama and I almost didn't train at all, I was just like 'uhhh, this sucks, like this is not what I want'.

But then for whatever reason I started training with Camp B and there were two girls in my group, one from Jamaica and one from St Vincent. Their goal was the Olympics, and they were training hard for that. My coach pushed me, and I'll give him a lot of credit because he had seen it in me even though at that time I didn't see it at all, it wasn't even on my radar. So he said, 'you can be up there too' but I was really far behind, but being able to be around their company inspired me. I'm not a person who is mediocre anyway, so even though that wasn't my

*goal, if I'm in an arena where everyone else is delivering excellence or everyone is
really competing, I rise to the occasion. I was in the environment to thrive and
because those girls were chasing something, my competitor juices got going and I
was like 'ok, me too, I'm going to chase it'.*

*I was challenged every day, and that's how that happened.*

**Kubi** *How did you have the discipline? What was required to have the
discipline to juggle the two? To be in the career you wanted and obviously at
budding stage as a trader, but also to be training to be an Olympian?*

**Idara** *You know that's a very good question! It's funny because I haven't really
thought about it until now . . .*

*My 9am–5pm, or like 7am–5pm, was focused on work, and then I would
compartmentalize that away. Maybe if I took an L [a low] during the day, in
the evening when I was training I could get a W [a win] at night. So I think
that really helped me to remain balanced. That is to say, I didn't put my entire
identity in being a trader and my entire identity wasn't in being a runner, so
the fact that I had both things working at the same time, it forced me just to
really be disciplined all around.*

**Kubi** *What techniques do you think you derived from training at that level?
What techniques have you pulled from that process and used in your ability to
navigate business and your career?*

**Idara** *One major thing is visualization. I've always been a good goal setter
but being able to visualize the win is everything.*

*There's a level of discipline and even research that's required to deliver at
that level. When I went to the Olympics I was 25 years old. I was three years
out of school and for those three years I didn't do any training. I was just like
a regular person, I would do three miles every day here and there but nothing
much more than that. The girls I was competing against were girls who were
either still in college, really young and had tons of energy, or coming out of*

college programmes. So while I'm older I probably had a little bit more strength but I was behind the 8 ball completely. I literally trained for the Olympics in nine months and made a team.

**Kubi** *Wow!*

**Idara** *So in order for me to do that, I recognized very early that talent alone wasn't going to get me there, so I guess to answer the first part of your question: self-awareness is key and being able to sense the competition. I knew that those girls were younger; they can recover a lot quicker, they don't have full-time stressful jobs that they are going to, they aren't adulting. I owned a place at that time, so I had to make sure that bills were paid, I had a new car and things like that, so I had a lot of outside stress that had nothing to do with running. Realizing this I made sure that if someone who was younger than me had a little bit more physical talent than me, they would not have more mental talent. What that meant was I got really anal and very military about my eating. I became literally like a mini scientist for my body, so I knew what supplements I needed, I knew when I needed to go to sleep, I knew where I was sufficient, I even got blood work done. Basically, I did everything I needed to do to maximize my chances, because I was very aware of the competition.*

*What I did then, I do now: it's the same way that I approach networking, attending events, applying for a promotion, mentoring kids ... it's an overall recipe that I have concocted in my mind to enable my personal brand to play at the highest level.*

*The other thing that track does, it gives you humanity. Staying in a business like finance for so long, it's so easy to be jaded by 'oh you know who has these Ferragamo shoes' or 'I have a Gucci or Hermès tie' or 'we're eating at Cipriani' or you're going to certain schools or you're wearing this, you're driving that, you're living here. Whereas when you do something like track that is so physical in nature, and you see people who don't have designer clothes or an education, and they're crushing you on the track like none of that works, then the fact I went to Stanford means nothing on the track!*

*People from community colleges, people from the village that don't even have real shoes are out there beating me. Nobody knew what I did, nobody cared that I went to Stanford. It did not matter. Nobody cared about what kind of car I was driving, it was 'are you gonna get this time?' or 'are you gonna get these reps?' and 'are you gonna survive this workout?' So that level of humility, it's a constant reminder that it's not just money, it's not just titles, it's not just – all those different things. Life is so many different things, and people can be successful in many areas. What success means to you may not be what success means to me. Success to a housewife might just be healthy kids that are respectful, you know? Whereas to someone else it might be closing up the big deal.*

**Kubi** *So true! Track gave you visualization, self-awareness; competitor awareness and humility . . . love it.*

*Let's talk about that some more. When you're doing your audit and you're looking at how you're navigating your career at the top level, how are you navigating competition? How are you navigating the politics? What are the tips you could give to people on how you do that?*

**Idara** *If I'm thinking of a corporate situation I am very keen on what motivates everyone around me. Here's an example. There was a guy at Goldman Sachs who asked the question 'do you live to work, or do you work to live?' He's like, you don't have to answer, you don't have to tell me, but once you can answer that for yourself and everybody around you, that is the key to success and the key to surviving this place, this place being Goldman. His advice was so true because when you're a bright-eyed, bushy-tailed first year coming into a place, a machine, like Goldman Sachs, and you have people who are working constantly, who are literally always there, you can classify that person as someone who works to live vs who lives to work. Once you start to create a narrative you understand people* better. There are some people who literally live to work, work is their identity, work is what makes them feel good, that's who they are; so if I know that, that is who you are. I can't treat you as someone who works to live. Let's say I'm a works to live person, and you are lives to work, we're never really going to see eye to eye. But now that I have that level of understanding, I don't think this person is just trying to show me up; this is just where that person gets their identity from, and I get mine from so many other different things. So now instead of me being resentful towards this person, now I just know how to interact and how to deal with them.

**Kubi** *Mmmmm.*

**Idara** *Right? So now you know. With this knowledge it helps me to understand and I won't be irritated. Not that I'm saying I like what they do, or don't do, it just changes the narrative. Now it's not really about me … it's about them. So it's taking that focus away from me and putting it on other people.*

*You spend so much time with these people at work and it helps to break barriers by understanding them better. Especially for someone like me who's always the 'token' in either gender or in race, in any room or any arena.*

*If I tied it back to track you do the same thing, especially if you're in a relay. In a relay you're trying to find the area when you can cut in front of people so you can get ahead. To do that you have to realize that they're not one size fits all. I was a speedrunner. Now I'm next to a power or 400 runner. If I tried to follow their path I'm always going to lose so I have to study them, but also know my strength.*

*It's important to study people, study the competition and then speak to someone's humanity. Watch people and assess how it is that we can make a better connection.*

**Kubi** *This is what your brand is about – mastering the connection, that's what I'm hearing, right? Whether that be on track and field. Whether that be in the corporate boardroom, whether that be in the charity, you really are brilliant at mastering the connection, that's powerful!*

**Idara** *Thank you!*

*I would also say know your 'why'. Knowing why you want to do something, why, you want to take certain steps, is essential. If you don't know your 'why', someone else will set it for you.*

*Early in my career, even when I was going against the tide, people tried to tell me 'you can be Edith Cooper, you can be MD at Goldman'. But that wasn't for me; I knew I didn't want to do that. It all ties back into the Brand Audit: if you know why you're doing something or why you want something it'll help streamline the right questions to ask yourself, and where to make the decision to get where you want to go. Because I knew what was driving me, I knew it was always my path . . . it was always my mistake to make, but it was always my success to have, and it's never anybody else's.*

# 4

# Branding Is Like Dating

Decision. Vision. **CLARITY**. Strategy. Tactics. Metrics. Ownership. Be Unapologetic

I often refer to branding like dating. The same way that you will find a life partner is the same way you will find a customer for life. How so? You start by aligning your Brand Values. Whatever you value is what your customers or clients should value. The values that underpin why you do what you do are the same values that your customers and clients should care about. For this reason I don't like to refer to them as customers or clients; instead I like to call them Your Tribe.

Your Tribe, also known as your target market, includes your customers, clients, hiring companies, employees, suppliers, partners, sponsors and other members of your stakeholder group. They are the ones who care about what you care about. They can be identified as those who care enough about your 'why' to buy into your 'what'. When your 'why' is communicated and your values are promoted, your brand becomes a magnet to the Tribe that connects with that 'why' the most. Your Tribe comes together under one common goal, to be part of your 'why'. They support your mission, they understand your vision and they harness your brand's success. As a Tribe they are rooting for you and you are serving them. It's a collective approach of like-minded people working together in line with one common goal: your personal brand success.

As identified in Chapter 2, your brand is an *emotional connection* with your target audience. All of your brand assets (Brand Logo, Brand Strapline, Brand Colours, Brand Promise, Brand Mission, Brand Vision and Brand Signature) should be used to connect your brand to the heart-space of your audience. The principle that *people buy from their hearts and not their heads* is important to remember, because people buy from a place of emotion.

Think of it like this: if you purchased using your head would you really have as many shoes as you do? The answer is probably no. We all have more than enough stuff. We buy not because we want it, but because we feel *we need it* and *we desire it*. We buy because the product or service, app or experience makes us feel connected and a part of something bigger than ourselves. For some, owning a luxury car is more about the elite group it makes them feel a part of than the car itself. For others, the technology in their bag is more about being part of a cool community than it is about the product features.

The same principle applies to personal brands: people buy people! Of course we care about the technical abilities of a person, but your abilities in and of themselves are not enough; it's the emotional connection that gets someone to say yes to you. Your skills, capabilities and abilities, your product functions and service attributes may change over time, but the desire and emotional connection to you, as a brand, should always be there.

As an example, when Steve Jobs co-founded Apple, one of his core values was innovation and changing the status quo. His 'why' was about disrupting the technology industry and those who cared for that 'why' became the Apple tribe. They got excited about the innovative ways that Apple used technology to create its products. They became exhilarated about the advertising campaigns that told them to 'Think Different'. They were eager to visit the new Apple stores, with their open-plan areas allowing them to touch and explore new products without restrictions. Steve Jobs' 'why' resonated with their 'why'. They, like him, saw themselves as disruptors, innovators and game changers and, as such, this connection is what drew them to the products, and once the products delivered excellence, they were hooked.

The same should apply to you.

Whether Your Tribe is the companies to hire you, clients to book you or customers to purchase from you, when Your Tribe engages with you, your brand should conjure up an emotive response that leads them to say yes. But far too often people find themselves in the wrong job, or not being able to attract leads, because they are solely focused on promoting their products or promoting their skills. They put all their energy into what they do, without first identifying *why* they do it. Why are you in the job you're in? Yes, I know you need to pay the bills, but you can pay the bills working for a number of different companies, so why are you in that company, doing that job? Once you identify why you do what you do, your 'why' attracts people to your 'what'. Not the other way around.

Your 'why' is therefore the utmost important part of building an effective brand. Without knowing your 'why', you are left with nothing more than your capabilities and skills, but they are simply not enough. There are too many people that share the same abilities and skills as you, so it's the who you are, not the what you are, that matters the most.

Just like dating, the more you love the real you, the more you attract someone who will love the real you too. But if you repel you, you will never attract the right person. To know and attract the right partner, you first need to know and love yourself. This is exactly the same with attracting Your Tribe.

# Personal brand journey

An effective personal brand is an authentic expression of the individual.

I often see clients trying to cover up who they are, and they have done this cover-up job for so long that they get lost in the manufactured brand they have created. But to really connect with Your Tribe, you first need to start with a true connection to yourself. It is too tiring to try to keep up the facade, and after a while Your Tribe will sift out the truth from the lie. It is best to show up as you, and not someone you think the world wants you to be!

There are signs throughout our lives that indicate what our personal brand really is; key moments that help us to see our true authentic selves. When we analyse the journey to date we can see patterns that emerge that show us, in the plain light of day, who we really are. It is then our job to learn how to package and sell this authenticity, to use our unique story to connect with our tribe, and get them to buy into or buy from us. When we are clear on who we are, we can start to be intentional on how we want to show up, which in turn enables us to attract the right tribe to us. Not everyone is going to connect with you, because not everyone is meant to. Your job is not to be liked by all, but to serve the ones that need your brand the most. The idea that you can 'fake it 'til you make it' is just as ridiculous as it is damaging. You can't fake it, because people can see a fake a mile off, and if you keep trying to make it with a fake brand, you will end up frustrated and burnt out.

The documentary *Whitney* (2018) chronicles the amazingly talented, but also very tragic life of the late great pop star Whitney Houston. In this documentary you see the tale of a personal brand curated from a place of inauthenticity. In the 1980s, Whitney Houston's brand was marketed as a 'church going, Sunday school singer, with a shy and very sweet persona, who came from a middle-class neighbourhood'. However, according to reports that have emerged since her death, and as detailed in the documentary, Whitney did take drugs, she understood and had experience of the inner-city ghettos, and loved RnB music more than pop. It has been said that it was this complete inauthenticity that led to such inner turmoil, and that serves as a painful reminder of the price that can be paid for not showing up as the real 'you'.

When I work with my clients I encourage them to take the time to own who they are and to fall in love with their truth. Before I even think about showing them how to market their brand, I spend lots of time getting them to own their brand's authenticity. But many are unsure of what that brand is or even where to start. One way to help reconnect is to undertake a Personal Brand Journey. As shown in the diagram below, the Personal Brand Journey is designed to get you to walk down memory lane. To explore who you have been, to see your patterns and uncover your truths.

The Personal Brand Journey has been created as a table, divided into columns.

The 'Areas of Interest' column includes key parts of your life:

1   *Hobbies and interests* – the things that you enjoyed doing and partaking in during your life or still enjoy to this date.

2   *Fun moments* – experiences that brought immense happiness to you.

3   *Down moments* – experiences that were particularly painful.

4   *Defining moments* – impactful events that helped to shape who you have become.

5   *Lessons learnt* – key lessons that you have learnt from the fun, down and defining moments.

6   *Emerged beliefs* – belief systems that you have as a result of the activities, moments and experiences in your life. Note our emerged beliefs might also have come from family, religious groups or our wider culture.

7   *Friendship values* – the values you saw in your friends and family that you really liked, and drew you close to them.

The 'Age' column is divided into age groups; how old you are will determine where on the table you stop. But I would recommend that you return to this exercise every decade of your life to summarize the journey you are on. Doing this will keep you in tune with your true self and help shape how you want to show up in the world.

Once you have completed the table it is important to take the time to actually analyse what's going on in your life. Identifying the patterns helps you to identify where you can take your brand next. As an example, when I turned 40 I started to wonder where I wanted to take my personal brand, and what I wanted the next phase of my career to look like. I knew I wanted to focus more on brand training and speaking, but I wasn't 100 per cent sure what I wanted my speciality within the Brand Marketing industry to be. So I did the Personal Brand Journey for myself and what I discovered gave me permission to do what I did next. Here is mine. I hope it will help encourage you to do your own:

| Areas of interest | Under 10 years old | 11–18 years old | 19–29 years old | 30–39 years old | 40–50 years old | 51–60 years old | 61 years + |
|---|---|---|---|---|---|---|---|
| Hobbies & Interests | Dancing – ballet, tap and jazz. Writing my journal. | Going to performing arts school. Reading and English Literature. | Going clubbing, concerts and cultural events. | Attending fashion shows, live music and poetry clubs. | | | |
| Fun Moments | Dance competitions. | Being on stage. Holidays with my family. | Living in New York City working in brand marketing. Having my own TV show. | Getting married in Barbados. Travelling for work. Holidays with my husband and daughter. Travelling and training for work. | | | |
| Down Moments | Biological father not being around. | Being told 'black girls can't dance in the corps de ballet'. | Struggling to pay my mortgage as a freelancer. | Not being 'on stage' enough. Feeling like I can't cope with the juggle of family and career. | | | |

| Defining Moments | Seeing 'Alvin Ailey' Ballet Company performing. | Injuring my knee and not being able to dance again. | Being in NYC during '9/11' and seeing the first tower hit. | Becoming a mother and wife. | | | |
|---|---|---|---|---|---|---|---|
| Lessons Learnt | Hard work pays off. | You have to be prepared to sacrifice something to get what you want. | You need to stay the course. Keep focused and keep at it, despite the hard times. | You need a support system. | | | |
| Emerging Beliefs | If they can do it, I can too! | I will show you – I do belong. | Life will try to knock you, your job is to get back up. | Happiness is your birthright. What you think you are, you are. | | | |
| Friendship Values | (can't remember!) | Creativity, fun, compassion. | Adventurous, risk takers, positivity. | Reciprocation, happiness, dependability, adventure, fun, positivity and kindness. | | | |

When I began to analyse my own Personal Brand Journey I recognized things about myself that I had ignored as I got older and needed to bring back for the next phase of my career:

1   *I needed to perform* – Being on stage wasn't just something that I needed as a child, it was something I needed as an adult too. Doing my Personal Brand Journey I realized that performance for me is more than just a hobby or interest, it's part of the core makeup of my being. Performing feeds my soul. I no longer care for dancing on stage, Lord knows I am too old to try to do ballet pirouettes in front of anyone! But my ability to perform makes teaching brand marketing and speaking on stage really easy. More importantly it brings me immense joy, more than any other area of my work. At the time of filling out my

Personal Brand Journey, speaking was about 20 per cent of my career. I decided that needed to change.

2   *I missed writing* – I started keeping a journal from the age of about 6 or 7 years old. I think as soon as I could write, I wrote! Literally every single day I put my imagination down on paper. I loved documenting the adventures of my day and I remember getting lost in books as a pre-teen and teenager. I especially loved fictions and autobiographies. At around the age of ten I was given *The Diary of Anne Frank* (the writings from the Dutch language diary kept by a young girl called Anne Frank, while she was in hiding for two years with her family during the Nazi occupation of the Netherlands). I loved this book as I could get lost in her stories and tales. Her imagination captivated me. By the time I was in my 20s, I still wrote in my diary but I also loved attending live poetry slams. Whilst living in New York City I would spend nearly every weekend at one poetry event or another; there was something about the wordsmith and intellectual banter that made so much sense to me. In remembering this I gave myself permission to write this book. I wasn't a first-time writer, I had actually been writing all my life! Even though I have dyslexia, writing has always been one of my first loves. So despite the fear, I decided to pick up my pen again.

3   *I had turned my pain into my mission* – As an 8-year-old I was told that whilst I could attend the Royal Academy of Arts, the ballet school I had auditioned to get into, I, as a black ballet dancer, was not allowed to audition for the main company. It was 1986 and I remember feeling distraught. All of a sudden I knew exactly what it felt like to not belong. I have since spent my entire adult life championing for the unseen to be seen. Whether that be women in the workplace, or dark-skinned models on the runway, I have been fighting for the little dancer in me – I turned into a warrior on her behalf. This realization, having looked at my patterns, made me decide that I was going to be intentional and

unapologetic about this mission. There are so many people in this world who have been told they are not the right fit. *I AM MY BRAND* is about giving them, and me, the tools to step into our light. *We all deserve to be seen* is my new mantra. As such, this has become my 'why'.

By undertaking the Personal Brand Journey, you get to see yourself. When you pull out the patterns of your life you begin to see the talents, interests and gifts you have hidden from the world. Normally your pain and personal struggles help to uncover your true 'why' and you can start to see who Your Tribe are. You can identify where you have historically fitted in, the people that you have connected with and the ones that have connected with you. It's a powerful tool that, when you take the time to do it, helps reveal the authentic version of you.

## LET'S DO THE WORK

Fill in the Personal Brand Journey for yourself. Go to SheBuildsBrands.com for a larger version of this chart.

| Areas of Interest | Under 10 years old | 11–18 years old | 19–29 years old | 30–39 years old | 40–50 years old | 51–60 years old | 61 years + |
|---|---|---|---|---|---|---|---|
| Hobbies & Interests | | | | | | | |
| Fun Moments | | | | | | | |
| Down Moments | | | | | | | |
| Defining Moments | | | | | | | |
| Key Lessons | | | | | | | |
| Emerged Beliefs | | | | | | | |
| Friendship Values | | | | | | | |

Once you uncover your truth, then you need the courage to market it!

# VIA Chart

Author and businesswoman Radha Agrawal wrote an amazing book called *Belong*, in which she describes the importance of your VIA Chart. The 'V' is your Values, 'I' is your Interests and 'A' is your Abilities. In her book she talks about the importance of creating a VIA Chart to help you establish who you are and how you fit into the world. The Values are key to identifying your principles: what standards of behaviour or judgement do you deem as important in your life? The Interests are put down to see what you like doing: what is fun for you? The Abilities are there to establish what you are capable of: what are your natural gifts and your learned skills?

To create a VIA Chart you need to draw three big circles for each element – the Values, the Interests and the Abilities – allowing the circles to overlap in the middle. Then brainstorm what goes into each area. By doing this exercise you begin to see what exactly is your makeup and also what overlaps for you. Unlike the Personal Brand Journey, this exercise takes you from who you are, to how you begin to package your authentic self. If you have never done something like this before it can be quite a daunting task because it forces you to really analyse you.

Let's do it together.

## Values

Think about your values as the things that define why you behave the way you do. For example, if you are the sort of person that worked extremely hard in university and then decided to go and do a Masters degree, the chances are you value formal education. If you are the sort of person who gets mad when your colleagues leave work dead on time, rather than staying to finish the task at hand, maybe you value commitment. Often when we are struggling to identify our own personal values we can look to what makes us upset or frustrated;

usually it's because we feel a core value is being violated. Whatever you despise, try to identify where the value might be in that feeling.

Another way to establish what your values are is to look at values in general, and see if any resonate with you. Here are some generic examples to help you along the way.

| | |
|---|---|
| Dependability | Motivation |
| Reliability | Positivity |
| Loyalty | Optimism |
| Commitment | Passion |
| Open-mindedness | Respect |
| Consistency | Fitness |
| Honesty | Courage |
| Efficiency | Education |
| Innovation | Perseverance |
| Creativity | Patriotism |
| Good humour | Service to others |
| Compassion | Environmentalism |
| Spirit of adventure | |

Do any of the above values resonate with you? If so, highlight them from the list above. We will put them into the VIA Chart in a bit.

Once you have established your Values, move on to your Interests.

## Interests

What do you enjoy doing? If you are unsure of what you're interested in, maybe you have got into a rut of just going to work and coming back home with no social activities. If so, go back to your Personal Brand Journey to review what activities you enjoyed as a youngster and maybe revisit some of them again. Or maybe there are clues in the programmes you watch on TV – if you constantly watch travel programmes maybe you secretly want to travel more. To help you, here is a list of Interests with examples of what they might say about your personal brand:

1  *Individual sports* (e.g. marathon running or going to the gym) – You're fit, self-motivated, enjoy pushing yourself and relish the challenge.

2  *Team sports* (e.g. netball or football) – You excel at teamwork, work well with others, like having fun and have leadership skills.

3  *Extreme sports* (e.g. motocross or skiing) – You are a risk taker, open to new experiences, adventurous, emotionally stable and extremely conscientious.

4  *Tech hobbies* (e.g. computing and gaming) – You are tech savvy, possibly introverted, good at navigating, can tune out the noise, enjoy competing against yourself.

5  *Puzzles* (e.g. crosswords) – You're an analytical thinker with problem-solving skills.

6  *Board games* (e.g. chess or Monopoly) – You're an intelligent strategist, practical and logical.

7  *Social hobbies* (e.g. mentoring or volunteering) – You're a great communicator, connect well with people and care about others.

8  *Creative arts* (e.g. singing, vlogging, performing) – You are extremely creative, an extrovert, a good communicator, bold, a risk taker and enjoy breaking the rules.

9  *Literary & Arts* (e.g. painting, blogging, writing) – You are expressive, lead with your heart, curious and work well independently.

10  *International explorations* (e.g. travelling or learning new languages) – You are adventurous and like pushing yourself with new challenges and exciting things.

Do any of these sound like you? If so, highlight them from the list above. We will put them in the VIA Chart in a bit.

# Abilities

Finally, you will need to complete the Abilities circle. What are you naturally good at? What skills have you acquired over the years? What capabilities do people always commend you on? Sometimes it is difficult to see your own natural abilities, so here is a list to get you started. Go through the list and highlight the words that seem natural and easily describe a trait you have.

| | |
|---|---|
| Athletic | Open-minded |
| Artistic | Investigative |
| Creative | Reasonable |
| Friendly | Resourceful |
| Funny | Positive |
| Organized | Confident |
| Leadership | Genuine |
| Logical persistence/diligence | Innovative/technological |
| Analytical | Motivating/motivated |
| Hard working | Disciplined |
| Problem solving | Intellectual |
| Ethical | Forgiving |
| Listening, honest/trustworthy | Visionary |
| Detail oriented/attentive | Compassionate |
| Computer savvy | Writing |
| Spontaneous | Inspiring/empathetic |
| Studious | Musical |
| Imaginative | Communicating ideas/concepts |

Now that you have highlighted your Values, Interests and Abilities, put them into the VIA Chart below.

If you find an overlap of words, those words should go into the centre parts of the circle. For example, if there are words in your Values that are the same as your Interests those words should go in the inner circle between Values and Interests. The same applies with words in your Values and Abilities; the same or similar words should go in the inner circle between Values and Abilities. Equally this applics to Abilities and Interests; where words are the same or similar, put them in the inner circle. The words in the inner circles are key to discovering the makeup of your personal brand.

Here is an example of mine to help you on the way:

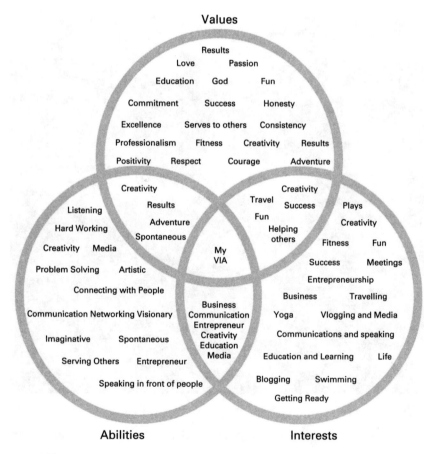

FIGURE 4.1 *Example VIA Chart.*

## LET'S DO THE WORK

*Complete your VIA Chart.*

Write down what you Value, what you are Interested in and what are your Abilities.

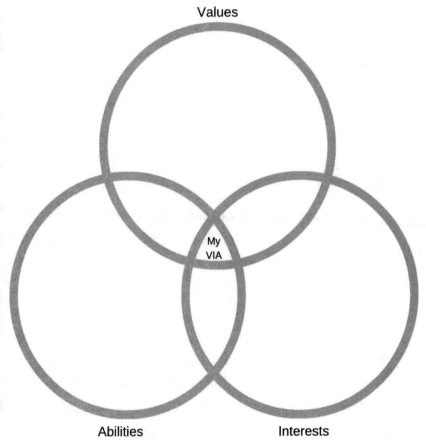

FIGURE 4.2 *My VIA Chart.*

# Who's Your Tribe?

When thinking about Your Tribe you need to consider the entire ecosystem of people who engage with your personal brand. If you are running a business these could be customers, clients, suppliers, prospects and media (such as journalists, influencers, bloggers, editors). It could also include potential partners and collaborators, suppliers, plus what I like to call the 'money people' (advertisers, sponsors, funders, investors). It also includes your staff (both freelancers and core teams) as well as your advisers (mentors, coaches and consultants). All of these people make up the ecosystem of Your Tribe.

A coaching business, for example, might have the following in their tribe: clients, potential clients, freelance staff, collaborators, funders, influencers and journalists.

If you work for someone and are building your career, your brand stakeholder groups could include the existing company you are working for, plus future hiring companies, your colleagues in the department you work in, but also colleagues from across the organization at large. The owner of the business, the organization's customers, creditors, shareholders, sponsors and directors. It might also include government (and its agencies), trade unions and the community from which the company you work for draws its resources.

As an example, a Partnerships Director for a bank might have the following in their tribe: their existing company, prospective hiring companies/hiring managers, colleagues in the Partnership & Business Development department, co-workers from other departments such as Marketing & Sales, plus potential partners, funders and government agencies that they are trying to do business with on behalf of the bank they work at.

The key is to be clear on who sits within the ecosystem of Your Tribe. Who does your personal brand engage with as part of the day-to-day running of your career/business?

## LET'S DO THE WORK

*Who's in the ecosystem of Your Tribe?*

Write down as many areas that you can think of:

_____

_____

_____

_____

_____

_____

_____

_____

_____

_____

_____

_____

_____

# Solving problems

When developing and marketing your personal brand you need to think about how your brand connects with each facet of Your Tribe. To do this you need to be clear on each person's 'pain-points' (their greatest pains or problems) within

Your Tribe, asking yourself the question: 'What problem is my personal brand solving for this person or stakeholder group?' If you are trying to engage potential partners, what problem is your personal brand solving for them? Is your personal brand helping them to reach their own commercial targets or is your personal brand a bridge for them to connect with new audiences? Why should these partners work with you?

Unlike the Brand Promise, which is designed for *all* stakeholders acting as the overarching *feeling* that's connected them to your brand, the Brand Solution is specific to each of your stakeholder groups. For example, the problem your brand is solving for your clients might be different from the problem you are solving for your staff. The problem you are solving for your boss might be different from the problem you are solving for your co-workers. With each of your brand stakeholders you need to break down their pain-points, and how your brand acts as a solution to their pains. To achieve this you should seek to understand what their greatest pain is, and how your brand is helping to alleviate that pain, i.e. what problem is the brand solving for them? To get Your Tribe to say 'yes' to your brand, you need to be able to communicate the problems you are solving for them.

As an explanation, I once had a junior member of my staff prepare a draft press release on behalf of my brand. Before she started, I asked her to outline what problem she felt this press release was going to solve for the business media she was hoping to get coverage from. She seem perplexed by this question, so I asked it another way: How was me coming on their show going to help alleviate their 'pain'? Again she didn't seem to understand the question.

What my colleague didn't recognize was that all stakeholders have a pain-point. For business journalists, their pain-point is failing to hit their viewing targets. Like all media, they have a number of viewers that they want engaged with their shows. Therefore the press release she was preparing needed to outline how having me on their show was going to assist their need for getting more people to watch the show. Now, we can't possibly put on the press release that we will bring in a specific number of eyeballs to watch the show, but what we can do is write a release that is topical and newsworthy. One that will add value to the content of their show. By adding value to the content, we in turn help them to attract or sustain their existing audience base, and thus increase or sustain their viewing figures. The opposite of this would be to write a press release that merely talks about how good our product or service is, without showing how that product or service is of relevance to the show at hand. Or, worse still, to write a press release that talks about the launch of our product or service without outlining how that launch is newsworthy or topical and of relevance to the show's viewers.

I have seen many clients get this wrong. Whether they are trying to engage funders or press, influencers or hiring companies, they don't take the time to ascertain how what they do is going to solve a problem for the stakeholder at hand. How are they part of the jigsaw? To do this, you need to be clear on each one of your stakeholders' pain-points. You can identify these pain-points by filling out a Stakeholder Grid, which outlines who the stakeholder is, what their pain-points are and how your brand is the solution to their pain. To illustrate this further, I will use as an example a client that I worked with who is the owner of a digital marketing agency. Below is a copy of their Stakeholder Grid with all names removed for client confidentiality:

| Stakeholder | Their pain-point | Your solutions |
|---|---|---|
| Potential clients | They don't have time to manage their own digital marketing campaigns. | The agency has experienced digital executives who can run innovative campaigns to client briefs and budgets. |
| Existing clients | They want ideas for new ways to better run their existing digital campaigns that drive higher profits for their business. | The agency has award-winning digital experts with innovative ideas for business growth, and a proven track record of doing this for other clients. |

*(Continued)*

*(Continued)*

| Stakeholder | Their pain-point | Your solutions |
|---|---|---|
| Marketing trade press | They need new story ideas for digital trends globally. | The agency senior managers travel internationally to digital conferences to gain up-to-date trade information that can be shared via tips and expert advice in the publications. |
| International partners | They want exposure of their products and services to global audiences. | The agency's media coverage is a platform for the potential partners, to talk about their products to global audiences. |
| Junior staff | They want experience as they start their careers to take them from theoretical knowledge to practical implementation. | The agency has a breadth of clients that gives junior staff hands on experience, coupled with in-house training. |
| Senior staff | They want to expand their international portfolio. | The agency has offices in New York, London and Shanghai giving senior staff experience with clients from multiple cultures and regions. |

When you are clear on Your Tribe's specific pain-points and you are seen as the solution to their problems, you will find that people within your stakeholder groups act as brand ambassadors on your behalf. I have had previous staff open doors to new clients and I have had suppliers introduce me to potential partners. The clarity of messaging is what helps them understand how you are the solution, but the evidence of results helps them to believe that *you* (not just your industry) are truly the solution to the problems at hand. When Your Tribe, across all stakeholder groups, believes this about your brand, you have complete brand buy-in from Your Tribe. This level of buying reduces the amount of work you need to do to convince people because Your Tribe then acts as your mouthpiece, providing introductions via word-of-marketing, which, as we are all aware, is by far the best form of marketing there is.

## LET'S DO THE WORK

*Fill in your Stakeholder Grid below.*

Write down who is in Your Tribe. What are their pain-points and how is your personal brand a solution to their 'pain'? Go to SheBuildsBrands.com for a larger version of this chart.

| Stakeholder | Their pain-point | Your solutions |
|---|---|---|
|  |  |  |
|  |  |  |
|  |  |  |
|  |  |  |
|  |  |  |
|  |  |  |
|  |  |  |
|  |  |  |
|  |  |  |

# Target audience profile

Once you fully understand who fits into Your Tribe's ecosystem you can then break down a more detailed target audience profile. Your target audience consists of those who are the primary 'buyers' of your brand; these could be your core customers, main clients or specific hiring managers.

To be able to effectively market to your target audience you first need to know your target audience. One way to achieve this is by producing your target audience profile. In my masterclasses I often refer to your target audience as 'Your Friend'. I say this as an illustration of how well you need to really know this person/group of people. Like a friend, you need to be clear on how they are feeling, where they go, what they do, what they believe in and how they like to be spoken to. When you start to think of your target audience as more of a friend than a distant consumer group, you are able to build an authentic relationship between you and them.

Key questions you need to ask and to know about your target audience are:

- *What is their age group?* – This should be no more than ten to fifteen years apart. The reason being, the psychology of people at different ages varies drastically. For example, the psychology of an 18-year-old is very different from the psychology of a 58-year-old. Where they go, the media they consume, the problems your brand is solving etc. are too varied to try to capture such a wide audience. Whilst you might think you want 'everyone' or 'all women', the reality is that everyone doesn't need what you have and, even if they do, how can you possibly keep the communication concise when you are trying to talk the language of such a broad audience? Additionally, where you communicate that message will be too broad based on the lifestyle habits of the age of your target audience. For example, a Saturday afternoon for a 20-year-old is different from that of a 70-year-old; they go to different places and enjoy different things. It is therefore imperative to keep your audience group to no more than ten to fifteen years in age range.

- *What is their gender?* – Depending on where your brand is operating in the world this could be male or female, but it could also be transgender or 'other'. Whilst you can have multi-genders in your target audience, it is recommended that you seek to narrow down the age group within the gender group.

- *What is their geographic location?* – This again should not be broad, particularly if you are just starting out. If for example you say the UK, I would ask you to review whether or not everyone, everywhere in the UK, really needs your brand. Or could the geographics of your target audience be major cities in the UK such as London, Manchester or Glasgow? The more specific you are, the easier it will be later when you are trying to market your brand and promote it to the audience based on their locations.

- *What is their ethnicity?* – Culture and ethnicity play such a large role in the reception of brand messages; the words you use and the images you portray can easily alienate your target audience if you have not considered their culture and ethnicity. In recent years we have seen brands attempting to factor ethnicity and culture into their marketing messages, some with great success whilst others have missed the market. As a personal brand you too need to think about how the perspective of the 'buyer' is going to change depending on their background, and their ethnic and cultural grouping, as these will impact what they do and do not value.

- *What is their sexual orientation?* – Similarly with gender, this answer may vary depending on where your brand is positioned in the world. It is also something to bear in mind when you are seeking to take your brand into international markets. To ensure your brand messages are non-offensive, you need to research the countries' views on 'sexual orientation' and make sure your brand messages are not repelling the very audience you are trying to connect with.

- *What is their profession?* – Being clear on your target audience's profession will assist you to understand their income and spending power. These factors are critical when it comes to identifying your brand's price points and sales strategy.

- *What is their monthly income?* – Knowing what they earn helps you to effectively position your brand. Based on their income, your brand would be perceived by them as either a luxury brand, affordable luxury, premium, affordable or low-end.

- *What is their monthly spending power?* – Their spending power is the money they have left over once they have paid all of their bills. If, as an example, your desired customer group gets £5,000 per month as their income, but after bills and tax they are left with £1,000 per month, then their spending power is £1,000. What's key here is that you are then competing in the marketplace with your direct, aspirational and non-direct competitors for that £1,000. If your brand's product or service is priced at £800, the chances are you will be deemed as a luxury brand to them, because your brand is not something they can afford every month. Being a luxury brand means that their frequency of purchase might be less than if you are an affordable or low-end brand.

- *What are their religious views?* – Knowing this will help with your brand marketing messages. Being aware of any religious views within your target audience will help ensure that your brand is not offending the audience it is trying to market to.

- *What do they value?* – As mentioned earlier in this chapter, matching your audience's values with your own is the best way to create a tribe. So understanding what they value is extremely important to your brand success.

- *What is their media consumption?* – With the advancement of technology your target audience's media consumption might be changing swiftly. Are they on social media? If so, what platforms do they spend the most amount of time on? Do they read print media or do they consume their print media via the publication's website as opposed to physical paper? Are they watching TV? If so, what type of programmes? Do they listen to the radio? If yes, what time of the day and what are they doing when they are listening? Or have they moved away from TV and radio, and now watch all their 'TV' via YouTube and only listen to music through Spotify or another music platform? Understanding the specifics of their media consumption will help you know which platforms to put your brand on and what time of the day to advertise/post. (We will cover this in more depth in later chapters.)

- *What is their lifestyle?* – Understanding what your target audience does and when they do it will help you know which partners to collaborate with and when during the week or day to advertise or promote your brand. For example, if you have a fashion line and your target audience goes to the spa once a month then your local spa would be a natural partnership fit.

- *What is their emotional state?* – It is important to know the emotional state of your target audience as it pertains to your brand. When it comes to *your brand* are they currently happy, sad, neutral, frustrated or indifferent? Because branding is about solving problems, you need to know how deep the problem runs for them. As an example, my SheBuildsBrands Academy clients are frustrated. They have tried to build their businesses and now recognize the importance of spending money on their brand. Or they have spent money but with the wrong person so they want someone with a proven track record to help them. By understanding their emotional state I can do a number of things: a) create products that alleviate this state; b) use messages that speak to the emotions; and, in this specific case c) produce ample evidence to convince them that and my team and I are the ones for them to buy into.

When you create a profile of 'your friend' you are able to better connect with them, better solve their pain-points and get quicker buy-in. Below is an example of a client – she has a wellness brand. Here is her target audience profile:

**FIGURE 4.3** *Client target audience profile.*

## LET'S DO THE WORK

*Complete your own target audience profile and name your friend!*

FIGURE 4.4  *My target audience profile.*

# To love me, you need to know me

Once you have identified a Your Friend profile, you then need to think about what sort of relationship you want to develop. For some their brand is formal and thus their relationship with their tribe is conventional. For me, and the SheBuildsBrands team, we enjoy having a professional but very approachable relationship with our entire tribe. The audience segment who are Academy Members, those who buy our books, watch our Lives, attend our masterclasses etc, we tend to call them the BossSquad. I even have a weekly personal letter that goes out to the entire mailing list, designed to give them branding tips that will help them conquer their week. The letter starts with 'Dear

BossSquad'; it is written by me, signed by me, and talks in the same way that I would communicate with my girlfriends. When I am out at events I am more than happy to make time after a speaking engagement (as long as my diary permits), talking to members of the audience and helping them with their brands. Why? Because in listening to their feedback and conversations I get to learn more about their needs and how SheBuildsBrands can be a solution. With our corporate clients I schedule in regular dinner parties to cross-promote relationships and 1-2-1 coffee meet ups to get to know them better. Whenever I travel I try to reconnect with old corporate clients and take them out on 'client dates' and send them personalized gifts at Christmas.

I operate from the principle of givers-gain: it is my duty to give first, knowing that the way the world works, the more you give, the more you get back. This manifests itself in many ways: there are times when I will give a discount the first time someone is booking me to speak, knowing that once I deliver, they will book again. The regularity of the information I put out on social media is done from a place of 'give as much as you can', knowing that once they taste my knowledge, they will want more. Even if it doesn't happen straight away, twenty-plus years in this game has taught me that at some point it will happen. My job is not to focus on when, but to focus on the relationship and delivering my best the minute the opportunity arises. Therefore the relationship I have created with my tribe is personal and professional, with delivery and results at the core.

The idea that as long as you just work hard, you will acquire success is not true. The relationship you have with Your Tribe is what will enable or disable your success. You can be extremely skilled but if no-one is rooting for you, supporting you, opening doors for you and buying into you, your talents, gifts and skills will amount to very little. So taking the time to think through what you want your relationship to look and feel like is imperative.

## LET'S DO THE WORK

*Fill in the table below.*

| Your Tribe (list them) | The relationship you want to create is . . . | What actions do you need to take to make this relationship happen? | By what date will you start actioning this? |
|---|---|---|---|
|  |  |  |  |
|  |  |  |  |
|  |  |  |  |
|  |  |  |  |
|  |  |  |  |

# What's the Promise?

As identified in Chapter 2, the Brand Promise is an idea that articulates what all of your stakeholders will experience when doing business with you. When done well it engages the buy-in from all facets of Your Tribe as it aligns your Brand Values, your Brand Vision and your Brand Mission. It goes beyond the benefits of your product or your skills and capabilities, as it represents so much more. It is the core of what you promise you will deliver when every single one of Your Tribe engages with your brand.

As a personal brand you need to be clear on what you are promising. What will they experience from you? What will they get when they engage with you?

One way to establish your Brand Promise is to review your Stakeholder Grid and identify the common theme between each of the solutions you bring to each stakeholder. Whatever the common theme is, is ultimately your Brand

Promise. For example, the owner of the Digital Agency above has different Brand Solutions for each of his stakeholder groups, but the overarching theme is: *innovation, global experience and on-trend expertise*. Once you have identified the theme, then you need to hone in on which one of the words you have written is the main one. For example, out of innovation, global experience and on-trend expertise, he could choose global experience. This would mean that everything his brand does needs to have a global and international focus, with experiences at the heart of his delivery.

When you analyse the wider picture you begin to see a pattern; what you deem as your core Brand Values are also what Your Tribe see as their core values. These values then end up feeding into and becoming part of your Brand Promise. At the beginning of this chapter I said *Your Tribe comes together under one common goal, to be part of your 'why'*. The interesting thing is, not only does Your Tribe come together, and is attracted to you by that one common goal, but your entire brand also becomes about servicing Your Tribe with that one common goal. When done well, your brand becomes a beautiful circle of connecting the dots: you serving Your Tribe and Your Tribe serving you.

A perfect illustration of this is Mark Zuckerberg and Facebook. In July 2003, Mark Zuckerberg, alongside fellow Harvard University student Eduardo Saverin, launched FaceMash, the predecessor to Facebook. Initially designed as a membership site for Harvard university students, the site later became open to other Ivy League universities in the Boston area. The success of this opened the site to universities across the United States and Canada, before being open in 2006 to anyone over the age of 13 years with a valid email address. According to the movie *The Social Network*, Zuckerberg was a computer genius who felt disconnected from fellow students at Harvard University, particularly girls. Based on this, it would appear that his initial pain-point was a lack of connection. Assuming this is true, it would not come as a surprise that he started a university membership site, enabling him to do what he could not do in the physical, but could now do on the net. This pain-point is the exact same pain-point as the Facebook tribe; anyone who wants to connect and feel connected joined Facebook. Fast forward to today: Facebook has 2 billion users per month and 'connectivity' has become its 'why'. According to the Facebook website, their mission is to:

> Give people the power to build community and bring the world closer together. People use Facebook to stay connected with friends and family, to discover what's going on in the world, and to share and express what matters to them.

This Brand Mission interconnects the 'why' with every facet of the Facebook tribe, from advertisers who want to connect better with their consumers, to people who want to connect with lost friends, to businesses who want to connect better with their staff via Workplace by Facebook. Mark Zuckerberg's 'why' started Facebook, but now this 'why' is the reason Facebook still operates today. The dots have been connected; his tribe is serving the brand by using the platform and the brand is serving the tribe by delivering on the promise.

## LET'S DO THE WORK

*Complete the sentence.*

What is your Brand Promise? (What one thing are you promising to deliver for all stakeholders?)

_____

What is your 'why'? (What is the mission behind your vision? Why are you doing what you are doing?)

_____

# 5

# Your Difference Is Your Strength

The second part of gaining real brand clarity is understanding that your Brand Identity is one of the most critical components needed for personal brand success. Also known as your Brand ID, your Brand Identity is how you want to present yourself to, and be perceived by, Your Tribe. I often hear people say that their Brand ID and Brand Image are the same thing, but they are not. Your Brand ID is what you choose to be your name, colours, logo, typography, style, tone of voice, story, personality and core differentiators. It is your intent; your Brand Image is the results, successful or unsuccessful, of that intent.

Having become clear on your Decision and your Vision (as discussed in Chapters 1, 2 and 3) we now need to gain Clarity on your Brand ID. We started this process in Chapter 4 by reviewing your Brand Vision, Brand Mission and Brand Values, noting that: your vision is where your brand is going; your mission outlines why you do what you do; and your values are what underpin your daily actions. We navigated the importance of identifying your Brand

Colours and Brand Signature, as they help to create brand recognition. Lastly we evaluated your Brand Promise, reviewing what you are promising to deliver when Your Tribe engages with your personal brand.

A powerful Brand ID is where all of the elements listed above are cohesive, consistent and concurrent with your true, authentic self. When communicated effectively, your Brand ID builds trust, harnesses recognition and secures buy-in from Your Tribe, whilst simultaneously differentiating you from your competitors.

Before we go any further, let us review what you have outlined about your Personal Brand ID so far.

## LET'S DO THE WORK

*Complete the statements below.*

My Brand Vision is

_____

(This is where you are going. What is the vision for your personal brand?)

My Brand Mission is

_____

(This is your 'why'. Why are you developing your personal brand? What is its purpose?)

My Brand Values are

_____

_____

(These are the things that define why you behave the way you do.)

My Brand Promise is

_____

_____

(This is what you promise Your Tribe you will deliver when they work with you or experience your brand.)

My Brand Colours are

_____

(These are the key colours that represent your brand.)

My Brand Signature is

_____

(This is your distinguishing sign, feature or personality trait.)

My Tribe is

_____

(Your Tribe is your target market, those who sit in the ecosystem of your brand; the people and companies that your brand engages with, or seeks to engage with, on a day-to-day basis.)

My 'Friends' are

_____

_____

_____

_____

(Your 'Friends' are your target audience, the people who will directly buy from or buy-into your brand. I call them your friends so that you can focus on the human engagement and relationship building needed to truly gain their trust and buy-in. Your target audience needs to be seen as more than just numbers, a pay cheque or money in the till!)

*Note: If you are unsure of any areas, I would advise you to go back to previous chapters, re-read the sections and complete the exercises so that you are able to fill in the above.*

# Branding is the *pull*, Marketing is the *push*

Most people don't spend the time to create a personal brand; instead they jump straight into brand marketing. This is because they think that branding and marketing are the same thing, and, in fact, they are two completely different things.

- The *brand* is the *who you are.*

- The *brand marketing* is the *methods used* to get to who you are, in front of Your Tribe.

- To put it another way: branding is the *pull* – marketing is the *push.*

When done well, branding is the *pull* that gets people interested in you, your products and services. It's the magic that makes them curious and wanting to learn more; whereas marketing is the *push*. It's the series of activities and channels used to promote your brand. To be effective you need a combination of both *pull* and *push*. Too often people are pushing messages before they have worked out what their pull actually is. When you do it the wrong way round, it leaves Your Tribe confused and uncertain of what you are all about. It provides miscommunication of your brand, and ends up with you doing a lot of work, without seeing the fruits of your labour. Too many times to count, clients have come to me asking why their brand marketing is not working; why their social media is not gaining traction or their résumé website is not being taken seriously. The reason is: they need to stop promoting what they think others want to see, and start creating a personification of their best selves. A winning Brand ID is rooted in your truth and packaged from a place of authenticity.

> You can't effectively promote your brand if you haven't first created your brand.

In this chapter we will break down each element of your Brand ID, with the understanding that, once they all come together, they are the *pull* that will make people come to you, so that you can *push* the right messages, with the correct activities, across the appropriate channels.

# Brand History

During my business radio show, *Ask Kubi*, I often get questions such as 'Kubi, how long will it take to build my brand?' or 'Kubi, I have been doing this for three years and it's still not happening, should I stop?'

These questions derive from the person believing that the process of creating a brand happens quickly. They see what appears to be overnight success on social media and in the press, and then assume that these brands have appeared from nowhere. My answer is usually: if you love what you're doing and truly believe that you're solving a real problem in the world, why would you want to stop? If you know in your heart that your talents, gifts and abilities are needed, then stopping shouldn't be an option.

If your brand is not working, undertake a Brand Audit; review your skills, up your education level, change your products or services, examine your price points, distribution channels, business model, route to entry etc. But the idea of stopping the process of building your personal brand, that shouldn't even be an option. I understand that you might have days, weeks or even whole seasons when you think it's not working. It's hard work. It's taking too long. You want to quit. I understand those feelings because I too have been there. But giving up isn't the answer. Because, the reality is, brand building takes time.

How much time?

As long as it needs to take.

For me, the focus should not be on how long it's taking, it should be on the day-to-day journey of learning and growing, refining and mastering your personal brand. What are you doing every single day to make your brand thrive? How can you be better? What do you need to do to deliver brand excellence? Who should you partner with? Which strategic steps should you be taking to reposition your brand for success? Is your Brand ID authentic and working? These are the questions you need to focus on. Not how long will it take.

Richard Branson has famously said: 'There are no quick wins in business – it takes years to become an overnight success.'

I couldn't agree with him more.

When you actually analyse some of the world's most recognizable and profitable brands, they have been going for decades, if not centuries:

- Deloitte started in 1845 in London, England.

- Louis Vuitton started in 1854 in France.

- The Coca-Cola Company started in 1892 in Atlanta, USA.

- Ford Motor Cars started in 1903 in Detroit, USA.

- Marlboro was registered in 1908 and the brand was launched in 1924.

- L'Oréal started on 30 July 1909 in France.

- Chanel started in 1910 in France.

- BMW started in 1916 in Germany.

- The Disney Company started in 1923 in California.

- Mercedes-Benz started in 1926 in Germany.

- Revlon started in 1932 in New York.

- Adidas started in 1949 in Germany.

- Nike started in 1964 in Oregon, USA.

- Dove started in 1955 in England.

- McDonalds started in 1955 in California.

- Apple started in 1976 in California.

. . . and the list goes on!

All of the household brands that we know today have taken time to become successful. It is this longevity that has cemented the brands in the minds of consumers and enabled such strong brand recognition. When a brand is able to deliver despite the test of time, loyalty is created and trust is formed.

This principle is just as true for personal brands. You may have an instant success, but that doesn't mean that you will be able to sustain that success. Just think of all the one-hit wonders that are out there! Successful people with personal brands that last have had to spend years developing their brand, honing their craft and receiving endless 'No's before they got any success. Irrespective of what social media might lead us to believe, brand building takes time.

To illustrate this, let's review some of the most popular personal brands in the world:

- *Oprah Winfrey* – Oprah took her first presenting job in 1971 at the age of 17, but she didn't start the *Oprah Winfrey Show* until 1986, aged 32. It took her 15 years to master her craft as a presenter before she signed a deal for her own show. The *Oprah Winfrey Show* went on to air for 25 seasons, with its final broadcast attracting 16.5 million viewers. Her other successful ventures include the *O The Oprah Magazine*, which she didn't launch until the year 2000, at the age of 46, and the OWN Network, which wasn't founded until 2011. As the timeline shows, her own TV network took a total of 40 years since she embarked on a career in television to launch. Oprah is an example of 'luck' being preparation meets opportunity, with a whole lot of hard work and dedicated time as well.

- *Richard Branson* – He dropped out of school to begin his magazine *Student* on 1 July 1966. It took two years before the first issue of *Student* was even released. Following the release of his first issue, he founded Virgin two years later on 8 September 1970, selling records through mail order to cover the costs of his magazine. The magazine was unsuccessful and three years later he started Virgin Record Label. Whilst he signed notable artists such as Mike Oldfield, The Sex Pistols and Genesis, it took him 17 years to convince the Rolling Stones to sign with him. He has also had enormous failures, including: Virgin Student, Virgin Cars, Virgin Brides and Virgin Cola. In 1992 Branson made one of the most difficult decisions in his life, when he was forced to sell Virgin Records to Thorn EMI to save Virgin Airlines. Branson has opened more than 60 companies (to date) in the time span of 53 years since he dropped out of school in 1966. Branson is a classic example of 'you lose some, you win some', but if you keep going and learn from the lessons, the odds are you will win more than you lose.

- *Sheryl Sandberg* – COO of Facebook and Founder of LeanIn.org, co-founded an organization called Women in Economics, which was her first business venture whilst at Harvard College at the age of 18. But she didn't publish *Lean In: Women, Work, and the Will to Lead* until 2013 at the age of 44. It took her 26 years to master her expertise in gender equality in the workplace before she launched her first book, which then went on to sell 2.25 million copies worldwide. Today she sits on the Board of Directors of Facebook and is the first female employee to become a billionaire, with a net-worth of $1.6 billion. Sandberg is an example that it takes time to call yourself 'an expert'.

- *James Dyson* – started the Dyson technology company, which today has machines in 65 countries around the world and over a thousand engineers working for it. But it started with just one man. In 1978

James Dyson became frustrated with his vacuum cleaner's diminishing performance. As an inventor, he took the machine apart and discovered that the bag was clogging with dust, causing the suction level to drop. He then went about attempting to create a bagless vacuum cleaner. It took him five years and 5,127 prototypes to create the Dyson machine. He is the personification of 'try, try and try again'.

As shown above, every great brand has a history; a journey that took years and years, filled with a timeline of immense struggle, lessons learnt, highs and lows. Just like a diamond requires high pressures and temperatures to form, and is delivered to the surface of the earth by deep-source volcanic eruptions, your personal brand also becomes exceptional when it has gone through its own journey of fire. When your personal brand has shown resilience throughout the knock backs and, despite it all, still delivers with a consistency of excellence, that is when you have a brand. The regularity, the constancy, the repetition of delivering – these are the things that build trust and harness that emotional connection that gives life to your brand.

One brand that has an interesting history is Lady Gaga. When I saw her win eight out of the 13 nominations for the 2010 MTV Awards I was captivated by the creative expression of this artist and the sheer power of her voice. What I didn't know then was that she had spent nearly 19 years cultivating her talent before that win.

Lady Gaga, whose real name is Stefani Joanne Angelina Germanotta, started learning to play the piano at the age of 4. By the time she was 11, she was accepted into the Juilliard School of Performing Arts in Manhattan. By 14 years old she had undertaken her first performance in a New York City nightclub. She was granted early admission to New York University's Tisch School of the Arts (one of only 20 students in the world to receive an early admission). To make ends meet she took several jobs, including that of a go-go dancer. In 2005 she was signed by Def Jam Records only to be dropped three months later. Desperate to make it, she performed in several rock bands and began experimenting with fashion. In 2007, at the age of 20, Gaga was signed by Interscope Records as a songwriter for other artists including Britney Spears, New Kids on the Block and The Pussycat Dolls. Nearly 17 years from when she started embarking on her journey to brand success, she was still unsigned as an artist in her own right; she was a songwriter for others. It wasn't until 2008 that she was signed as an artist to Akon's label KON Live, under the Interscope umbrella; 18 years after she started trying, she finally gained commercial and artistic acclaim when her debut single 'Just Dance' went to number one in the US charts. This song was nominated for a Grammy Award in the Best Dance Record category and I am sure that those looking on would assume that she was an 'overnight success' with her first single. But, as this timeline shows, she was grinding and crafting for over 18 years before she received the popular acknowledgement or commercial success for her talent.

What happened during those years was that Gaga discovered Electric Pop music (part of her differentiation as a contemporary artist). She created her brand (her name Lady Gaga was taken from the Queen song 'Radio Ga-Ga'). She crafted her fashion style (making contacts with stylists, designers, makeup artists, hairdressers and creative directors, some of whom eventually worked under her House of Gaga creative team). She developed her performance style (through the necessity of earning a living by dancing in night clubs across New York City). She mastered her songwriting skills (gaining industry recognition for songs she wrote for other award-winning artists) and she worked on her acting skills (both in school and through amateur plays to pay her bills). Nothing happens before its time. This 18-year process turned her from Stefani Germanotta to Lady Gaga.

# Brand Story

Your history gives birth to your Brand Story. All its highs and lows are the 'good stuff' that makes people want to pay attention to your brand. Through the journey, your brilliance is moulded and the characters of your story are created. Without the journey there is no Brand Story. Without the 'No's and rejections, without the lessons of getting it wrong and trying again and again, how can you carve out a compelling brand message? How can you know what to say if you haven't taken the time to find out what people want to hear? You only discover what they want when you have gone through the process of listening and learning. This is why it takes as long as it needs to take. The journey is necessary.

A Brand Story is a cohesive narrative that encompasses the facts, experiences and feelings that are created by your Brand History; as such, all great brands use their history to cultivate a compelling Brand Story.

Let's look at the Dyson story. Undertaking 5,127 tries at a bagless vacuum cleaner before he found the one that worked is used in every brand touch point to reinforce the message that Dyson is unique. This very struggle is the differentiator that creates superiority positioning over its competitors. On the Dyson website they say:

> At Dyson, it's invention that sets us apart. Cyclones that generate 79,000g to separate dust. Pioneering digital motors that are smaller, faster and more powerful than anything before. It's our obsession. That's why nothing else really works like a Dyson.
>
> JAMES DYSON, www.dyson.co.uk

The word 'obsession' references the Brand History and justifies their competitive edge. The struggle of the past is at the core of their Brand Story today. Even the idea that you have to be smart to create a Dyson is used in their advertising messages. Outlined in their 'Dyson – the smart room' campaign, which was created by Livity Agency London (2017), a short animation was produced with a call-to-action for viewers to crack the code in the film to win a prize. Everything about the brand builds from the struggles of its founder and the story propels the message that this company is smarter than the rest, more obsessed and dedicated than its competitors and thus leading the market.

Another example of how one's Brand History creates its Brand Story can be found in that of supermodel and businesswoman, Iman.

Born in Somalia, Iman was from a middle-class family where her mother was a gynaecologist and her father was a diplomat. Iman was sent to an all-girl Catholic private school and by the time she was 18 she spoke five different languages and was a student of political science at University of Nairobi. Discovered by renowned fashion photographer Peter Beard in 1975, Iman negotiated a US $8,000 fee for her first fashion shoot from Beard as she wanted to pay off her tuition fees (her father's diplomacy skills clearly taught her something).

Propelled by her exotic looks, Iman was invited to New York City in the October of that year and landed her first international shoot on the front cover of American *Vogue*. However, it was on this shoot that she discovered that none of the makeup artists had foundation to match her black skin.

'They made me look greyish' was what she later told Essence TV when recalling that first day in the modelling industry. Recognizing that she had to learn everything about the industry, Iman started mixing different foundation colours to be able to match her own dark brown skin tone.

'I had to be my own brand. My image is my currency – if they don't know how to make it look right, I would make it for them.'

This decision would later be the birth of her own cosmetics line in 1994 with the strapline: designed for All Women with Skin of Colour. The Iman Collection sold an impressive US $12 million worth of products in its first year, and grossed US $35 million by the following year. Despite the expansion of other mainstream brands launching lines for women of colour, the success of the Iman Collection was deeply rooted in her Brand History as a model from Somalia. Being one of the first black supermodels in the world she had a story that gave her collections undeniable authenticity and connection with its audience. By 2001 she had written the book *I am Iman* and in 2005 she wrote *The Beauty of Colour*, a makeup guide for women of colour. Every facet of the Iman brand has originated from the struggles in her early career as a model and thus gives the brand a foundation that, at the time, was unique and groundbreaking (Biography.com, 2014).

When you start to understand the power in your history and take ownership of the journey you can use it to your advantage. By seeing the gems in what would appear to be the struggles, you can create impactful brand messages and compelling Brand Stories. These messages and stories help direct the tone of your promotional content and marketing images. Whether it's your CV, website, social media platforms or marketing collateral, you can use your history to identify the characters and key themes of your story. However, a word of caution: your Brand Story should *always* be 'on-brand'.

'On-brand' is a term I often use with clients to encapsulate what they have said are their brand values, brand mission, brand vision and brand promise. In other words, if the characters in your story and the essence of your message do not align with your brand values, then they should not be used – they are not 'on-brand'. Equally, if the tone of your story does not reinforce your brand promise, then it should not be used – it is not 'on-brand'.

The term 'on-brand' is imperative when creating your Brand ID. Everything you do should be 'on-brand' to ensure you stay focused and on track of where you are trying to take your personal brand. It can be too easy to create a story that is steeped in sorrow that just makes you look like the victim. On the contrary, your Brand Story should be powerful, engaging and making Your Tribe want to lean in to you more. If it distances Your Tribe, then it is not 'on-brand'. Since we have already established that branding is an emotional connection with your desired audience, it is your job to find the right highlights in your story that will touch people at their heart-space and reinforce what you say you are all about.

---

## LET'S DO THE WORK

List five to ten key moments in your history that could be used in your Brand Story:

_____

_____

_____

_____

_____

---

# Brand Personality

Successful brands have strong and uniquely identifiable personality traits that run through all of their brand messaging, packaging, content and promotions. These traits are known as Brand Archetypes.

Divided into genres based on universal symbols, Swiss psychoanalyst Carl Jung defined 12 Brand Archetypes. According to Jung, attaching your brand to a universal symbol that is understood everywhere is necessary for brand success as these symbols are primal and instinctive. They are part of a 'collective unconscious', which then makes your brand easily identifiable and recognizable globally.

Effective brands increase their brand equity when they adapt one of the 12 Brand Archetypes that align with their Brand Values and Brand Promise. With immense consistency, brands that harness their brand personality and allow it to come alive via their Brand Story better connect with their desired audience and secure buy-in.

As a personal brand, you, too, have a Brand Archetype that should be concurrent with your personal Brand Values and personal Brand Promise. When deriving from a place of true authenticity, your Brand Personality will resonate with the personality of Your Friend and key members of Your Tribe.

The 12 Brand Archetypes are as follows.

# 1 The Sage

Also known as the expert, scholar, advisor, thinker or guru – the Sage personality believes that 'your truth will set you free'. Aiming to celebrate curiosity, these brands seek to spread their knowledge with an unwavering desire to uncover and comprehend the truth. Sage types enjoy learning and understanding the world around them, they encourage customers to think, deliver knowledge and expertise, and see it as their purpose to set their tribe free by seeing the world objectively.

Corporate brands that hold this personality trait include: The BBC, CNN, *The New York Times* and the University of Oxford.

A primary example of a personal brand that has the Sage archetype is financial guru Suze Orman. An American author, financial specialist and TV host, Suze Orman's story is one of rags-to-riches: from waitress to Merrill Lynch stock broker, Suze learnt the hard way of how to build, sustain and grow wealth. Radiating the Sage personality, Suze's brand is that of authority, experience, knowledge, teacher and guru. This trait is exemplified in her daytime talk show *The Suze Orman Show*, where she is often delivering blunt but highly informative financial advice.

## 2 The Innocent

Also known as the traditionalist, saint, dreamer or utopian – this personality trait is optimistic and honest, spontaneous and often child-like. Brands with this trait are associated with goodness, morality and straightforward values. They offer a simple solution to a problem. Their goal is to 'be happy', their strategy is to 'do things right' and their motto is 'the glass is half full (not half empty)' or 'be young and free'.

Corporate brands that hold this personality trait include: Disney, Dove, McDonalds and Coca-Cola.

Whilst it is somewhat easy to identify corporate brands that demonstrate the Innocent brand archetype, it appears to be harder in personal brands. However, one that jumped out at me was Warren Buffett. An America business mogul and investment billionaire, Warren Buffett has often been referred to as a man that can provide simple, obvious and wise advice on some of the most complex investment opportunities. He has been described as humble and frugal, magical and cheerful (CNBC Make It, 2018; ValueWalk, 2015). In fact, author Nic Liberman (2015) exemplifies this character trait with the title of his book, *Being Warren Buffett: Life Lessons from a Cheerful Billionaire.*

## 3 The Explorer

Also known as the seeker, iconoclast or individualist – the Explorer is someone who is constantly seeking self-realization. They value freedom to be whoever they want to be and encourage others to do the same. They do not want to be confined and they are keen to help others to be nonconformists, and pioneering. They seek to discover self through exploring the world. To be more, do more and experience a fulfilling, authentic and better life. Brands that encapsulate the Explorer trait are in pursuit of answering the big questions: 'Why am I here?' 'What is my purpose?' They believe that it is better to know and be disappointed than to never know and always be wondering. The Explorer brand produces products that are ideal for the outdoors or in dangerous settings. Designing items that can be purchased for consumption on the go. They create adventurous brand experiences and a culture of excitement.

Corporate brands that hold this personality trait include: Range Rover, Jeep, Lloyds TSB and Marlboro.

An example of a personal brand that had the Explorer archetype was the 'The Crocodile Hunter'. Born Stephen Robert Irwin, this Australian zookeeper, conservationist, and television personality was famous for fighting off hundreds of predators. He built his brand through TV documentaries that showed his unconventional approach to wildlife and endless adventures. Broadcasting for eleven years, until his untimely death in 2006, his series *Animal Planet* became the second longest running programme on the Discovery Network. He was a prime example of a personal brand that loved the outdoors, as utterly nonconformist and created enjoyment through triumphing over the dangers around him.

# 4 The Ruler

Also known as the boss, leader, manager, role model, politician – these brands don't believe that power is everything, they believe it's the only thing. They strive for domination and help people to maintain or enhance their positions of power. They are confident, competent and responsible. The Ruler takes control and is motivated by high standards of excellence. Brands with this trait pride themselves on being a leader in their industry and in creating an environment of prosperity. As personal brands they offer security and stability in a world that is often seen as chaotic.

The Ruler creates high valued products and services used by powerful people, or by those seeking to create illusions of power. With moderate to high price pointers this brand helps people to be organized, effectively positioned and perceived as successful.

Corporate brands that hold this personality trait include: Rolls Royce, Rolex, IBM and Merccdes-Benz.

Editor-in-Chief for American *Vogue*, Anna Wintour, is the perfect illustration of a personal brand that is the Ruler. She is astute, confident, intelligent and extremely powerful. Her influence can make or break careers in the fashion industry and her ability to deliver excellence has been consistent for over 31 years as Editor-in-Chief at *Vogue* and Creative Director at Condé Nast. According to *The New York Times* she has a reported $2million USD per year salary and a net-worth of a reported $35 million USD (CNBC, 2017). As explained later in this chapter, even Anna Wintour's style or 'packaging' is one of absolute dominance.

# 5 The Creator

Also known as artist, inventor, muse, innovator, writer, musician – Creators believes if you can image it, you can create it. They use creative thinking to solve problems and, as stated by Oscar Wilde, their motto is 'You can't use up creativity; the more you use it, the more you have'.

Brands that are Creators promote self-expression, and give their clients choices and options. They help foster innovative ideas and have products that enable customers to 'do-it-yourself', giving them the space to be creative. The Creator can be seen across multiple industries, including marketing, the arts, public relations and technological innovation.

Corporate brands that hold this personality trait include: Apple, Lego, Instagram, Adobe, Burberry, Nintendo and Sony.

Retail executive, author, and businesswoman Martha Stewart is a brilliant example of a personal brand that embodies the Creator archetype. Since starting her catering business in 1976, Martha Stewart has written several books that enabled her tribe to create meals and host dinner parties. When you review her book list, which includes titles such as *Entertaining* and *Martha Stewart Quick Cook Menus*, her brand personality fosters the ideology: if you can imagine it, you can create it. Her brand expansion projects – ranging from *The Martha Stewart Show*, which won 32 Daytime Emmy Awards, to her *Martha Stewart* products that were sold in stores such as Walmart – have all encompassed the principle of self-expression through cooking.

# 6 The Caregiver

Also known as the helper, supporter, parent and saint – the Caregiver pursues protection and safety for others. With compassion at the forefront of their approach, caregiver archetypes seek to meet the needs of the people around them to ensure that everyone feels appreciated and safe. Brands that embody this trait care about their customers' wellbeing, and tend to be driven towards education, family or public service. These brands support people to take care of themselves. Generous and compassionate, they believe that you love your neighbour as you love yourself; as such, Caregivers are not interested in the hard sell but rather focus on deeply emotive heartfelt brand narratives in their brand storytelling and content.

Corporate brands that hold this Caregiver personality trait include: Johnson's Baby Shampoo, Amnesty International, Volvo, Green Giant and Pampers.

Nun and missionary Mother Teresa, spiritual leader The Dalai Lama and civil rights activist Martin Luther King are all historic Caregivers who built personal brands and legacies from a place of supporting and helping others, whilst Oprah is a current Caregiver whose entire brand essence is supporting and nurturing. As an example, in 2004 during her daytime show *The Oprah Winfrey Show*, Oprah gave away 276 cars to everyone in the audience. Hearing her screaming her infamous line 'You get a car! You get a car!...', the audience was stunned at the magnitude of the prize, which provided an epic TV moment for the show's producers. But her caregiving spirit did not stop there, by the time her show ended in May 2011, Oprah had given away 570 cars across the 25 seasons. The authenticity of this personality resonated throughout her career. When she started the show in 1996 she gifted the entire audience (and their families) with a trip to Disneyland, gave away a reported US$ 13,000 in gifts to teachers around the United States and, during her final season, Winfrey invited her audience to accompany her on an all-expenses-paid international vacation to Australia (Witter, 2018).

Brands that fall within the Caregiver category live and breathe it with their actions, not just their words or their marketing messages.

# 7  The Magician

Also known as the charismatic leader, visionary, catalyst and inventor – the Magician enjoys being responsible for making things happen, their goal is to make dreams come true. Brilliant at being the catalyst for change, turning problems into opportunities and reframing difficulties, they empower people, teams and networks. Creating win/win solutions for all involved, the Magician embodies amazement and wonder.

Brands that have this trait promise transformation for their customers, consciousness expanding and have a new age quality. Possibly contemporary in nature or user-friendly, their motto is to turn dreams into reality. These brands relish making the impossible possible.

Corporate brands that hold this Magician personality trait include: Disney, Dreamscape Multimedia, Oil of Olay, Dyson, Tesla, MAC, Mastercard and Smirnoff.

A personal brand with the Magician archetype is Apple co-founder Steve Jobs. From his majestic speeches, to his mesmerizing presentations, his ability to persuade and allure, and his immense talent of marketing the impossible, Jobs was one of the most high profile and successful Magician brands. In his authorized self-titled biography *Steve Jobs*, which was written by Walter Isaacson, it was said that:

> Jobs could seduce and charm people at will, and he liked to do so. People such as [former Apple CEOs] Amelio and Sculley allowed themselves to believe that because Jobs was charming them, it meant that he liked and respected them. It was an impression that he sometimes fostered by dishing out insincere flattery to those hungry for it. But Jobs could be charming to people he hated just as easily as he could be insulting to people he liked.
>
> ISAACSON, 2011; cited in *Independent*, 2017

This extract is a reminder that the Magician brand will be driven, charismatic and healing but on a bad day might be dishonest, disconnected or sometimes manipulative to its customers and stakeholder groups.

# 8 The Hero

Also known as warrior, crusader, rescuer, superhero, saviour, soldier, dragon slayer, the winner and the team player – the Hero relishes winning. Heroes encourage their customers to be more, and have more, and believe that you should prove your worth through acts of courage. Whether on the battlefield or political stage, the Hero is determined to leave a mark on the world. As such, there is nothing subtle about the Hero archetype. Heroes strive to inspire others to overcome obstacles, play for the win and will shout from the rooftops when success has been achieved. Motivated to prove their worth, the Hero's greatest fear is failure and showing weakness. Brands with the Hero archetype will position themselves as the best in their field, with a perceived superiority to their competitors. They deliver good quality products and marketing campaigns with extremely powerful messages, images and colours.

Corporate brands that hold this Hero personality trait include: Nike, US Army, AA, Mr Muscle, Duracell and Amazon.

Motivational Speaker and Life Coach Tony Robbins is a perfect example of a personal brand that embodies the Hero archetype. With self-help books such as *Awaken The Giant Within* and *Unlimited Power*, Robbins is known for his larger-than-life persona, energetic delivery style and dynamic presentations. His high-energy seminars have been attended by celebrities such as Oprah Winfrey and Al Gore, whilst his coaching clients include President Bill Clinton and Hugh Jackman. Known for taking ice-baths and jumping on a trampoline before delivering his seminars, Robbins has built several businesses with an annual revenue of more than £6 billion per year, from harnessing and marketing the Hero personality and teaching people that their own hero is within.

# 9  The Rebel

Also known as the outlaw, revolutionary, wild man, the misfit – this archetype believes that rules are there to be broken. Rebels thrive on carving out their own paths and challenging the status quo. They will often push the boundaries, creating unique products or marketing campaigns that are unusual or that pivot thought. They are unconventional thinkers who can create new cutting-edge approaches with a desire to shake things up. The Rebel is a countercultural force capable of releasing society's taboos (sex, drugs and rock 'n' roll) and does so by tapping into the shadowy part of human nature. These brands often attract employees or customers who feel disenfranchised from society and want to make revolutionary change.

Corporate brands that hold the Rebel personality trait include: Virgin, Harley Davidson, MTV, Diesel and Sparta Chicks.

A personal brand that fits the Rebel archetype is Gordon Ramsay. UK TV chef and Michelin-starred restaurateur, Ramsay is known for his outlandish ways in the kitchen. From swearing at junior chefs, to getting into public spats, Ramsay has carved out a career, especially on TV, known for his unapologetic brand personality. TV titles such as *Hell's Kitchen* and *Ramsay's Kitchen Nightmares* have proven to attract global audiences, with four top-rated FOX shows that air in more than 200 territories worldwide.

# 10 The Lover

Also known as partner, friend, intimate, enthusiast, sensualist, spouse, team-builder – this personality type helps people get along, have a good time, feel good, and find love or a partner. Focused on intimacy and experience, brands with the Lover archetype focus on creating relationships and evoking emotions. Lover brands promise passion and promote themselves as glamorous with an emphasis on sensual pleasures. They concentrate on how the product feels to the customers, and customers who buy into these brands value the aesthetic. They want to feel as if they are the only one.

Corporate brands that hold the Lover personality trait include: Victoria's Secret, Dior, John Paul Gaultier, and Secret Escapes.

The Kardashian-Jenner family is a powerhouse of personal brands, who unapologetically personify, market and sell the Lover archetype. With Kylie Jenner as the world's youngest billionaire, Kendall Jenner currently being the highest paid model in the fashion industry, and Kim Kardashian ranked 54th of America's Wealthiest Self-Made Women, this family has been embodying the Lover archetype trait since *Keeping Up With The Kardashians* aired in 2004. Ever since the infamous sex tape scandal surrounding Kim Kardashian and then boyfriend Ray J, the Kardashian-Jenner brand has launched endless products designed to make younger consumers feel attractive. These products have included their Glam and Fitness apps that have almost 900,000 subscribers (at the time of writing), Kim's mobile game *Kim Kardashian Hollywood*, Khloe's *Good American* clothing line, which in 2016 made US $1 million on its first day, and Kylie's cosmetics company *Kylie Cosmetics*, which is worth a reported US $900 million. The Kardashian-Jenner family has mastered the Lover archetype and harnesses its power without apology.

# 11  The Jester

Also known as the fool, trickster, joker, practical joker, entertainer or comedian – this brand personality believes you can only live once and strives to live in the moment with full joy. Jesters want people to feel good, lighten the mood and enjoy themselves. Brands that align with this personality want to give people a sense of belonging, implore their audiences to have fun and not take life too seriously.

Corporate brands that hold the Jester personality trait include: Skittles, The Muppets, Geico Insurance, M&M's, CompareTheMarket.com.

Comedian Kevin Hart has made a staggering US $150 million as the Jester archetype. Earning a reported US $1 million per stand-up show, he is ranked one of the top comedians in the world. He sold out his *What Now?* show at Philadelphia Stadium with more than 53,000 attendees, and has over 35 million followers on Twitter, 23 million on Facebook and a breathtaking 70.7 million on Instagram (at the time of writing). A family friendly brand, he exemplifies the Jester archetype through his movies, shows and merchandise.

# 12  The Regular Guy/Girl

Also known as the good old boy, everyman, the person next door, the realist, the working stiff, the solid citizen, the good neighbour, the silent majority –

this brand personality likes to have the common touch, believes that all men and women are created equal, and therefore wants to be on the same level as their customers. Expressing traits of unpretentiousness and humbleness, these brands want to get the job done, and do it properly. As down to earth realists, brands with this archetype deliver an everyday functionality and are normally at lower price points.

Corporate brands that hold the Regular Guy/Girl personality trait include: PG Tips, The Gap, Persil, Levi's, VW Cars, Walmart, Wendy's and Home Depot.

Actor Will Smith is a good example of a personal brand that demonstrates the Regular Guy archetype. He is deemed to be honest, approachable and down-to-earth. In press interviews, he comes across as a regular family man with an attractive humbleness. This persona has been reinforced by the characters he has chosen to play in his blockbuster movies and TV shows, from his 1990s sitcom 'The Fresh Prince of Bel-Air', to the down-to-earth cop in 1995's *Bad Boys* and flawed superhero in 2008's *Hancock* movie. With each role he has chosen, he has, for the most part, stuck to a version of the Regular Guy, even down to the animated voiceover of the underachieving character Oscar in the 2004 *Shark Tale*. This personality trait has recently been reinforced across his YouTube and Instagram videos, as he gives viewers an insight into his world by showing them such things as him ticking something off his bucket list by attempting to swim with sharks. He is the everyman; funny, warm, welcoming and kind, he symbolizes the Regular Guy with ease.

Personal Brand archetypes list:

| Archetype | Personal brand | Corporate brands |
|---|---|---|
| The Sage | Financial Guru – Suze Orman Actor – Morgan Freeman | CNN, University of Oxford, BBC |

| Archetype | Personal brand | Corporate brands |
|---|---|---|
| The Innocent | Investment Guru – Warren Buffett<br>Princess Diana | Disney, Dove, McDonalds, Coca-Cola |
| The Explorer | Natural Historian – David Attenborough<br>Actor – Will Smith<br>Steve Irwin – 'The Crocodile Hunter' | Jeep, Marlboro, Lloyds TSB, The North Face |
| The Ruler | Editor-In-Chief – Anna Wintour<br>Businessman – Sir Alan Sugar | Rolex, IBM, Mercedes-Benz |
| The Creator | Businessman – Richard Branson<br>Businessman – Bill Gates<br>Businesswoman – Martha Stewart | Apple, Lego, Sony |
| The Caregiver | Media mogul – Oprah, Gandhi, Martin Luther King and Mother Teresa | Johnson's Baby Shampoo, Amnesty International, Volvo, Green Giant and Pampers |
| The Magician | Author of *Rich Dad, Poor Dad* Robert Kiyosaki<br>Businessman – Steve Jobs | Disney, Dreamscape Multimedia, Oil of Olay, Dyson |
| The Hero | Motivational speaker – Tony Robbins<br>President Obama | Nike, USA Army, |
| The Outlaw | Chef – Gordon Ramsay<br>Actor/Comedian – Russell Brand | Harley Davidson, Virgin |
| The Lover | Music artist – Prince<br>Actress – Marilyn Monroe | Victoria's Secret, Chanel, Christian Louboutin |
| The Jester | Comedian – Kevin Hart | Skittles, The Muppets, Geico Insurance |
| The Regular Guy/Girl | Ellen DeGeneres<br>Rio Ferdinand<br>Anthony Joshua | PG Tips, Walmart, Wendy's, Home Depot |

## LET'S DO THE WORK

Write down what you believe is your brand archetype and why:

_____

_____

_____

_____

_____

# Brand Voice

How does your brand 'speak'?

Your Brand Voice embodies and expresses your brand archetype through words and phrases. It helps to bring your brand personality alive and allows Your Tribe to hear it as well as see it.

It is important to take time to think about how your brand speaks across all brand touch points. Your website, social media, business cards, promotional collateral – what will be heard and how will Your Tribe hear it? How does your brand sound? Are the words you use humorous, creative, blunt, intellectual? All great brands have a Brand Voice that is in line with their brand values, promise and archetype.

US President Donald Trump – blunt, unapologetic, provocative – part of his brand marketing strategy was that he used his Brand Voice during his campaign to capture the headlines and to keep his name in the press. Even his speaking style, which has often been mimicked by comedians, plays into a consistent Brand Voice that adds to the brand's perception and recognition. Whether you agree with his politics or not, his ability to build a personal brand is a lesson to many and the way he has used Twitter as a mouthpiece has carved out a brand tone that supported his winning of the 2016 Presidential Election.

UK Boxing Champion Anthony Joshua – calm, warm, welcoming and often funny – his Brand Voice is nonaggressive. Despite being a boxer and Heavyweight Champion, he has chosen to come from a place of being polite, respectful and speaking about his dedication to the sport. This Brand Voice has been no accident. In an interview with American radio show *The Breakfast Club*, as part of his US debut in early 2019, Joshua spoke about the strategy of his boxing career. During the interview he explained that 'big corporations do not want to be associated with a blood sport and some of the aggression in the sport'. To combat that and make his brand more appealing to the endorsement deals that could derive from large corporates, he opted for a Brand Voice that was enduring and nonaggressive. He talks quietly, he hardly ever swears, he appears intelligent and polite; these traits are unlike those of previous boxers such as Mike Tyson or even Muhammad Ali.

American Internet Personality Gary Vee – abrupt, rude, in your face – known for his social media rants and seminar presentations that include the 'F' word, Gary is the Rebel archetype and his Brand Voice matches it to a tee. He doesn't care who is around, what he is talking about or who it might offend; he will speak in whatever manner he sees fit. His personality comes alive, with force, when he opens his mouth.

The way you speak is important when creating your Brand Voice: the tone and style, but also the catchphrases or specific words that you adopt are equally influential.

From the 'You're Fired' catchphrase first shouted by Donald Trump and later by Lord Alan Sugar in the *Apprentice* TV shows, to Tyra Banks' made-up word 'SMIZE', which means models should smile with their eyes, as seen on her *America's Next Top Model* franchises: all these phrases help to cement the Brand Voice in the mind of its tribe. In the case of Tyra, you can also turn your distinctive words for use as merchandise and businesses in their own rights.

To create your Brand Voice, you need to have a Brand Voice chart. First, think about keywords that you want associated with your brand. Think of these words as your voice characteristics, such as 'passionate', 'fun' or 'quirky'. Then you need to add descriptions on how you will use these words. How would they appear in sentences? Finally, you need to be clear on what you and your team should and should not do when it comes to your Brand Voice.

Here is an example of a Brand Voice chart:

| Voice characteristic | Description | Do | Don't |
|---|---|---|---|
| Passionate | We are obsessed with innovation and challenging the norm. | Use strong verbs. Be champions of industry. | Be wishy-washy or unenthusiastic. |
| Confident | I have been told I am a leader in my field. With 15 years' experience and ten trade awards, I own that title. | Speak with authority. Use data to back up your claims. Introduce new concepts. | Come across kooky. Express uncertainty. Be passive. |
| Reliable | We stand by our products and our customers can count on us to deliver. | Be honest. Take responsibility. Follow through. | Don't oversell. Leave conflicts unresolved. |

Once you have created your Brand Voice chart, you need to think about how your Brand Voice will be executed across your marketing messages and promotions materials. As discussed later in this book, your Brand Voice will be critical when creating branded content. From videos to social media posts, PR to internal communication documents, your Brand Voice needs to be consistent and aligned with all other facets of your Brand ID. With this in mind, what you don't say is just as important as what you do choose to say. But more on that later.

In the interim, let's review how President Obama has mastered his Brand Voice and how it ties into all other elements of his Brand ID.

Obama's personal brand falls under the Hero archetype. As mentioned in Chapter 2, his brand promise was 'Hope and Change' and his logo was an 'O over a rising sun', demonstrating the dawn of a new day in America. These Brand ID elements all come together when you listen to his speeches, where even his voice and writing style embody that of the Hero, as demonstrated in his 2008 speech on race and his 2012 election victory speech:

I chose to run for president at this moment in history because I believe deeply that we cannot solve the challenges of our time unless we solve them together, unless we perfect our union by understanding that we may have different stories, but we hold common hopes; that we may not look the same and may not have come from the same place, but we all want to move in the same direction: toward a better future for our children and our grandchildren.

And this belief comes from my unyielding faith in the decency and generosity of the American people. But it also comes from my own story. I am the son of a black man from Kenya and a white woman from Kansas. I was raised with the help of a white grandfather who survived a Depression to serve in Patton's army during World War II and a white grandmother who worked on a bomber assembly line at Fort Leavenworth while he was overseas.

I've gone to some of the best schools in America and I've lived in one of the world's poorest nations. I am married to a black American who carries within her the blood of slaves and slave owners, an inheritance we pass on to our two precious daughters.

I have brothers, sisters, nieces, nephews, uncles and cousins of every race and every hue scattered across three continents. And for as long as I live, I will never forget that in no other country on earth is my story even possible.

It's a story that hasn't made me the most conventional of candidates. But it is a story that has seared into my genetic makeup the idea that this nation is more than the sum of its parts – that out of many, we are truly one.

President Obama's 2008 'A More Perfect Union' speech on race

Tonight, more than 200 years after a former colony won the right to determine its own destiny, the task of perfecting our union moves forward.

It moves forward because of you. It moves forward because you reaffirmed the spirit that has triumphed over war and depression, the spirit that has lifted this country from the depths of despair to the great heights of hope, the belief that while each of us will pursue our own individual dreams, we are an American family, and we rise or fall together as one nation and as one people.

Tonight, in this election, you, the American people, reminded us that while our road has been hard, while our journey has been long, we have picked ourselves up, we have fought our way back, and we know in our hearts that for the United States of America, the best is yet to come.

President Obama's 2012 victory speech; *Guardian*, 2012

But it doesn't stop there. In the later years of his Presidency he demonstrated consistency of voice through his speeches right up until the end of his farewell speech:

God bless you. Thank you, everybody. Yes we can. Yes we did. Yes we can. God bless America.

President Obama's 2017 farewell speech; *New York Times*, 2017

What we see here, from the beginning of his campaign to the end of his two terms, is a consistency of tone, messaging and voice. The words 'Hope, Change, Us, We' resonate throughout. The phrase 'Yes we can' finished with 'Yes we did', to demonstrate that hope continues even after Obama finished his term in the White House.

Whether you believe him or not, whether you buy into his politics, is secondary, the key is that great brands, both personal and corporate, create a uniformity and continuity that runs through their brand promise, vision, mission, personality and voice.

## LET'S DO THE WORK

Fill in the Brand Voice chart for yourself to start to create your Brand Voice.

| Voice characteristic | Description | Do | Don't |
|---|---|---|---|
|  |  |  |  |
|  |  |  |  |
|  |  |  |  |
|  |  |  |  |

# Typography

The use of typography and symbols is important when creating your Brand ID. As a personal brand you might not have a logo *per se*, but it is important to think about which fonts best reflect your Brand Archetype. This is because your brand typography will be used in every single communication tool, from your emails to your CV, your blog posts to your presentations. Being clear on what typographic works for your brand will create further recognition and connection with your desired audiences. Your fonts can be simple and non-obvious or they can be dramatic and enhance your brand personality. The keys are: what typographic you use, why you have chosen the fonts and how they will be interpreted by Your Tribe. In the same way that your image and colours will forge part of your Brand ID, so will your choice of typography, as it will help to manipulate the significance of your communication.

Corporate brands have understood the power of typography when creating their Brand ID, as outlined below.

## Ella's Kitchen

Popular baby food brand Ella's Kitchen uses uneven, varied sized text on their products to connect with their core demographic of mothers. The 'childish text', which looks like it has been written by a young child with its colourful packaging appeals to mothers because it reminds them of their child/children. The font is playful, the graphics are fun, whilst the innovative packaging is designed to reduce the mess of feeding your child. Both appealing and practical at the same time, this typography is ideal for this tribe.

## Disney

'Waltograph', designed by Justin Callaghan, was born through the inspiration of Walt Disney's handwriting. From 1985 Disney underwent a logo change to harness its young, innocent and magical brand personality, whilst keeping the connection between its founder and the brand.

## *The New York Times*

*The New York Times* uses a gothic Victorian style font to show their history and sophistication of content, which was embedded in the newspaper's launch in 1851. Their font suggests intellect, heritage and expertise.

## Coke and Pepsi

Spencerian Script Penmanship was the standard script taught from the 1860s to the 1920s. Coca-Cola adopted this script style writing in the early 1900s. Its competitor Pepsi used the same script style for their branding from the very beginning but changed their typography in 1962. Whilst it would appear they did this to help create brand distinction and differentiation from Coke, it actually resulted in them losing brand cognition; whereas Coca-Cola, who continue to use this style to this very day, has gained unimaginable brand recognition as a result of the consistency of its typography.

History could have a huge impact on your brand's typography. Depending on the font, you can tell in which era that brand was founded. Cleaner, easier-to-read fonts could suggest a more recent founding date. Nike, which was founded in 1964, opts for a clear, bold and easy to read typography. From the 1960s onwards the fashion trend was all about the future; the future was sleek so the typography matched this. Script writing was seen as old and vintage, so when Nike used the more clean and blocky letters in 1974 it fitted their brand perfectly. Because of this trend a lot of brands underwent a logo change in this era. A few examples of brands using a similar typeface are: McDonalds, who underwent a logo change in 1961; Levi's, whose logo changed in 1969; and Pepsi, whose logo changed in 1962.

Whilst some brands may use specific fonts to distinguish their brand, others use shapes to form letters for their typography. This is seen as both creative and abstract. Gaming company Pac Man, which is revolutionary in the gaming industry, used shapes to create words in the 1980s, and Tesla incorporates this in some of the letters in their logo, enabling them to become synonymous with innovative and revolutionary technology.

Here are some fonts and their associated brands:

| Font Psychology | | |
|---|---|---|
| Type | Font | Personality |
| Serif | Times New Roman | Respectable |
| SansSerif | **Helvetica Bold** | **Stability** |
| SlabSerif | Rockwell | Bold |
| Script | Bickham Script | Elegance |
| Modern | Futura | Progressive |

| Rounded | Arial Rounded | Friendly |
|---------|---------------|----------|
| Geometric | **ƎFOUR DIGITAL PRO** | **RETRO** |
| Geometric Sans Serif | Montserrat | Chic |
| Old Style | Antic Didone | Heritage |

## LET'S DO THE WORK

Choose from these font styles to help you identify a typography that might match your brand archetype. What is your typography?

_____

_____

_____

_____

_____

_____

_____

# Brand packaging and style

Italian fashion designer Miuccia Prada once said, 'What you wear is how you present yourself to the world. Fashion is an instant language.'

I love this statement because it is so very true. Eighty per cent of communication is nonverbal and therefore what you wear plays into how people perceive you. How you act is important but what you wear is critical to creating a brand impression that is 'on-brand' for you.

I remember when I first started working with corporate clients. I was probably 25 years old when I returned from the USA back to the UK and started going to business networking events in the City of London. One day my mother happened to see me before I left to attend an event and she was astounded by my dress sense.

'Aren't you going to wear a suit?' she asked. I honestly wasn't. Coming from an entertainment-marketing background I had no intention of wearing a suit; in fact I hated black and grey suits, especially grey. But not wanting to fail at my first corporate business event, I decided to go back and change.

Whilst at the event, I distinctly remember meeting an older chap, I can't remember his name, but I do remember what he said to me. After possibly 20 minutes of engaging in business small talk, he said, 'I hope you don't mind me saying this, but why are you trying to be older than your years?'

I was shocked by his statement. Curious, I asked, 'What do you mean?'

'You're clearly young, yet you're wearing a suit that seems older, somehow stuffier than the person in front of me. I just think you should embrace your youthfulness. After all, it's this unique perspective that you have on the world that people like me will be interested in.'

Seeing the perplexed and probably vexed expression on my face, he quickly said 'I am just saying. . . you should never be afraid of being you.'

That statement left a lasting impression on me. I was young, I was different from everyone else in the room, so why would I want to pretend to be older? I didn't have their years of experience, but I did have an energy, a hunger that came with my age. From that day onwards I never wore a grey suit again. In fact, as the years have gone by, I have found that colours, bright colours particularly, have helped to personify my Sage with a little Creative brand archetype. Whether that be the colour on my nails or a bright lipstick, a pop of colour on my shoes or big afro hair. The colour brings out my effervescence and my eagerness to be a different version of a traditional brand consultant. But I am not the only personal brand that has taken the time to think through its brand style. Below are examples of others who have made lucrative careers out of their expertise but also their recognizable style.

As mentioned earlier in this book, the late Karl Lagerfeld was well known for his pulled-back white hair, black shades and a pristine tailored black suit. As creative director for luxury fashion houses such as Balmain, Chloe, Valentino, Fendi and Chanel, Lagerfeld oozes luxury and is the essence of being suave. In celebration of his own unique viewpoint – 'fashion is an attitude more than a clothing detail' – his style has become so iconic it became his own fashion label logo. Many of his designs sport the synonymous effortless, rock-chic style that everyone has come to know and love.

Apple's co-founder Steve Jobs' distinct designs for clean, minimalistic aesthetics not only worked for Apple products but also his own personal brand style. Known for saying 'simplicity is the ultimate sophistication', this statement translated to his simple black turtlenecks, jeans and trainers, which became a statement of a new type of CEO styling.

Editor-in-Chief for American *Vogue*, Anna Wintour, owns her Ruler archetype. Known for saying that 'trends is a dirty word', her never-changing hair has always remained a short bob with bangs since the early days of her career. Fond of 1960s styling, her wide-framed glasses are a staple during London Fashion Week as she sits on the front row of fashion shows. It could be said that these glasses are an important part of her not giving away how she feels about the designers whose careers she can make or break with one swoop of an inclusion in American *Vogue*.

To start to create your own Brand Style, I sat down with personal brand stylist Alex Agboke. Our conversation was extremely interesting and insightful. Here's what was said about how she works with clients to get them to own their style:

**Alex** *One of the things I would ask my clients is, what is good style? The answer is a visual appearance that can grow in line with your core values, your character and your complexion.*

*There are five main basic style personalities and people tend to be a mixture of two. The main style personalities are:*

1   Dramatic

2   Classic

3   Natural

4   Creative

5   Romantic

## Dramatic personality

- Loves to make an entrance, loves structure, creates drama and adventure with their clothes.

- Clothing type – Highly structured, leather, sharp contrast. Dresses for impact rather than comfort. Will tend to be high fashion and super on-trend (or just before it hits the high street).

- Examples – Kris Jenner, Sharon Osbourne, Dita Von Teese.

## Classic personality

- Simple cuts, quality, no loud colours, often wears neutrals, nothing that shouts too loudly.

- Clothing type – Chooses timeless cuts and styles.

- Examples – Victoria Beckham, Meghan Markle, Angelina Jolie.

## Natural personality

- Dresses for comfort more than anything else. Tends to wear natural fabrics, unfussy and simple.

- Generally hates all things fashion. As stylists we must be careful not to make them feel uncomfortable about their style personality.

- Example – Cameron Diaz.

## Creative personality

- Likes to look different and edgy but not necessarily high fashion. They're more in touch with how clothes express their personality.

- Will feel like they have lost their mojo in clothes that are too classic and plain and they're not afraid to wear what they want, whether it's fashionable or not.

- Examples – Gwen Stefani, Carrie Bradshaw from *Sex and the City*.

## Romantic personality (can be boho)

- Loves everything feminine, from fabric, to cut, to style.

- Loves the ethereal elements of clothes that are very lady-like, often feathery and gentle in demeanour, almost gamine in appearance.

- Fabric choice: Lace, silk, pearls and dresses

- Examples – Kate Middleton, Katie Holmes.

*There are a lot of different fashion theories but I like to keep it simple; people tend to be a mixture of two, one which will be dominant and the other subordinate. Those are people's style personalities and they really work well when people learn to connect them to their personalities.*

*For example, one of my clients came to me a year ago – a retired teacher in her early 50s. Her children were now older and she wanted to follow her passion of teaching Indian cookery and make it a successful business. I liked her immediately, as she was serious about making change and bringing her personal style in line with her vision. But her style was safe and bland, pleasant and inoffensive. She wore very little makeup and her style was slightly mindy. Then I tasted her cooking and experienced first-hand her love, passion and enthusiasm for the flavours and culinary delights of her homeland. She came alive! But where was any of that in her personal presentation? Not one bit. I had met her at a networking event where she was really friendly and warm but instantly forgettable. I didn't take her seriously (first mistake) and dismissed her as a nice lady with a hobby. We had some work to do but she was up for the challenge – starting with her personal style statement.*

*We found words to describe her – passionate, vibrant, enigmatic. Then her cooking, which was strong, not overly complicated, and authentic. Her colour analysis showed that she best suited bright and warm colours (funny that!) and her style was classic and elegant. A million miles from the jeans, floaty shirts and cardigans she had been wearing on a daily basis.*

*After an evening over the most beautiful dinner, we decided that her PSS (personal style statement) was: 'I project an image that is spirited, simple and elegant.'*

*Her logo was black and orange. So in turn we chose 'edible colours' like greens, oranges and yellows from her personal colour palette to complement her brand. Colours that would also have a physiological effect on her audience.*

*Even though she would be wearing an apron for many of her cookery presentations, her brand style was still strong underneath it. Instead of wearing a practical tee-shirt and jeans she would now wear a bright one-colour dress or a vibrant flowing top with black floor-length trousers – even a softly tailored jumpsuit. She would look strong, elegant, yet vibrant. At her networking events we worked on choosing understated styles but in bold colours, finished elegantly with statement pieces of jewellery to reflect her Indian heritage. We wanted her to convey strength and authenticity. We wanted people to leave her presence feeling warm, enthusiastic and maybe even curious about her business and services.*

**Kubi** *So what you worked on was conveying inner style personality through clothes, so then your outer style personality is your physiology?*

**Alex** *Yes, it would be your physique, so you're thinking about your proportions, your complexion and your shape. Those are the three main aspects to think of in relation to your physique. So you are asking yourself questions like: Are you tall? Is your body longer than your legs? Those kinds of things are really important to know, especially if you are doing any public speaking, you have to be aware of your proportions.*

**Kubi** *Why?*

**Alex** *Because, for example, when you are up on a podium, people are most likely looking up at you. So if you have shorter proportions – for example your legs are shorter than your body – you have to make people see balance, you don't want them to see short legs and huge body. Public speaking is a challenging area because you really have to manage your appearance for the space in which you are speaking.*

**Kubi** *Is there anything else that is important in your style personality within business?*

**Alex** *'You have 60 seconds to make a first impression': it's where we make a subconscious judgement about a person, thing or place, so it goes beyond what you look like. Did you know around 62–90 per cent of that is based on colour? So based on the colour you are wearing or the room you walked into it will impact 62–90 per cent of your first impression. Colour has physiological effects on all of us; that's the whole aspect of the psychology of colours.*

**Kubi** *How can we relate it to our personal brand style?*
**Alex** *One thing about personal colour is that it has to suit that person. Your eyes are built to see harmony. If you listen to a song and someone's tone is not quite right, you won't hear harmony. It's the same with colour and patterns,*

*so one thing I say to clients is that you want to display a harmonious feature, because that person is seeing a picture; that is why we remember more visually than we do verbally or audibly.*

*For example, I tend to wear green when I am going somewhere I don't know because it is the most neutral colour on your eye – it is mid-wavelength. If you think about greenery, how nature is green, it is creating balance. So I wear it as it not only balances me but it balances others; and, on the other hand if I want to walk into a room and announce my presence, I will wear a shade of red.*

*The functions of the colours usually go as follows.*

## Red

- Most powerful colour, great for networking.

- Longest wavelength.

- Colour of passion, excitement, sexuality and danger.

- Promotes appetite, increases blood pressure.

- Negative: Too sexy in the wrong context.

## Blue

- Second most powerful colour.

- Masculine, cool and calm.

- Colour of intelligence, strength and authority.

- Biggest corporate colour.

- Negative: Cold and impersonal.

## Yellow

- Warm, lively and stimulating.

- Will speak of confidence and enthusiasm.
- Negative: Frivolous.

# Green

- The most restful colour for the human eye.
- Universal colour of nature.
- Will put people at ease.

# Purple

- Colour of the spirit.
- Represents our higher being.
- Regality, luxury and strength.
- Often a royal colour denoting majesty.
- Will speak of regality and quiet professionalism.

# Pink

- Most gentle and feminine colour.
- Represents softness.
- Great for romantic dates.
- Negative: Must be worn in the right context or matched with another colour.

# Brown

- Associated with nature, trees and wood.
- Represents conservancy and humility.

- It's the most familiar colour to our subconscious and so denotes in a business sense trustworthiness and stability.

- Negative: Can look boring so choose a more luxurious fabric like crepe or satin.

## White

- Associated with purity, innocence and birth.

- Keeps you cool in a hot climate as it reflects the sun's energy.

- White makes a good neutral because it establishes clarity and contrast against other colours and images.

## Black

- Positively associated with elegance and class.

- Mostly associated with death, fear and mourning.

- A good and preferred colour to highlight and contrast other colours.

*After understanding the functions of the colours we would identify what your brand colours are, but we would then need to find the right shade of colours for you so that it is harmonious and doesn't distract from what you are trying to communicate.*

*What you are wearing is your visual marketing; you don't want to detract from your message. You don't want to say that you are bold but you are 'cheap' if you are wearing the wrong shades. If you want to say you are knowledgeable but yet you're not visible – you'll do that if you're wearing pastels that are too dull for you. You don't want to work against your brand messaging by contradicting it with what you are wearing.*

**Kubi** *When I was doing a talk in a private investment firm, a woman came up to me rather upset when I told her to own her authentic self. She told me* *that she had tried but the company wouldn't allow her to be herself. She was dressed quite punk with a touch of corporate; what would your advice be in these situations?*

**Alex** *Well, you need to start with people's perception of things, so what are people's perceptions of punk? You are basically having to manage people's perceptions of yourself within the boundaries of where you are. You have to think, 'ok, what is their perception of punk?' and there will be some things you won't need to change and some things you'll need to adapt. You have to work with their perception and pull them more subtly around to you. You have to take your creativity and work within the corporate boundaries. You have to deal with their limitations and manage that in a way you feel comfortable, otherwise it's not going to work and you shouldn't be there.*

**Kubi** *Ok. In developing your personal brand style, would it be important to have a vision board?*

**Alex** *Yes, use Pinterest to outline what you are drawn to, what feels like it is you, what has an essence of you? Now, you need to be careful; for example, people who are in their 40s may find something that is sexy, but that might have been sexy back when they were in their 30s but isn't necessarily working for their body type now. Sometimes I see pictures of women projecting how they want to look but that is not who they are now. You have to focus on the essence of the style and then work out how you adapt that to your colours, personality and figure. Use Style Icons: they are a good starting place to give yourself a sense of who you are drawn towards. For example, people who like Jackie O, they tend to like elegance and being regal, and when I see that I get a sense of what they are hoping to look like and I will think of ways how I can help them to achieve that. Having a style icon gives me clues.*

## LET'S DO THE WORK

*What is your style personality statement?*

_____

*What is your style colour?*

_____

*Who is your style icon?*

_____

*How can you adapt that style to your personal brand (remember to factor in your age, personality and body type)?*

_____

# Brand differentiation

*Be a different sound amongst the noise.*

Creating your brand differentiation is less about creating it, and more about uncovering it. I strongly believe that you shouldn't project what you're not, but instead harness what you already have. In a world that is cluttered with so much noise, we should be aiming to stand out from a place of owning our truth.

Whenever I talk about brand differentiation in a masterclass or conference, I often reference my 'afro story'. It goes like this:

A few years ago I was asked by a multinational professional services firm to deliver a brand training session for their midlevel managers. They wanted me to be on stage for a 90-minute session, teaching their staff how to build their personal brands and social capital. I was flattered by the invitation, but somewhat intrigued. 'Why me?' was all I kept thinking. After all, I am the Diddy-girl, the Justin Timberlake-girl ... the one with the celebrity, entertainment and fashion brand portfolio. I don't wear grey suits! After delivering the training, I pulled the hiring manager aside; I figured he was happy with my session, and might be open to providing some honest feedback. So I asked, 'Why me? Why did you choose to hire me for this conference?'

His reply was game changing: 'Historically, we've had male consultants, normally over the age of 50, mostly white, who have all gone to Ivy League universities, Cambridge or Oxford, and they have a background in finance. They are good. But this time we wanted something ... different.'

I nearly fell off my chair.

His bluntness shocked me and his candid answer ran through me like electronic waves in my body. All of a sudden the things that I was once told would hold me back – being female, being younger than most of my counterparts, being black, not having a masters degree from a top business school – now they were my strengths! My diverse experiences meant that I had something different to say and, what's more, people were ready to hear it. I didn't belong in the room because I assimilated; I belonged because I stood true to my authentic self. My image, history, story, personality and style were what made me relevant. My career path was not sidelined to just one thing, but embraced as an option for new solutions. It was as if my 'afro' had become my superpower! Today I unapologetically embrace 'me' and use my truth across every brand touch point. Even in my client pitch meetings I say: 'If you want the same old thing, if you want to do what you have always done, that is not me. But if you need something different, something with a unique perspective to help solve your unique problems, in today's globally diverse world, I am the girl for you.' Without justification, my Brand ID sits at the core of who I truly am.

Now it's time for you to do the same. What is it about you that brings something fresh to your industry? What is it about the way you do things – your processes, or innovations, your delivery style, history or background – that enables you to be different from your competitors? What does your industry need? How do your unique attributes help to solve the problem?

Dig deep.

What is yours? What makes you a cut above the rest? What do you dislike about you, that could actually be the very thing that makes you stand out and be desired by Your Tribe? What have you been trying to hide, that Your Tribe needs to see?

---

## LET'S DO THE WORK

*What is your superpower?*

_____

_____

_____

_____

_____

_____

_____

---

# References

Biography.com (2014). 'Iman Biography', 2 April 2014. https://www.biography.com/people/iman-9542466

CNBC (2017). 'Who Gets Paid Most at New York Fashion Week' by Karen Gilchrist, 9 February 2017. https://www.cnbc.com/2017/02/09/who-gets-paid-most-at-new-york-fashion-week.html

CNBC Make It (2018). 'Why Warren Buffett is Such an Influential Leader, According to 40 Years of Data' by Zameena Mejia, 24 February 2018. https://www.cnbc.com/2018/02/23/why-warren-buffett-is-such-an-influential-leader-according-to-data.html

Guardian (2012). 'Barack Obama's Victory Speech'. *Guardian* 7 November 2012. https://www.theguardian.com/world/2012/nov/07/barack-obama-speech-full-text

Independent (2017a). 'The Steve Jobs Guide to Manipulating People and Getting What You Want' by Dave Smith. *Independent*, 1 September 2017. https://www.independent.co.uk/life-style/steve-jobs-manipulation-guide-getting-what-you-want-a7924321.html

Isaacson, W. (2011). *Steve Jobs*. New York: Simon & Schuster.

Liberman, N. (2015). *Being Warren Buffett: Life Lessons From A Cheerful Billionaire*. Victoria, Australia and London, UK: Hardie Grant Books.

Livity Agency London (2017). 'Dyson "The Smart Rooms" by Livity' Campaign, 24 January 2017, https://www.campaignlive.co.uk/article/dyson-the-smart-rooms-livity/1421913

New York Times (2017). 'President Obama's Farewell Address'. *New York Times*, 10 January 2017. https://www.nytimes.com/2017/01/10/us/politics/obama-farewell-address-speech.html

Obama, Barack (2018). 'A More Perfect Union', speech delivered in Philadelphia, 18 March 2008. Available at: American Rhetoric, 29 September 2018. https://americanrhetoric.com/speeches/barackobamaperfectunion.htm

ValueWalk (2015). 'Revealing Seven Personality Traits That Have Made Warren Buffett A Cheerful Billionaire', 22 May 2015 https://www.valuewalk.com/2015/05/warren-buffett-cheerful-billionaire/

Witter, B. (2018). 'Why Oprah's Car Giveaway Is the Most Epic Talk Show Moment Ever', Biography, 11 December 2018. https://www.biography.com/news/oprah-car-giveaway

# Websites

'The Entertainer' by Debbie O. 2019. https://brandpersonalities.com.au/personalities/the-entertainer/

Marketing101. '12 Brand Archetypes' https://marketingideas101.com/idea-center/branding-idea-center/branding-101-12-brand-archetypes/

Retail Marketing Group. 'What Are Brand Personalities?' 15 September 2017. https://www.retailmarketing.com/what-are-brand-personalities

VisionOne. 'The Regular Guy Brand Archetype' https://visionone.co.uk/consumer/brand-research/brand-archetypes-2/regular-guy-brand-archetype/

Aspect Film and Video. 'What Are Brand Archetypes and Why Do They Matter?' by Evelyn Timson, 5 April 2018. https://www.aspectfilmandvideo.co.uk/brand-archetypes-matter/

# 6

# Hope Is Not a Strategy

Decision. Vision. Clarity. **STRATEGY**. Tactics. Metrics.
Ownership. Be Unapologetic

The first half of this book has been designed to give you the tools and confidence to create your personal brand and carve out your brand purpose, to give you further understanding of your brand identity and brand superpower. With clarity of who you are, now you need to devise a plan on how to take who you are to market. Having established your *pull*, it is time to focus on your *push*.

But before you can create a plan, you need a strategy.

It's common for people to confuse the difference between a brand marketing plan and a brand marketing strategy, often making the mistake that they are the same thing. On the contrary – a brand marketing strategy is an explanation of what you are trying to achieve. Deeply rooted in your business or career aspirations, your brand marketing strategy outlines what you want to accomplish with your marketing efforts. The brand marketing plan, on the other hand, is the *how* it will be done. It is the tactical approach needed to make the strategy happen.

I often tell my clients who are trying to market their personal brand that they need a 'GO-AA-TA' – Goals & Objectives, Awareness & Approach, Targets

& Application. When you put these together, your 'GO-AA-TA' becomes your personal brand marketing *strategy*. These elements give you the stepping stones to achieve your ambitions, whereas your personal brand marketing *plan* will include your marketing messages, your channels of communication (also known as the marketing mix), your marketing budget, timeframe for implementation, metrics and ROI (Return on Investment) calculators. The plan outlines what needs to be implemented to make the strategy work, so that your ambitions are met.

To help you understand this better, here is a breakdown of the 'GO-AA-TA'.

# Goals

To effectively market your personal brand you need to have a destination in mind. Your goal is a description of that destination. Ask yourself:

- What are my three-year goals?
- What results and desired outcome do I want to achieve?
- What am I trying to do, and by when?

Don't think about what you want in twenty years, this is too far away and could result in you going into day-dream land. Over-exaggerated goals and desires are common, but ultimately useless. So instead, keep it concise, with a clear outcome over a short period of time. I would always recommend starting with no more than three to five years.

If you are struggling, don't worry – a lot of people struggle to answer these questions because they believe that as long as they just put their head down and work hard, they will somehow magically become a success. Somewhere in their subconscious they think that hard work alone will act as the marketing tool to get them noticed. But it doesn't work that way. Your hard work will enable you to deliver results, but just because you deliver results does not mean you will be noticed. How many people have you seen in the workplace who do less than you, yet they still get promoted? This is because these people have realized that working hard is not enough; you have to have a strategy, and your strategy starts with you being clear about your goals.

Think of it like this: branding is a business driver, and since you are in the business of one, where do you want your brand marketing to drive you to?

If you are working in a company, this is particularly important, as you can easily be sucked into creating goals that are based solely on the organizational goals. Whilst it is imperative that you understand and align with your company's goals, you also need goals of your own. Once you have your own goals, the organizational goals should be assisting your personal brand goals, at the same time as you delivering theirs. If you have no goals, you will end up working for a pay cheque, with no focus on how that pay cheque enables you to thrive beyond just paying your bills.

Whilst some executives suffer from the 'I'll just work hard' approach, I tend to find the opposite with freelancers and budding entrepreneurs. Their answer to the question 'what are your three-year goals?' tends to be complex and highly convoluted. Ordinarily, budding entrepreneurs come to me with too many goals; they want to do everything, and as a result they are achieving nothing. I am a strong believer that you can do everything in your lifetime, but you can't do everything all at the same time. You need to focus your energy on an idea, a destination, not five or six! Just think what would happen if you put five different destinations into your SatNav – you would end up going nowhere fast. Your brand marketing is like your SatNav, in that it is helping you to navigate your way to your business or career aspirations. But to be effective, your SatNav must have a singular destination.

If you find that you have lots of ideas and are not sure what to do, then force yourself to make a decision, and *choose ONE*. Ideally the one that brings out the best in you; the one that utilizes your capabilities and skills in a way that makes you feel joy and brings in results. Don't try to reinvent the wheel, but instead stay focused on what comes naturally to you. Identify what capabilities you have and run with the ones that come easily. I always say, 'it's important to follow the path of least resistance'; in other words, go with what flows effortlessly. Usually the things that come to us the easiest are the ones we want to discard. We act as if the journey to success is meant to be super hard and so we try to find something else. I hear people saying: 'I want to find my purpose', but what does that really mean? For me, your 'purpose' is in your hands, it is the thing you do most easily. It's easy for you because it's what you're meant to share with the world; not everyone has that gift, so the world needs it from you.

*What you have been born to do can be found in what you have been born with.*

Don't make it harder than it is. Stop thinking about what you should be doing and instead go with what you naturally do best. If you are naturally good at convincing people and can sell ice to Eskimos, chances are you're meant to be working with that gift. If you were the joker at school and always making people laugh, chances are you're meant to be working with that gift. If you are naturally brilliant at drawing, chances are you are meant to be working with *that* gift. Acknowledge your natural gifts and align them to your career or business aspirations. Naturally good at drawing? You could launch a graphic design studio, focus on being an industrial designer, makeup artist, animator, illustrator, cake decorator or an art teacher. Naturally good at selling? You could master being an advertising account director, customer service manager, real estate agent, financial service sales agent, fashion modelling agent, software sales, insurance sales, retail merchandising. Naturally good at communicating and making people feel welcome? You could master broadcast journalism, customer service, or become a motivational speaker, a comedian or script writer.

I know this all sounds obvious, but trust me when I say this; I see so many people wandering aimlessly through their careers searching for their 'purpose' as opposed to making a decision to align their natural abilities to a career and mastering that. The key is to focus less on trying to find a purpose and more on mastering your gift; the channel that gift is used for can, and probably will, change over the course of your lifetime. But if you own your natural gifts and stop following trends, then you will find it easier to brand and market these gifts.

I know this is true, because I was once that person who completely missed this; I spent all of my 20s thinking marketing was just something I did because I could no longer dance. By the time I reached 30, I wanted to give up marketing. It bored me because it came too easy to me. It was so natural, that I thought it was meaningless. But actually my natural ability to brand and market things is why I'm able to do it so well. What's more, the pain of not being 'seen' as a child dancer aligns to my desire to see other people shine. Making them shine is marketing! It took me years to understand that. To align my purpose with my natural ability, and my pain with my mission.

When professionals come to me distressed over what their goals should be, asking which one of their talents they should use to get to their end destination, they do this because they mostly think their end destination is money. When I ask them: 'Where do you want to be in three years? What are your three-year goals?' They say things like: 'I want to be making more money!'

However, this is an illogical statement. Money is not a destination, money is a result of delivering a brand of excellence. Money is a result of fulfilling a particular demand. Money, and lots of it, comes as a result of being the best at what you do. Money is a tool to help you get to the destination, but it is not the destination itself.

Those with commercially successful personal brands focus on being known for something specific, and do not focus on just making money. They spend years developing their skills, capabilities, talents and gifts to master something. Once they do this, they get paid well because they are the best at what they do. Think of any successful personal brand, then think about what they are known for.

Here's my list and what I think their gifts are:

- Beyoncé – singing

- Tony Robbins – motivating

- Serena Williams – tennis

- David Beckham – football

- Nicole Kidman – acting

- Usain Bolt – running

- Albert Einstein – physics

- Nelson Mandela – leadership

Imagine if James Dyson had said, 'my goal is money'; we simply would not have the Dyson vacuum cleaner today. He would have stopped at the first hurdle. But because his goal was more than money, he tried 5,127 times before he got it right!

Your personal brand goals need to go beyond financial reward. When you serve others well, and bring the best of you to the table, then they will pay you well in return. What's more, those who focus on being experts at a particular thing get paid the most. Generalists get generalists' money: experts with niche skills, talents and abilities are in much higher demand. It is important to have financial targets (which we will cover later), but your goals should be much bigger than money.

Furthermore, just because you have lots of talents and interests, it doesn't mean you need to build a brand and market all of those talents and interests all at once. For example, Beyoncé – who is a phenomenal singer – first mastered her singing ability and then, once her singing career was established, she launched a clothing line. She didn't try to do both at the same time right at the beginning of her career. Tony Robbins is a motivational speaker who developed an online coaching resource once his brand as a speaker was established. David Beckham is a footballer, who went from football academy to professional football before he tried to secure endorsement deals. The contracts came off the back of his notoriety from football.

I can sing, in fact I love singing, but that doesn't mean I need to be a singer. My job is to find what my *natural abilities* are and *turn them into commercial commodities*. I am a much better talker than I am singer, so I use the art of communication to teach people how to build their brands. Combining my natural talent of communicating and marketing with a learnt skill of branding, I mastered the two, marketed the two, and then I got paid as a Brand Specialist. Take this book, for example: just because I have written a book and love the process of writing, doesn't mean I start marketing myself as an 'author' – I am no J.K. Rowling! On the contrary, I am a Brand Specialist who happens to have a book that teaches people how to build their brands. It is the expertise of being a Brand Specialist that needs to be marketed, not the author part. Of course it is ok to mention that I'm an author, but my income comes from my expertise as a Brand Specialist, and you picked up this book in the hope that my expertise would help you.

So you market the expertise, and set goals around it.

Why is this important? Because we as human beings innately trust people who have dedicated their time to mastering a particular thing. We admire the dedication. We're in awe of their 'superhuman ability' to be the best. We buy for specific reasons, and when someone has specific skills, to solve our specific problem, with a solution they've mastered and in their specific way, we buy from them, each and every time.

There is this myth that to be successful you need to be doing lots and lots of different things. You need multiple income streams and therefore it's ok to have your hands in different pies. Whilst I have nothing against multiple income streams (in fact, I think they're sometimes necessary), when *marketing* your personal brand you need to be focused. When setting goals for your personal brand, which will result in marketing activities, you need to be focused on being known for a thing, not everything. Whenever I see people trying to market two or three different things all at start-up stage, I wonder why they are doing this. Rome was not built in a day!

Remember, when we reviewed Oprah's career journey it took her years from starting as a presenter before she opened the OWN Network. What would have happened if she had tried to launch *The Oprah Winfrey Show*, the OWN Network and *O Magazine* all in the same year? She would not have had the knowledge, contacts, experience, or financial backing to make it all work. It sounds obvious but I see people doing this all the time. You look at their profile on LinkedIn and it says, 'Entrepreneur, Speaker, Yoga Instructor, Presenter & Author!' Honestly, there are people with such titles! The reality is that if you look like you do everything, no-one will take you seriously. When you start to set multiple goals, and marketing for multiple things all at the same time, you confuse Your Tribe. So focus on one thing, not everything, and create specific goals around it.

## LET'S DO THE WORK

***What do you want to be known for?***

_____

***What are your three-year goals?***
Take a moment to write them down:

*Year 1:*_____

_____

_____

*Year 2:*_____

_____

_____

*Year 3:*_____

_____

_____

# Objectives

An objective is a measure of the progress that is needed to get to the destination.

- What are you trying to achieve year on year to reach your goals?

- How can you take each goal and break it down into measurable outcomes?

Your goals will determine your objectives, but equally you can't have objectives without a clear goal. In other words, you can't have a breakdown of what you are doing if you don't know where you are going. People often use goals and objectives interchangeably, but they are not the same thing: a goal is the destination; an objective is the measured progress to reach the destination.

For example, if you say 'my goal is to be the number one salesperson in my company in three years', the objectives could be to win X number of accounts in year one, to increase this win by 20 per cent in year two and to be awarded 'Employee of the Year' in year three, with the wins announced in the company newsletter. Here you can see a clear destination and a breakdown of measured outcomes to get to that destination.

Once you have your goal, then you can work on your objectives. Here are some examples of objectives that you can use to help achieve your goals:

- *New customer acquisition* – Most entrepreneurs and freelancers turn to this objective first; they want to attract more leads and secure sign-ups from new customers. Whilst this is a brilliant objective, to be effective it needs to be broken down. Simply saying 'I want more customers' is not enough. How many customers do you want? What resources need to be in place to support the demand? The last thing you want to do is attract new leads, convert them into sales and then lose them because your brand failed to deliver due to a lack of resources and an ineffective infrastructure.

- *Retain customers* – 80 per cent of business should come from repeat business! When your brand is delivering on its brand promise, you should not lose existing customers to your competitors; instead you need to have a set of objectives that focuses on how you retain existing customers. How do you ensure your business keeps those who have already signed up? And how do you use those already engaged to be your brand ambassadors to generate new leads?

- *Increase brand awareness* – Brand awareness is about how well your desired customer can recall or remember your brand. The art is to communicate your brand promise, brand mission, brand personality, style and differentiation. What therefore is your visual stimuli? How will the brand penetrate the psyche of your audience? How will you be remembered? Awareness takes time and requires a great deal of consistency. Think of it like water dripping from a tap: you need the consistent, but small drops to eventually fill up the sink. If you turn off the tap, you have stopped the filling of the water. So never turn off the 'tap', because emotive brand awareness is one of the most effective ways to pull people towards your brand, without the need for a hard push.

- *Launch a new product or service* – This is often done when someone wants to solidify their position in the market or increase their market share. The prerequisite for success is ensuring the launch complements your existing products or services, and remains 'on-brand' with your overall brand promise. It is imperative to make sure the conditions are right for a launch and that you launch during your peak buying cycle, asking yourself – what time of year, or month, would be the best time to launch this product/service and why?

- *Increase market share* – This can be measured by calculating the number of sales you made within your industry over a particular time period, then calculating what percentage of your sales are based on the overall sells within that industry, over the same timeframe. For example, if you made £250,000 in 2018 and within that same year your industry sales were £2.5 million, then you have a 10 per cent market share that year. An objective to increase market share can be easily measured and clearly quantified, making it an effective part of your brand marketing strategy.

- *Attract collaborators* – The ability to attract partners, sponsors, affiliates, influencers, endorsers is vital for personal brand success. Identifying the right collaborators is essential as they help to reduce your marketing spend and act as effective stepping stones to brand expansion. I always advise my clients to ensure that this is a key part of their brand marketing strategy; however, a word of caution is to ensure you partner with the right collaborators – i.e. people who share your brand values, work ethic and professional principles.

- *Enter new markets* – It is continually presumed that entering new markets is strictly for large firms, but this is not necessarily the case. Personal brands can, and should, look at where the 'hungry markets' are and attempt to go there. Whether that be local or international markets, you can analyse that market to see if they would embrace your brand or help to propel it to new heights. Later in this chapter we will explore 'hungry vs saturated markets' but for now just remember that the world is very big, but also very, very small, so what is to stop you from travelling and working abroad? I advise my clients (and myself) that the adventure, even with children and a family, is one worth exploring.

- *Improve internal communications* – Your first and number one customer is your staff! Freelancers, interns, part-timers, contractors, permanent staff or even your mother – anyone who works for you needs to buy into your brand. Therefore one part of your objectives could be outlining how you will ensure staff buy-in. Which communication tools are needed as part of your strategy to get your team fully onboard and effective brand ambassadors? How do you communicate updates, progress and developments happening around your brand? This is particularly important for personal brands who are freelancers without offices, which means staff are working remotely and need mechanisms for effective communication flow.

- *Improve stakeholder relations* – Everyone within Your Tribe needs to buy into your brand: your boss, senior management team, colleagues across departments, suppliers and partners. You can't just be good, you need buy-in from those who engage with your brand in order for your brand to get things done and thrive. Word-of-mouth marketing is still the best marketing there is, so how will you get all of your stakeholder groups to buy-into you? There are lots of ways to achieve this, which we will cover under 'Tactics' later in this book.

- *Secure a new job or contract* – This could be a critical part of your strategic objectives. If you have a career aspiration, it might be that your current company can't help you grow and achieve that goal, so being brave and leaving to find a new role could be exactly what you need to do. It takes guts to move from a comfortable job, but if moving will help you achieve that goal, you have to jump!

- *Reposition your brand* – If you want to change how your brand is perceived by your customers, clients or wider tribe, repositioning might be a strategic objective. To do this effectively, you need to think through where you want to sit in the market, what your niche or specialism is, and plan key communication messages to support the transition.

- *Increase your social capital* – When developing your personal brand for both your career or business, your social capital is extremely important. The saying 'show me your network and I will show you, your net-worth', is so very true. As such, it's important to create marketing campaigns with the objective of increasing your business relationships. Finding the time to actively create a campaign that develops your contacts is necessary for career success.

## LET'S DO THE WORK

|        | Goal | Objective breakdown |
|--------|------|---------------------|
| Year 1 |      |                     |
| Year 2 |      |                     |
| Year 3 |      |                     |

# Awareness

Recently, I had a brand coaching session with a group of freelancers and asked them to list their personal brand goals and objectives. I was shocked by their answers, most of which were alarmingly vague. To give you an example, I will outline a conversation I had with one particular client.

Client A is a fashion stylist, with a background in teaching, but has decided to embark on a new career. She is in her early 40s and wants to follow her passion for fashion. When I asked her to outline her three-year goals, she explained that she wanted to work with corporates. 'Ok,' I said 'that answer is very broad.'

She paused, laughed and then said she knows, but what do I think?

'Well, it's vague for two reasons: firstly, you've not stated in what capacity you want to work with corporate companies; and secondly, you haven't outlined what type of corporate firms.'

After giving it some thought she explained that she wanted to work as a speaker helping employees discover their personal style. So I continued, 'Who needs this service? What type of organizations would deem this of value and why?'

Again she failed to have a complete answer. Then I probed further: 'Who's already doing this in your market? How successful are they? What would be your measurable objectives to let you know you are reaching that goal and achieving success?' She looked at me with a blank stare, completely unable to answer any of the questions. This is because she had very little knowledge of the market and was unaware of the industry trends; the needs of her potential customer or prerequisites of working as a fashion stylist. What's more, the title she had given herself as 'fashion stylist', as opposed to 'personal brand stylist', didn't naturally align with the demographic she was seeking to serve.

But Client A is not alone, and there are lots and lots of people who set goals in a vacuum. Normally people are unable to list specific goals and measurable objectives because they have very little knowledge of the sectors and markets they wish to work in. Instead of making blanket statements, they need to spend time studying the industries to ascertain where the biggest pain-points are, what the latest trends are and how their skills can fit in to it. But a lot of people simply can't be bothered, or are unaware of the need to research, study or become knowledgeable in their chosen industry, because they underestimate the value of it. They think that setting a goal and visualizing it is enough, and it simply isn't. Whilst I'm all for visualization, and I think vision boards are important, to be able to 'see the goal' clearly is essential. However, the reality is, if your goals are set without evidence of need, you will be visualizing a dream that may never materialize.

Don't get me wrong. At this stage you might not know *how* you are going to reach that goal, and that's ok; but you should be able to be specific on where you're trying to get to and why you think you are the person to deliver it. When you understand the industry you are trying to conquer, you are better equipped to explain to yourself and others why you are the one to do it.

As part of the process, here are some key areas for you to seek knowledge.

## Your market

What's happening in your market? As mentioned in Chapter 3, it's important to undertake a PESTLE Analysis. With all the global shifts, having an awareness of the Political, Economic, Sociological, Technological, Legal and Environmental landscape will help you to see what trends are emerging that will aid or hinder your personal brand growth.

You also need to know if you are operating in a 'hungry market' or a 'saturated market'. A 'saturated market' is one in which there is lots of competition and very little demand for what you have to offer. The opposite is a 'hungry market'; in which there is very little competition and lots of demand. Or there might be lots of competition but the demand is so high it doesn't impact your brand success. The concept of a hungry vs saturated market applies to both business as well as personal brands. As an example: a client of mine found herself working for a large multinational company in their CSR (Corporate Social Responsibility) division. Due to the size of the firm, their CSR activities were robust and the team was big, spread across three different countries. She observed that she had very little room to grow in this company. The 'competition' was high and so it was proving difficult for her to really shine or to win a promotion. She decided to leave and secure a job in another company, equal in size but without a vigorous CSR division. This then created demand for her expertise and knowledge. Not only was it a new company but she was also now part of a new sector that was trying to incorporate more CSR activities. As such, she was brought in to help grow the department and implement innovative new campaigns. In this environment she could thrive because the demand was high, and the competition was low.

Often people can find themselves in a saturated market but assume that the problem is them, when in reality the problem is not them at all, it's just that they are operating in the wrong market. I see people all the time questioning their skills, abilities, price points, service and products, thinking they have it all wrong, when, really, they are just operating in a saturated market. Having awareness of this both elevates the pain and provides the solution, which is sometimes to leave and go where there is a higher demand for you and what you have to offer.

## LET'S DO THE WORK

***Are you in a hungry or saturated market?***
Explain why and then write three things you can do to reposition your brand:

_____

_____

_____

_____

_____

# Your competitors

Success leaves a footprint; whose footprint do you need to follow? As mentioned in Chapter 3, you should spend time undertaking a Competitor Analysis across your aspirational, direct and non-direct competitors, so that you are aware of who they are, and what they are doing. It is recommended that you do this once a year to help reposition your brand for greater success. To undertake a competitor analysis you will need to identify the following:

1   Who are your competitors? Let's recap from Chapter 3: write down your direct, non-direct and aspirational competitors – try to list five in each category:

| Direct competitors | Non-direct competitors | Aspirational competitors |
|---|---|---|
|  |  |  |
|  |  |  |
|  |  |  |
|  |  |  |
|  |  |  |

2   Who are *they targeting* and why? Next to each of your competitors, list who their 'Friends' are and why you believe they have chosen this demographic of people. Knowing this will help you see potential opportunities in the market. If you work for a company, analyse who sits in their ecosystem; who within their Tribe is helping them grow? What mentors do they have, which associations do they belong to, which members' clubs do they attend? Understanding this will give you a path to learn from and emulate for yourself.

| Competitor name | Their friend | Why are they targeting them? |
|---|---|---|
|  |  |  |
|  |  |  |
|  |  |  |
|  |  |  |
|  |  |  |

3   *List their pricing, fee or salary* – you can always find this out by requesting a brochure, reviewing their website or estimating based on industry knowledge. If you are in contact with any of their customers, you can ask them, or if they have an off-the-shelf product you can review the retail price. If you're trying to ascertain their salary, you can do some desktop research to see what people get paid in their positions, with their level of education, skills and experience. When you know what they are being paid, you can work out how you can price your brand and what your pricing strategy might be.

| Competitor | Price point | Pricing strategy |
|---|---|---|
|  |  |  |
|  |  |  |
|  |  |  |
|  |  |  |
|  |  |  |

4  *Itemize their marketing activities* – What are they doing and, most importantly, how are they doing it? Don't just write – they have a Facebook page, so analyse what they are specifically doing on their page. How many likes do they get, engagements or shares? How is the quality of their pictures and what are their key marketing messages within their posts? How often do they post? How are they using their page for digital CRM (customer relationship management)? How many blogs do they write? When do they post these blogs? What topics do they cover? Analyse in depth!

| Competitors | Marketing messages | Content approach | Channels used |
|---|---|---|---|
|  |  |  |  |
|  |  |  |  |
|  |  |  |  |
|  |  |  |  |

5  *Undertake a Competitor SWOT Analysis* – Strengths, Weakness, Opportunities & Threats. Start by listing what you believe to be your

competitors' strengths and weaknesses. Then list where there are opportunities for your brand and, equally, where they pose potential threats. Undertaking a competitor SWOT analysis is so insightful because it gives you a detailed awareness of the potential to penetrate and make your mark. It shows you where there are gaps and also it presents openings for strategic partnerships with competitors.

| Competitor | Strengths | Weaknesses | Opportunities | Threats |
|---|---|---|---|---|
| | | | | |
| | | | | |
| | | | | |
| | | | | |
| | | | | |

I've heard clients in the past say that they've become overwhelmed or jealous when they do a competitor analysis. They feel that they can't keep up or compete. But the reality is, you do not need to compete but you do need to be aware. You might not be able to do everything they are doing – you might not have the team in-house to churn out phenomenal digital graphics, or secure press coverage – but you can do something, even if it's only one thing. Utilize what you have learnt from your competitors and apply the lessons. To understand what the path to success looks like is better than not understanding at all, because with each day you can get closer to executing your version of that path. Never feel defeated, but be inspired by your competitors, and, if you are anything like me, you'll find a way to turn even your most direct competitors into your partners!

## LET'S DO THE WORK

*Based on the above, which competitors could you potentially partner with and why do you believe the collaboration will work?*

_____

_____

_____

_____

# Your Tribe

In Chapter 4, 'Branding Is Like Dating', we looked at who is in Your Tribe and we created a comprehensive list of all the people who sit within Your Tribe's ecosystem. As part of your personal brand marketing strategy, it is important to think about who in the ecosystem are the gatekeepers. Who can open doors for you to help drive the success of your personal brand? These gatekeepers could include associates, colleagues, ambassadors, influencers, journalists, editors and power-brokers. When you identify who your competitors are utilizing as gatekeepers, you can start to identify who could be relevant for you. If they are not currently in Your Tribe, then one marketing objective would be to secure their buy-in. To do this you need not only to be aware of who they are, but where you need to go to connect with them. What membership clubs do they belong to? Which online forums are they a part of? Which trade events do they network at? Which associations are they members of? Being aware of this will help you when you're creating your marketing plan. If you don't have the immediate answers, research, research, research!

## LET'S DO THE WORK

Fill in the table below.

| Who are the gatekeepers in Your Tribe? | Where do you need to go to connect with them? | When will you start doing this? |
|---|---|---|
|  |  |  |
|  |  |  |
|  |  |  |
|  |  |  |
|  |  |  |

# Your Friend

As mentioned throughout this book, it is important to have clarity on your 'Friend Profile' – understanding the true profile of your target audience including their ages, spending power, lifestyle habits, gender, belief systems, etc. When you understand your desired audience, you are better equipped to market to them. Awareness of who they are enables you to know what messages to put out that will fall in line with their beliefs. It will give you an understanding of when to post on social media, based on what they are doing at any given time of day. It will give you clarity on where to market, based on their daily activities and lifestyle. But there is more to be aware of when it comes to Your Friends. As outlined below, you need to know when they are buying, what their buying triggers are and where you sit in the buying cycle.

## *When are they buying?*

There is a myth that people buy all the time but this is simply not true. No one is interested in buying every day, or every week or every month. Your Friends buy in seasons and as such there are peak buying seasons and off-peak buying seasons that will determine when Your Friend will buy-in to or buy from your personal brand. You can start to look at this based on four criteria:

1   *The time of year* – Seasonality affects buying. For example, if you are looking for a new permanent senior level job, depending on your industry, Christmas might be the worst time of year to start looking, as the hiring managers might be more interested in the Christmas parties than they are in reviewing your CV. However, if you're looking for a part-time retail job, then pre-Christmas might be the best time as retailers are looking to hire more staff for their busy Christmas period. Understanding the seasonality will determine what activities you put on your marketing plan. For budding entrepreneurs and freelancers in the UK, Christmas is perfect for networking, but not necessarily for selling (depending on the industry you work in). In this case I would encourage you to go to as many Christmas networking events as possible to start developing new relationships for the post-tax-year period, when people will have new budgets to include you in. Other key seasons to consider are Valentine's Day, International Women's Month, Mother's Day, Pre-Christmas, Christmas, New Year, Chinese New Year, Ramadan, Summer and Spring. Understanding the seasons determines the action.

## LET'S DO THE WORK

*What are your peak buying seasons and why?*

| Season | Why will Your Friend buy from or buy into your brand at this time? |
|---|---|
|  |  |
|  |  |
|  |  |
|  |  |
|  |  |

2   *Month on month* – Similarly to seasonality, it is important to know which
    months are the peak buying months for your brand. For example, August
    is usually a poor buying month in the United States and the UK for those
    looking for a new job because the hiring managers tend to be on holiday.
    Equally, in those territories, January is a month when many people don't
    have a lot of money to purchase consumer goods, which is why so many
    brands have January Sales. Your peak months indicate when to push your
    brand marketing with a call-to-action that will convert marketing to
    sales, whereas your off-peak months are ideal for branding activities that
    focus on building relationships and brand buy-in.

## LET'S DO THE WORK

Highlight the months in the buying wheel to signify which are your peak buying months.

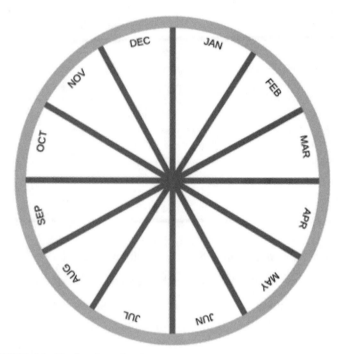

FIGURE 6.1 *The buying wheel.*

3  *Days of the week* – Which days of the week are people most likely to buy from your brand? Are they fired up about taking action in their lives and therefore most likely to buy at the beginning of the week, say on a Monday or Tuesday? Or are they seeking relaxation and will want to purchase from your brand on the weekends? The key to understanding the days of the week is understanding the lifestyle of Your Friend. How are they feeling, when? Depending on their emotional state, your brand can be the solution to their problem, and knowing which day that falls on, is crucial. For example, I always laugh

at the fact that Sunday and Monday are my biggest buying days of the week for my BossSquad (the ones who tend to buy our academy membership, books and tickets to our SME masterclasses). It's the time when that demographic are thinking about the new week and want to 'conquer it!' As a result, Sunday and Monday are the peak days for them to buy my products. However, come Friday, they don't care as much; they are tired from the week and the last thing they want to do is read about branding! So instead of posting about an e-course on a Friday, I give insights into my week, which clients I have worked with, and post videos to show me in action. These Friday activities are the *pull* towards my brand as they evidence and reiterate what I do, but there are no calls-to-action as my audience is not interested in buying on that day.

You need to know when Your Friend is buying.

## LET'S DO THE WORK

Fill in the table below.

| Day of the week | Which day will they be buying? Write yes or no in the box: | Why is that? |
|---|---|---|
| Monday | | |
| Tuesday | | |
| Wednesday | | |
| Thursday | | |
| Friday | | |
| Saturday | | |
| Sunday | | |

**4**  *Hours of the day* – It is not enough to just know the day of the week; you also need to know the time of day. For example, if you're targeting professional women and you try to market with sales calls-to-action at 11 a.m. on a Thursday morning, the chances are this demographic will be at work. But you might find that this same demographic will be interested on Thursdays at 1 p.m. when they go out for lunch and want a 'quick purchase'. The time of day needs to mirror their lives and their physiological state.

## LET'S DO THE WORK

Add to the table your peak times of day.

| Day of the week | Which day will they be buying? | What time of the day is the peak buying time(s)? |
|---|---|---|
| Monday | | |
| Tuesday | | |
| Wednesday | | |
| Thursday | | |
| Friday | | |
| Saturday | | |
| Sunday | | |

## *What are their buying triggers?*

A buying trigger is when your desired audience has a clear need, which converts into a sense of purpose and urgency, and triggers their buying from you or buying into you. When developing your personal brand marketing strategy it is important to be aware of what the buying triggers are for Your Friend. Here are some examples:

1  *Pain release* – As mentioned throughout this book, business is about solving problems, and your brand is designed to execute how you solve the problem for Your Friend. With this in mind, the biggest buying trigger is when potential leads can clearly see how you are a solution to their problem. When communicated in a simplistic way, they can equate your brand, not just your industry but your specific brand, to the solution they need. It is important to make sure that you're communicating how *you* specifically can solve their problem. Being generic might lead to them choosing a competitor over you. For example, you might say 'As a personal trainer I can help you lose weight!' but that message is generic and alludes to something that is a solution for your entire industry and not specifically you. Whereas if your marketing messages said 'My personal training will let you lose weight using my specific X programme', that is something that says only you can do it.

2  *Social proofing* – A brilliant way to trigger the buying process is to use social proofing. In other words, to have other people saying how well you solve the problem. Or having others evidence your consistency of being the solution. Human beings are social creatures and we look to others to tell us what action to take. In his book *Influence: The Psychology of Persuasion*, Professor Robert Cialdini says: 'If you can get people who are similar to the person you're trying to persuade to speak on your behalf, it's a lot easier for you than if you have to try to hammer your message one more time into a reticent mind.' Who can you find to speak on your behalf that Your Tribe will respect and listen to?

3   *Tell a story* – One of the best ways for buyer triggering is to tell an
    emotive story about your brand. One with clear characters, storylines
    and resolution is perfect when seeking to impact buyer behaviour.
    According to Gerard Zaltman, the author of *How Customers Think:*
    *Essential Insights into the Mind of the Market*, 95 per cent of cognition
    happens outside of our conscious brain and inside our subconscious,
    emotional brain. This innate driver has been exemplified for thousands
    of years as humans told stories to spread the word and pass on
    messages from generation to generation. How can you tell a consistent
    story across your brand touchpoints?

4   *Create novelty and inspire curiosity* – People love new things, they love
    the anticipation of something new happening. This is the reason why
    Apple have so successfully launched so many new products; just when
    we think we have had the latest iPhone, another one pops onto the
    market. This ability to keep your brand marketing messages new and
    to push something different is an important buying trigger. If you're a
    personal brand, you might create an e-course for purchase on your
    website and then drip feed one-minute clips to create anticipation and
    a feeling of something new coming as part of the launch strategy.

5   *Example 'why'* – I will give you a free access to my e-course if you
    complete this book. Do you believe me? Do you wonder why I am
    doing this? The chances are you would ultimately want to know why.
    Without an explanation, your questioning of the promise would
    increase, so in good marketing you need to explain why you are doing
    X thing. By doing this you feed into human desire to learn more and be
    informed. Our brains are always searching for answers and always
    looking for reasons to say no; so explaining why you are doing a
    particular thing will help the conversation move from marketing
    message to sale guaranteed.

6   *KiSS – keep it simple, stupid!* Try not to over complicate your brand marketing messages or purchasing process. Put yourself in the shoes of your customer and make sure you KiSS. To achieve this you might need to produce a Customer Journey Map, outlining what steps they have to complete from seeing the message, being triggered to buy, and through to actually purchasing. For example, how many steps from your social media post do they need to take before they buy? Do they need to click on your bio, then go to your website, then go to your about page, then go to your services page, then find the sub-service page and read the information on your website, then click on the 'contact us' page, then call or email you, then fill out an enquiry form, then sign your purchase agreement, and then finally pay! If so, this is *long*! There are way too many steps and it leaves too many opportunities for the customer to drop off. So review your messages and buying process and make it KiSS.

## LET'S DO THE WORK

*Which of the above buying triggers will you use as part of your next brand marketing campaign and why?*

_____

_____

_____

_____

_____

_____

_____

## *Where are you in the buying cycle?*

Sometimes known as the sales cycle, the buying cycle is the series of steps a customer has to go through when contemplating a purchase from you. These steps are as follows:

1  *Awareness* – Customer becomes aware of the problem and a need. They also become aware of your brand or someone might refer them to your brand as a potential solution to that problem.

2  *Consideration* – When a customer starts evaluating solutions to their problem. They search for options in the marketplace and start to compare your brand with those of your competitors.

3  *Intent/Research* – They are intending to buy but want more evidence to support their decision. This is particularly true for high-ticket purchases such as buying a car or senior management positions. The more they have to spend on you, the more evidence they are going to want to convince them.

4  *Selection* – Narrowing down between competitors to find an 'emotional favourite'. They may even negotiate with you at this stage, and seek deals or other incentives to purchase.

5  *Purchase* – They buy into or buy from you. They consume what you have to offer and become a customer/client/hiring manager.

6  *Repeat purchase/Advocacy* – They tell others about your brand. They repeat buy from you and/or they become an ambassador of your brand and recommend you to others.

As shown in the diagram overleaf, you need to match your marketing tactics to the correct stage of the buying cycle. We will cover this in the next Chapter, 'What's The Plan?', but for now it is important to be aware of the buying cycle and how your brand might need to navigate customers through it.

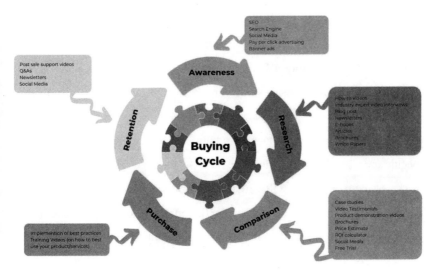

FIGURE 6.2 *The buying cycle.*

# Approach

What is your strategic approach to getting Your Tribe to buy into or buy from your brand? Now that you are aware of the industry trends, audience needs, buying triggers and competitive landscape, how will you strategically approach your brand marketing?

## Tribe hierarchy

One way to do this is to understand the hierarchy of Your Tribe. There are some within Your Tribe who have more influence than others: who are they? Who sits at the top of Your Tribe's hierarchy with the most power and influence to propel your marketing efforts and increase the chances of your success?

I recently had a conversation with an associate who works for a technology firm. She was telling me that when she first arrived at the company she thought the power brokers and gatekeepers were the senior management team; she soon realized that actually it was the engineers. This changed everything about how she marketed her personal brand, how she networked and whom she networked with, what she wrote about in her blog posts and which trade events she attended. In Chapter 9, 'Know Your Worth, Then Add Tax', we will talk about how to reposition your brand for success, but for now just note this – your brand marketing strategy needs to factor in all stakeholders but there are specific people, based on their hierarchical levels of influence and power, who need specific messages or a specific approach. Understanding who these people are will help you navigate and market to them effortlessly. Often, the very people we think have the influence are not the ones with influence at all, so take the time to study your environment to gauge where the influence lies. This is particularly important for those who work as freelancers or contractually for a company. When you are working remotely, it's more difficult to ascertain where buy-in needs to derive from, so think through how, strategically, you can make this achievable. Maybe you could go into the office one day a week, or be instrumental in organizing colleague lunches or be in charge of the Friday night drinks. The key is to position yourself so that you're building relationships with those of influence.

## Collaborations

Who do you need to collaborate with to push your brand forward? This isn't just about sponsors or partners, it also includes colleagues, associates and gate-keepers. I have spent my entire career building success through the power of collaborations. When I started as a freelancer and had very little money to pay project staff, I used collaborations to get people onboard. When I wanted to enter new, international markets to teach branding, I used collaborations to get me through the door. When I had the most success with brand launches on behalf of clients, it was through the power of collaborations. For example, the launch of herRUNWAY (a London Fashion Week Show that featured eight female designers from all over the world) was successful due to the collaboration I worked on with the Aston Martin dealership on London's Park Lane. At every single stage, collaborations have been the name of my game. In Chapter 9 we will go into how you do this, but for now ask yourself who needs to align with your brand?

## PPS approach

The PPS approach is all about how you strategically execute your brand marketing messages: *Pull, Push* and *Sale*. Depending on what time of year (whether it's your peak buying months or off-peak buying months), you should have a rotational PPS approach.

During my clients' off-peak buying months, I usually get them to do three *Pull* messages (these are messages that get their audience engaged and understanding their brand; there is no hard sell or call-to-action), two *Push* messages (these are message that are pushing particular products or services) and one *Sale* message (these are messages that include direct selling of a particular thing with a clear call-to-action for sales). For example, I had a client who is a musician; her three *Pull* messages included a) showing her at gigs, b) live tutorials and c) behind-the-scenes videos of her in rehearsals. Her two *Push* messages promoted her piano tuition and her new single. Her *Sale* message was a direct call-to-action to purchase a ticket to her gig, since this was the product driver she was focused on at the time. This strategic approach impacts what marketing activities you do, and when you do them. You can't be selling all the time, and neither can you just push products with no conversions. Equally you can't, and never should, build a brand with no business on the backend to drive income! This PPS approach is for both personal brands with services or products, as well as personal brands that are working inside of a company.

## Evidence building

A very important part of your strategic approach should be evidence building. As mentioned previously, it is important to garner evidence to illustrate your excellence. Now that you are pulling together your brand marketing strategy, evidence gathering should be part of it. For example, you might have a new book coming out. As part of your strategy, you could implement ways to ask everyone who purchased the book to do a video testimony in exchange for a complimentary or discounted service. This ensures that you are evidencing your customers' enjoyment of your book. Or when you successfully deliver on a project, ask your colleague to write a short endorsement on your LinkedIn page in exchange for you doing the same for them. Whatever you are doing, evidence your work.

I often get laughed at when I turn up to events with a camera person following me and filming my every move, but when we turn that footage into a one-minute wrap-up video it becomes part of our marketing evidence. It goes in our next newsletter, gets posted on social media, is stored on YouTube and is featured prominently on our website homepage. This translates to people seeing what I do, and getting a feel for my teaching style and brand knowledge, which has resulted in an 80 per cent increase in speaking bookings! Evidencing is key to your success.

## Power and influence

As part of your strategy, does your brand need to acquire power and influence? If so, here are two key things to consider:

- First, you need to carve out your niche and be unafraid to 'own' a space that is micro-targeted and micro-niched. For example, if you are a personal trainer, you might want to narrow that down to personal training for people embarking on a vegan lifestyle, or personal training for busy mums. You then become the go-to person and know everything as it pertains to training women, eating a vegan diet for example, or managing work stress with physical activity. When you narrow your niche you have a better opportunity to master the space.

- Second, recognize your influencing style. Are you the type to dominate, bridge, negotiate or inspire? Do you apply the same style to every situation? If so, you should look at how you adapt your influencing style to match the audience you are trying to influence. For example, if you are trying to gain influence with your CFO (Chief Financial Officer), you might want to use data, stats and information to drive a negotiation approach. If, on the other hand, you want to gain influence over the junior Digital Executive, you might want to use storytelling, creative thinking and inspiration to get the desired outcome.

## LET'S DO THE WORK

Write down your strategic approach:

_____

_____

_____

_____

_____

_____

# Targets

Now that you have your Goals, you're clear on your Objectives, you have researched and become Aware of what's happening in your sector, you have listed your strategic Approach – you need your Targets.

The targets are designed to put quantifiable numbers next to your objectives: it is important to have something to measure the success of your marketing efforts. Based on the objectives, here are some example targets that you could match with each:

- *Objective: New customer acquisition* – Target: increase my customer base by 30 per cent within the next year.

- *Objective: Retain clients* – Target: retain my existing clients with a maximum of a 5 per cent drop-off rate, and up-sell a new service to 25 per cent of those who stay.

- *Objective: Increase brand awareness* – Target: increase my brand awareness within the UK market by doubling my press exposure in trade publications within my industry, over the next two years.

- *Objective: Launch a new product or service* – Target: I want to launch my new product line for pre-Christmas selling with a lunch event on 1 November, attracting 500 attendees.

- *Objective: Increase market share* – Target: within the next three years I want to double my existing market share, which currently stands at 1.3 per cent of the market.

- *Objective: Attract collaborators* – Target: within the next six months I want to collaborate with ten micro-influencers within the US beauty industry who operate specifically in New York, Chicago and Boston.

- *Objective: Enter new markets* – Target: by 2022 I want to have entered the Latin American market with a focus on Colombia, Brazil and Argentina, having secured one major distributor per market, selling via wholesale and retail.

- *Objective: Improve internal communications* – Target: by Q4 of this year I want to have more than 60 per cent of my staff effectively using the internal communications platform.

- *Objective: Improve stakeholder relations* – Target: over the next 12 months I want to have visited all of my key stakeholders and obtained feedback from them regarding the development and commercialization of my brand.

- *Objective: Secure a new job or contract* – Target: by October this year I want to be in a new Customer Relations Directorship earning no less than £85,000, within a technology company that has a global expansion strategy.

- *Objective: Reposition your brand* – Target: over the next two years I want my brand to be seen as both luxury and affordable luxury, with the implementation of a new premium line.

- *Objective: Increase your social capital* – Target: by the end of the summer period I want to have joined a members' club and attracted over 50 new leads for my X business.

As you can see above, the key with the targets is to be specific in your timeframe and desired results. This is critical, as your brand marketing activities will be created to help you achieve them. Without clarity of targets you could end up creating marketing material or undertaking marketing activities that do nothing for you, whereas you want every bit of your marketing – from videos, graphics, wording, materials, press release, networking, events and coverage – to drive the specific targets you have set.

Branding is your business driver; where do you need this car to take you?

# Application

What physical resources, money or people do you need to turn this strategy into an actionable plan?

People have great goals most of the time, but what turns a goal into results is the application: the consistency of doing what you say you are going to do to make that goal a reality. To achieve this, you need in advance to think through what is needed. What key things can you put in place to ensure that you're able to execute the strategy? There will be hard days, boring days, times when you want to stop doing it and can't be bothered, so what do you need for you to stay focused?

This many include any of the following:

1   *Resources* – What resources do you need to enable your day-to-day execution? For example, do you need an office, or do you have a space at home where you can work? Do you need an electronic diary planner to better prioritize your personal brand marketing activities? Do you need a CRM (customer relationship management) system to organize your contacts and keep track of your sales leads? Do you need a car to get to your appointments? Do you need to renew your passport so that you can deliver on international bookings? Do you need a printer so that you can reduce the cost of external printing of your presentation documents? Do you need a design application such as Canva so that you can produce more professional-looking artwork for your social media posts? Do you need business cards for networking?

When thinking about what you need, also consider what resources you don't need. There was a time when I realized that, actually, I don't need an office. It was an unnecessary expense in both rent, business rates, lunches and travel. It also took time away from my ability to juggle being a mum and a consultant, so I got rid of it. It was purely my ego that made me think that one was necessary, but, instead, what I really needed was a large home office and access to some good private membership clubs.

2   *People* – What people do you need around you to enable your personal brand to thrive? Do you need an after-school nanny or au pair to support with child care? Do you need a VA (virtual assistant) or PA

(personal assistant) to manage your diary and administrative tasks? Do you need a good accountant and lawyer? Do you need a business partner to add strengths to your weaknesses? Do you need a mentor or coach to keep you on track? Do you need investors to buy into the vision or sponsors to give resources to enable growth? Do you need regular meetups with friends so that you can let your hair down and not think about work for a minute! They say it takes a village to bring up a child, but I also think it takes a village to support an adult! There is no shame in needing support. I for one know that I will not wear a superhero cape 24 hours a day. I can't; someone else needs to take the cape and wear it for me, so that I can rest, rejuvenate and start again. So never be afraid to ask for help and get the right people around you.

3   *Money* – What finances do you need to help your personal brand grow? How much money, specifically, do you need and over what timeframe? Do you actually need money at all, or can you partner with someone and leverage on them to combat the financial necessities? For example, I had a client that who said she needed money for a website to make her personal brand more attractive to her Tribe. Once she calculated the amount, she didn't have it, and was unsure of how and where to get it from. I proposed she contact a graphic designer and use an open platform such as WIX or WordPress. After all, the website she was creating was a basic brochure site and didn't need a developer to code anything complicated. This slashed the required budget by more than half and allowed her to create a brand new site. Often, we think we need more than we actually do. I will cover this in more detail in later chapters, but, for now, the important thing to remember is that money should never hold you back; instead, ask the question 'Who can I partner with to reduce the costs and achieve the same results?'

## LET'S DO THE WORK

Write down your targets:

_____

_____

_____

_____

_____

# Her GO-AA-TA

Now that you understand the principle of a GO-AA-TA, here is an illustration of how it all comes together. For the purpose of client confidentiality, we will call this client Client B. Here is Client B's GO-AA-TA.

*Background – Client B was working as a Partnerships Manager in the charity sector and wanted to transition into the creative industry with a focus on music. With a love of all things entertainment, her desire was to transfer her skills and abilities to a sector that would allow her to combine her passion with work. Strategically she wasn't trying to change her career, i.e. she wasn't trying to transition from Partnerships Manager to Music Producer. Instead, she was trying to transition her career; remain working in partnerships but in the music industry instead of with a charity.*

*Her GO-AA-TA needed to be rooted in her career ambitions:*

- *Goals – She had a four-year goal to be working for one of the top record labels, music venues or music management firms in the UK. To ensure clarity of direction, we helped her come up with a concise wish-list of* companies that she wanted to work with. But for her transition to be a success, every firm on her wish-list had to have robust partnerships and events divisions to enable her career to thrive.

- *Objectives* – Her goal was divided into yearly objectives. Year one was to start a part-time Masters degree in Music Business Management. Whilst doing this she would continue to work full time in her current job to save enough money to be able to stop working by the end of year two. In year two she would continue with her part-time degree course whilst saving money from her full-time job. Simultaneously, she would join and or attend events at private members' clubs within the creative industry, such as Soho House, Shoreditch House Library or the Century Club to build up her contacts. In year three, she would leave her current job and undertake a lower paying job within an entertainment or music brand. Taking this pay drop, whilst difficult, would allow her to gain real experience and exposure in the industry. In year four, she would complete the course and get a job as a Partnerships Manager for one of the firms on her wish-list.

- *Awareness* – To achieve her career ambitions she needed to increase her knowledge of the industry. She simply could not have jumped straight from the charity sector to the music industry without having in-depth knowledge of the sector at hand. She also needed to have contacts and a mentor to help secure a placement and gain insights into how the entertainment world works. She was willing to sacrifice a year's salary to get the awareness she needed. Lastly, she undertook desktop research to discover routes of entry into the partnerships divisions that she wanted to work in. This awareness was imperative for her to sell her brand, knowing what she brought to the table to secure the job she wanted.

- *Approach* – Her approach was three-fold: a) learn the industry via the degree and show passion for the industry through her commitment to *completing the degree; b) network to develop her contacts and opportunities; c) gain support via a mentor whom she would find from her university guest lecturers or industry talks.*

- *Targets – To achieve all of the above she needed clear financial targets: she had to save £30,000 over two years to be able to stop working and take the lower paying job. This meant that she would have to save £1,250 per month. To accomplish this she needed to rent out the second room in her flat, reduce the number of times per month she would eat out and stop any international holidays during the course of her degree.*

- *Application – The last part of her GO-AA-TA was the application: on days she couldn't be bothered, what would help her to apply herself and keep going? The solution was made up of various parts: creating a vision board, as a reminder of what she was trying to achieve and why; securing a peer-to-peer buddy with someone else on her course, so she had a safe place to vent frustrations and seek advice over the four years; and setting up a separate savings account so that she could track her money and make sure she was on target each month to save up for the industry year out.*

As you can see above, Client B's personal brand marketing strategy has nothing to do with her marketing plan; there isn't anything on there about updating her LinkedIn profile, creating a résumé website, what to put on her CV, what interview techniques she might need, or the importance of writing a monthly blog on partnerships in entertainment – those things are not meant to be outlined on the strategy. The strategy is the strategic approach of what needs to be done. Once she has strategically identified how to position her brand for her desired outcomes, then a plan will outline *how* to take herself to market.

## LET'S DO THE WORK

Review your GO-AA-TA. Have you been clear at each step? Is there anything you need to add or amend?

_____

_____

_____

_____

_____

# Resources

Mahoney, M. (2003). 'The subconscious mind of the consumer (and how to reach it)'. Harvard Business School, 13 January 2003: https://hbswk.hbs.edu/item/the-subconscious-mind-of-the-consumer-and-how-to-reach-it

# 7

# What's the Plan?

Before we begin creating your brand marketing plan, let's remind ourselves of what it is: a brand marketing strategy is *what* you will do with your brand marketing efforts, and the brand marketing plan is *how* you will do it. Once you're clear on your strategy, you are ready to create your marketing plan with defined tactics.

To create a brand marketing plan, you start by dividing your goals (as outlined in your strategy) into brand marketing campaign objectives. (A campaign is a short burst of marketing activity that acts as stepping stones to the wider plan and overall strategy).

The reasons you need to run campaigns are as follows. A campaign:

1  gives you a focused approach;

2  is specific and time sensitive;

3  helps create a framework to deliver your objectives;

4  provides clear metrics;

5  allows room to change and adapt as you go, to ensure the wider plan is working.

To illustrate this, let's go back to Client B from the previous chapter:

| Client B – Brand marketing strategy | Client B – Brand marketing plan | Client B – Brand marketing campaigns |
|---|---|---|
| To transition her career in Partnerships from the charity to the entertainment industry, over a four-year period. | To execute the strategy objectives via three brand marketing campaigns. | Campaign 1 – to *launch* herself in the entertainment business scene in London as a seasoned Partnerships professional looking for a career change. |
| | | Campaign 2 – to *position* her brand and secure a lower paid job, which would be her entry into the entertainment industry.<br><br>Campaign 3 – to *promote* her brand and secure her dream job with one of the companies on her strategy wish-list. |

When you are creating your brand marketing plan, think of it working together with your strategy as a funnel system to achieve your desired results.

As illustrated in Fig. 7.1, you have your desired results at the top of the funnel, with each of your specific campaigns delivering marketing efforts to

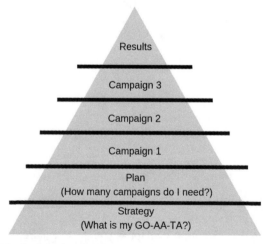

FIGURE 7.1 *Marketing planning.*

achieve the results. The plan is the forward thinking that frames the campaign structures, and the strategy is your GO-AA-TA.

# What goes into a campaign?

For each specific campaign, there are seven key points to follow for the campaign to be a success:

1 Campaign objectives

2 Campaign targets

3 Marketing messages

4 Campaign budget

5 Marketing tactics or channels of communication

6 Lead times

7 Campaign calendar

## Campaign objectives

Your campaign objectives should state:

1 What you intend to do.

2 Who you need to do it with.

3 Why you want to do it.

Referencing Client B again: her Campaign 1 objective states that her *what to do* is to launch herself into the entertainment business scene in London; her *who you need to do it with* is to hire managers, HR, marketing, events and comms professionals from companies on her wish list (as outlined in her strategy); and her *why* is to secure a career change within the next four years.

# Campaign targets

Similarly to strategy targets, when people think about their campaign targets they normally focus on the money; Client B might say: 'I want to secure a £50,000 a year role as a Partnerships Manager as a result of this marketing plan and my campaign efforts.' However, I would recommend that, in addition to money, you also create other campaign objectives.

For example:

- How can you use this campaign to increase your social capital?

- How can use it to increase your power and influence?

- How can it be used to position you as an expert in your field?

- How can you use it to strengthen your digital footprint?

Having financial and non-financial targets adds layers to the campaign, which will result in an overall plan that is robust and multifaceted. Additionally, the non-financial targets tend to be great stepping stones to the bigger financial goals.

Let's look at another client example to help explain this further. This client we will call Client C.

Client C is a husband-and-wife duo working in technology, who want to launch a new dating app. To launch this, they have identified in their strategy that they need to attract two stakeholder groups: a) end users to test their prototype, and b) investors to launch the final product.

Their marketing plan is then divided into three campaigns, each with clear objectives and specific targets:

- *Client C, Campaign 1* – The objective is to launch the app by 1 February, just in time for Valentine's Day, and the target is to attract 50,000 followers across their social media platforms. These followers should fall within their target audience profile.

- *Client C, Campaign 2* – The objective is to secure users to test the app's prototype and the target is 5,000 people (10 per cent of their social media followers), testing it by 1 September.

- *Client C, Campaign 3* – The objective is to secure investment, and the target is £250,000 in raised capital within one year from test date.

As you can see, Campaigns 1 and 2 have targets that are non-financial but they are important milestones to increase their chances of securing investment. Without the test users for the prototype, they have no 'proof of concept' to show investors that the app works, and, without the followers, they can't prove demand for their app.

## LET'S DO THE WORK

Fill out the table below.

| What are your marketing strategy goals? | What are your marketing strategy objectives? | How many campaigns could go into your marketing plan to meet the strategic objectives? | What are the targets, both financial and non-financial, for each of your campaigns? |
|---|---|---|---|
|  |  |  |  |
|  |  |  |  |
|  |  |  |  |
|  |  |  |  |

# Marketing messages

Part of your plan is to ensure you have a consistent brand marketing message that resonates across all stakeholder groups. You can't have one message for your sponsors or investors, and a completely different message for your end users, or a conflicting message for your colleagues. This inconsistency only creates confusion.

For example, if your brand promise is that you 'deliver innovation' then your brand marketing message needs to illustrate this. Your presentations at pitch meetings should be unconventional, and your approach needs to feel fresh, energized and unorthodox. Your input at staff meetings requires innovative ideas. Your social media posts should have creative designs that differentiate you from the rest, and your blog posts need to include original thought. Your promise of 'innovation' needs to permeate everything you do in order for Your Tribe to believe you, and it should to be consistent!

I once went to a networking event and met a chap whose business card said: 'Innovation Is Our Thing'; a bold statement to make, but then he stood up and delivered the blandest presentation I'd ever seen. Whilst the content of the presentation and his thought process were quite inventive, his messaging, delivery style and brand experience were uninspiring. As he continued his presentation, I looked up his website and found the same strapline: 'Innovation Is Our Thing'. But the website itself looked like a template from a standard WordPress format, with little innovative thinking or design. His LinkedIn profile included no video content or innovative posts, and his Twitter page was full of reposts and lacked original commentary. His brand messaging was inconsistent so I stopped believing in his brand promise! This is why, when creating your marketing plan, it's important to think through how your brand promise will resonate across everything you do, as this is how you secure buy-in from Your Tribe. It's not just what you say but how you say it and how you make your audience feel, that needs to be consistent and coherent with your brand promise and brand personality.

Your 'brand touch points' are all the different ways Your Tribe can engage with your brand: your website, social media pages, emails, newsletter, office decor, business cards, presentation materials, promotional activities, etc. Being consistent with your brand marketing message across all of your brand touch points is critical. At each touch point you want to be able to identify how the promise comes alive and what the end user's experience will be. Once you have established this consistency of message, then you need to identify how you tailor your brand marketing messages to secure buy-in from specific stakeholders, within each of your separate campaigns.

For example: Client B might have an overall brand promise of 'being a connector'. As a Partnerships Manager transitioning from charity to entertainment, she may want her Tribe to see her as the person who is the 'go-to girl'. She has the contacts, she makes the connections, she secures the partners and she delivers on the deals. If this is her promise, then everything about her and her brand needs to illuminate this. Her strapline might read 'connecting the dots', which will then be on her email signature. Her website might have cool graphics that use animation to show connectivity between clients, projects and results. Her LinkedIn profile might have blogs analysing how companies are using international connectivity to deliver commercial results. Her Instagram videos might give evidence of her working behind the scenes as the connector at networking events that she puts on once a quarter. Her newsletter might outline results of how her Tribe, through her, have been connected and are now doing business. Everything about her brand should scream 'connecting the dots'.

When it comes to specific campaigns, she would identify how to make this message resonate to each stakeholder group. For example, as part of her Campaign 1 marketing messages, she might go to trade and networking events in the entertainment industry and use her contacts in the charity sector to be seen as the person who can connect entertainment brands to charity activities, in order to harness their PR efforts. Rather than going to these events and simply saying: 'I want to transition my career, please give me a job', she would go there saying: 'I have the contacts you need, so hire me to make it happen because I'm the person who can connect the dots between charity and entertainment companies.' Of course, she might not use those exact words but the overall message is that she can deliver exactly that. By doing this, she puts her brand in a position of power.

---

## LET'S DO THE WORK

Fill out the following:

My brand promise is _____

| List Your Tribe | Which brand touch point will they engage with? | How will your promise be executed? | What will be the brand experience? |
|---|---|---|---|
|  |  |  |  |
|  |  |  |  |
|  |  |  |  |
|  |  |  |  |
|  |  |  |  |

---

# Marketing budget

Generally speaking, 10–20 per cent of your annual revenue should go back into your brand marketing. This includes internal communications, brand assets and external brand promotions. Normally, a company will have an annual marketing budget that they've calculated from the previous year's revenue. If, however, your previous year's revenue has been low or you're just starting out, you would seek to create a marketing budget that is 10–20 per cent of your projected revenue. To achieve this, it is important to know:

1　What is your projected revenue? How much do want to make this year?

2　How many sales do you need to meet your revenue goal? How many products or services do you need to sell to hit the revenue target?

3 How many leads does your marketing effort need to secure in order for you to convert the right number of sales? (Every industry has a typical conversation rate – what is yours? If you are unsure, research your sector and niche area of expertise.)

Typically, when I'm working with a client, I will create a brand marketing strategy with a one-year marketing plan. This plan is then divided into key campaigns that are normally centred around specific buying cycles or buying periods. The 10–20 per cent of their annual projected revenue will then be divided across the campaigns within that year.

Sometimes, however, the 10–20 per cent budget might not come from their projected annual revenue, but instead might be from their projected project revenue. As an example, if Client B is expecting to secure a £50,000 job, then she should be allocating £5,000–£10,000 from her first year salary 'project revenue' to her marketing budget, and she would spread this money across all three of her campaigns. If Client C is expecting to raise £250,000 then they would not allocate any more than £50,000 to their marketing budget, again to be spread across all three of their campaigns.

---

## LET'S DO THE WORK

*Complete the sentences below.*

If you are a freelancer or entrepreneur:

1 How much do you want to bring in this year (your projected revenue)?

_____

_____

2 How many sales do you need, to hit that number (client or customer sales)?

_____

_____

3  What is your marketing budget (calculate 10–20 per cent of your projected revenue)?

_____

_____

*If you are a professional working for a company:*

1  What is your current salary? _____

2  How much of a salary increase would you like to receive at your next performance review? _____

_____

3  How much would you like to make if you left the company and secured a new job?

_____

4  What is your marketing budget (calculate 10–20 per cent of your projected salary)?

_____

## Campaign budget

When producing your marketing budget for each of your campaigns, consider the following:

- How much money will you allocate to marketing collateral, e.g. business cards, brochures, flyers, e-flyers?

- How much money will you allocate to content creation, e.g. videos, graphics, images, photographers, hair and makeup teams for photo shoots and videos?

- How much money will you allocate to events marketing, e.g. travelling to and from networking events, fees for membership clubs, trade shows?

- How much money will you allocate to advertising, e.g. social media boosting, LinkedIn Premiership, PPC (pay-per-click advertising)?

- How much money will you allocate to collaborations e.g. influencer fees, partnership deals, sponsorship spend etc.?

- How much money will you allocate to press activities, e.g. launch events, meet-and-greets, PR agency fees etc.?

- How much money will you allocate to CRM (customer relationship management), e.g. client dinners, coffee meetings, CRM systems, e-marketing tools etc.?

- How much is the management cost – what is it costing you for the staff who are working on the campaign?

- Cost of sale – what is it costing you if you do a freebie, i.e. if you give away something as part of the promotion (you need to identify how much this will cost you)?

Having clarity on how the money will be allocated throughout your marketing plan will help later when you're analysing the effectiveness of your efforts and marketing spend. Too often I see clients who are not thinking about every facet of their marketing budget. They may know how much they spend on PR agency fees, but they don't always know how much they're spending on all the coffees and glasses of wine they buy when entertaining clients and building new relationships. As a result, they're unable to measure the success of this particular spend. I often ask questions like: 'Out of the ten events, pitch meetings and client dinners you had this month, which one brought in the most money?' or 'Were all of the networking events you attended this month worth it?'

To which they may reply 'Oh yes, I brought in a new project from those events.' But when I ask: 'Does the income from that marketing activity justify the spend?' they normally can't answer that question without pulling out all of their receipts and a calculator! This is because they haven't, in advance, budgeted how much will be spent on these activities, so they have no idea if they're really worth it or not.

One client spent nearly £5,000 going to trade and networking events over the course of two months, and at the end of it brought in a £1,000 project. At first she was ecstatic because she had secured her first project, until I asked her what it had cost her initially and to review her spend! What's more, because she had failed to have clear non-financial targets, she didn't even manage to secure non-financial results. Had she secured both financial and non-financial results, the £5,000 might have been worth the money. Worse still, she had failed to use a CRM System to store contacts for all of the business cards she received. As a result, the business cards she collected were not easy to identify or turn into future clients. So, the £5,000 was actually a waste of money! But she is not alone; so many people are spending money, getting little return on investment, and are left wondering if their marketing is working.

Numbers paint clear pictures, so create a marketing budget!

If you're unsure of how much things will cost and are therefore struggling to create your budget, go back to your GO-AA-TA and do some research so that you have more awareness. There are endless ways of finding the costs of things to create a comprehensive budget. You can:

- Call potential suppliers and get a cost for your marketing collateral and content creation.

- Visit coffee shop websites to estimate how much their coffee/food costs.

- Email membership clubs to get their fees.

- Request agency rate cards to know their fees.

- Go online to see how much the various CRM and e-marketing tools will charge.

- Contact trade shows to get advertising rates and entry ticket prices.

- Contact media houses to identify their advertising rates.

Finding costs to create a budget is easy; you just need to do the research, put in the effort and create a concise budget that ensures you are making money from your marketing efforts. When doing so, be sure to also add in your time. You might think that writing a blog is 'free' but your time is not. So add in your hourly rate to demonstrate exactly how much time that blog cost you. Then, when you are analysing later, you can identify if writing blogs is actually a good marketing activity that's helping to generate leads, or not!

## Marketing tactics

I often smile when I ask clients what they've been doing for their marketing campaign and they tell me, with lots of pride, that they're on Facebook and Instagram. That is not a marketing campaign! This is just them being present on two social media platforms. A marketing campaign uses a number of tactics to position a brand in front of its audience. These tactics are also known as Channels of Communication.

Channels of Communication are broken down as:

- *Above-the-Line (ATL)* – Tactics that reach mass audiences and traditionally cost a lot of money.

- *Below-the-Line (BTL)* – Tactics that reach niche audiences and traditionally cost less money.

- *Digital* – All online tactics across the digital landscape.

- *PR* – Tactics that involve public relations and usually cost very little money or require no budget at all.

- *Partnerships* – Tactics that involve collaborations.

- *Events* – Tactics that include some form of events marketing.

The following table shows most of the tactics used for each Channel of Communication.

| ATL | BTL | Digital | PR | Partnerships | Events |
|---|---|---|---|---|---|
| TV & radio adverts | Business cards | Social media – Facebook, Instagram, LinkedIn, Snapchat, Twitter, Tumblr | TV & radio interviews | Sponsorship | Exhibitions |
| Magazine adverts | Samples | Video sites – YouTube, Vimeo | Magazine interviews & features | Endorsements | Networking |
| Billboards | Brochures | Display ads | Newspaper interviews & features | Brand ambassadors | Trade shows |
| Tube adverts | Point-of-sale advertising | Banner ads | Print reviews | Strategic alliances | Launches |
| Bus adverts | Merchandise | Pop-ups | Expert commentary | Influencers | Premieres |
| Bus shelter boards | Tele-sales | Content marketing (videos, graphics, gifts, images, blogs, webinars, podcasts, Lives) | Competitions | Affiliates | Listening parties |
| Newspaper ads | Direct marketing | SEO (search engine optimization) | Expert tips and advice | Strategic partners | Tasting/sample sessions |

| Building and car ads or branding | Sales promotions | PPC (pay-per-click) advertising | Appearances | Product placement | Speaking at conferences & seminars |
| --- | --- | --- | --- | --- | --- |
| | | SEM (search engine marketing) | Editorial | Brand partnerships | Brand activations |
| | | Online affiliate marketing | Advertorials | | Festivals |
| | | E-marketing (emails, e-flyers, newsletters) | | | Experiential activities |
| | | Online influencers | | | |

An integrated approach is where you choose tactics from multiple channels to carry out your campaign, the best result being that you use a combination of offline and online tactics across traditional and non-traditional marketing.

For example, you could have a personal brand campaign that uses one ATL (local newspaper advert about your service or expertise), social media platforms (LinkedIn, Instagram and Twitter), a number of e-marketing efforts (monthly newsletter, email signature and an e-flyer at Christmas), several PR activities (expert commentary, profile feature piece, interviews, tips and advice articles), one Partnership (a Strategic Alliance with a gatekeeper in Your Tribe) and several events marketing tactics (networking, speaking at conferences and exhibiting at your local 'Women in Business' meet-up).

People often ask me how brand marketing works: it works when you use multiple channels to reach your desired audience, within a very specific timeframe.

---

## LET'S DO THE WORK

List the tactics you will use in your next brand marketing campaign – and remember to try to make it more than just Facebook and Instagram!

_____

_____

_____

_____

---

# Lead times

What timeline will you need to make your marketing campaign work? It is important to remember that each marketing channel requires different lead times for implementation and execution.

## *Digital*

Digital has a short lead time. This is because people's attention span online is very, very short. You should be doing no more than a one- to four-week period for each of your digital campaigns. When it comes to content planning I advise my clients to do no more than four weeks' advance planning because you want your content to be relevant to what is happening in the wider world, or your wider industry. This is particularly important for social media and e-marketing campaigns.

## *PR*

PR has various lead times – short lead titles (these are normally your weekly newspapers, daily reports, online publications and radio interviews) and long lead titles (these are your monthly magazines, bi-yearly or yearly subscription magazines and TV shows). Depending on the title's frequency, this will determine the lead time of execution. You need to contact the editor, journalist or producer around three to six months before the title goes to print, or the show is created, to ensure your story is featured or the interview takes place. The best way to know the required lead time for any media outlet is to do your research: contact the editorial or production team and find out what their specific lead times are.

## *Partners and events*

Generally, partnerships and events have longer lead times, especially if you are a small business trying to connect with a larger organization. Don't get frustrated; it's not you, it's just that they have bigger internal processes to go through before they can say yes to you. I have worked on partnership deals and events marketing campaigns that have taken up to two years to execute. The process for partnerships and events is as follows: you prepare your proposal, send it and get them to say yes to a meeting, secure a pitch meeting date, then pitch, negotiate the deal, undertake the contracts, create the marketing collateral and then execute. So give yourself time – at the very least you need six months' upfront planning, but I would always aim for more.

Also, remember that the partner is going to be using part of their marketing budget for your campaign, so you need to find out when their financial year starts because that's when they will have new budgets to play with.

## *ATL*

Above-the-line marketing is changing; it used to cost a lot of money to do and a long time to execute, but the growth of digital is changing how ATL works. I would always advise that you research in your desired area as to how much it might cost and how long the buying agency normally takes to execute their ATL activities, as well as how long an advertising run you might be able to secure. Do all of this before you say it's not for you. Honestly, as a personal brand, it might just be something you can do for yourself, especially if you are looking at local platforms in your local area as opposed to the big cities in your country. For example, if I wanted to reach the 'yummy-mummy' market and have billboards in the countryside or in the home counties, it would be a lot cheaper than reaching the same demographic in the centre of London. So do your research, and see what's changing across ATL in your areas of interest. As a general rule of thumb, and very much dependent on the platform, you would be looking at anywhere from a one–four week campaign across ATL, plus the lead time to create your photoshoot and/or graphics.

## Campaign Calendar

Once you know the individual channel lead times, you then need to create a Campaign Calendar. On this calendar you need to factor in the time it takes to pitch (if it's partners or events), the time it takes to create the assets (such as videos and graphics), the time it takes for placement (such as interviews and printing) and the timeframe for execution (such as a one-week billboard or a five-day Instagram countdown campaign). To make the whole thing work together coherently, you should start from the campaign start date and work backwards.

Here is an example: A jewellery designer has a new collection that she wants to have ready for Christmas sales. Her consumer Christmas campaign will start from 1 October and will be executed until 25 December (giving her a sales period of two and a half months).

The tactics she will use are:

- *Digital* – E-store via her website, Facebook posting and Facebook Shop, Instagram posting, Live, and Instagram shoppable items, affiliate links, promo videos for YouTube, Facebook and Instagram, monthly e-newsletter, SEM and influencers' IG posting.

- *PR* – Product placement with micro-influencers, for them to wear at key events between 1 October and 24 December, and exhibitions at local high-end women's networking events during the same timeframe. Profile interviews with fashion magazines and product reviews with lifestyle magazines to come out in the October issues.

- *Events* – A two-week pop-up shop in conjunction with other jewellery and fashion designers during the first two weeks of December.

- *ATL* – Advertising in the local newspaper close to where the pop-ups will take place.

- *BTL* – Business cards, point-of-sale materials in the pop-up, branded T-shirts for the team to wear at the events, flyers and a Lookbook of the entire collection for people to review at the pop-up and exhibitions.

In this case, her Campaign Calendar would start in April and continue until the end of September in time for the campaign to launch on 1 October, as follows:

## Campaign calendar

| September | August | July | June | May | April |
|---|---|---|---|---|---|
| Website updated with new collection images, product information and price to buy. | Promotional videos edited. | Affiliates secured and terms agreed. | Pop-up venue secure. | Magazine interview delivered. | Pitch to Fashion and Lifestyle magazines for long-lead titles and print editions. |
| Social media graphics created. | SEM started. | Pop-up partners secured and terms agreed. | Newspaper advert designed. | Newspaper advert placement and terms agreed. | |
| Promotional videos edited. | Exhibitions confirmed. | Influencers secured and terms agreed. | Lookbook images edited. | Lookbook photoshoot. | |
| e-Newsletters designed. | | | | | |
| Business cards, POS, t-shirts, flyers and Lookbook printed. | | | | | |

## LET'S DO THE WORK

Use the calendar template below to create your next campaign – remember you always go from your launch date backwards. In the example grid below, I have given you a six-month period but you might want longer; if so, just add extra months. Go to SheBuildsBrands.com for a larger version of this chart.

What is your launch date?

_____

| Month 6 | Month 5 | Month 4 | Month 3 | Month 2 | Month 1 |
|---------|---------|---------|---------|---------|---------|
|         |         |         |         |         |         |
|         |         |         |         |         |         |
|         |         |         |         |         |         |
|         |         |         |         |         |         |

# 8

# #DoIT

*Stop selling. Start helping.*

ZIG ZIGLAR

This statement by author and motivational speaker, Zig Ziglar, sums up the power of good brand marketing. In a world that is full of competition, it's imperative to be seen as the brand that either solves problems, helps, inspires or entertains. The era of hard selling is over. We are in the age of the brand doing the selling for you. This means that you need to connect emotionally with your audience and be agile in your approach. The challenge for both businesses and personal brands is to understand that the marketing efforts you implement today will not necessarily work in three years' time, and that's ok. Your focus is less on the marketing channels but the brand delivery within those channels. With the advancement of technology, your marketing channels have become, and will continue to be, interchangeable; therefore you need to focus on how your brand consistently connects with your audience and builds trust, irrespective of the channel you use.

Recently, I was booked as a keynote speaker for a Facebook event. I stood up and the first thing I said to the audience was that, when I started my career in 1996, there was no Facebook! The millennials looked at me with complete confusion, shock and horror: *No Facebook or Instagram, no Snapchat or even Google!!!* Yes, when I started it was all about the Yellow Pages! If you wanted to know how to connect, you had to open a book. I went on to explain that in this game called 'brand marketing', the marketing channels you use will forever be evolving and changing, but the brand must always remain the same.

As such you can't sit back and wait to master how to market your personal brand, nor wait for the right channel, the right event, the right moment. You can't wait to learn everything about Facebook advertising before you start advertising on the platform. You can't master LinkedIn before you upload your first blog. You can't wait to be an expert at networking before you get out there. You just have to get out there, and #DoIT! It's in the doing that you'll learn, grow and become better at getting your brand in front of your desired audience. You need to see this as a game, one that involves doing, measuring, learning and doing it again. You will fail; that's the point, because in the 'failing' you'll be learning. As the channels evolve, you need to evolve with them and keep adapting and improving as you go along.

Jaz Rabadia MBE, a Senior Manager of Energy & Sustainability at Starbucks, describes her love for learning in such an elegant way:

> For me, life is about the 4 L's; Living, Loving, Learning and leaving a lasting Legacy. Everything I do is in service of this.
>
> Many of us focus on the living and loving, as it's what comes naturally to most of us. But often, we neglect the abundant learning opportunities out there and even more so the passing on of those learnings to leave a legacy. My hunger to learn something new every day and pass that learning on, is what helps me to push forward; you'll be amazed how infectious it can be!

How do you apply this to your personal brand marketing? You allow yourself to see every marketing activity and marketing platform as a learning opportunity for your brand, one that, when complete, means you have something new to pass on. You should see your marketing efforts not as a chore that you simply hope goes well, but as an adventure. If you're not seeing engagement on Twitter, or you have a fear of networking, or hate speaking to journalists, make it your mission to see this as an opportunity to learn something new, and do it with the spirit of joy. Have fun with your marketing efforts. Life is hard enough, so don't make marketing your brand more difficult than it needs to be.

This is particularly true when it comes to building your brand across the digital landscape, particularly on social media. The art of being 'social' on social media, instead of over-promoting and over-selling, is very much required for brand success. I know it seems like an obvious statement, one you have probably heard before, but there are still people using social media as a tool to promote themselves and their products, rather than recognizing that you have to be social on social media and engage with relevant content. Your audience visits your page because they want something more from you and your brand: they want to interact, to read, or watch something that will add value to their day. Start having fun with being 'the page' that gives your audience what they're looking for. Entertain them, inspire them, motivate them, help them, support them. It's your job to connect, not to sell.

Of course, it's ok to promote yourself and your products, but generally speaking (and depending on the buying period), you should be looking at a 20:80 rule: 20 per cent of your posts are promotional, while 80 per cent are adding additional real value to Your Tribe. Always remember to do the PPS (pull, push and sell) but only 20 per cent should be selling and promoting. No one wants to scroll through a Facebook page full of sales pitches, links to your site and demands to sign up to your newsletter. Having social media pages that are interesting is what will encourage likes, shares or engagement.

To achieve this, I ask my clients to start by auditing their current social media pages, asking the following questions:

- What are the objectives of your social media pages?

- What is your social media mission statement?

- Which platforms and content style generate the most value?

- What does your audience need?

Let's take a look at these questions in more detail.

# What are the objectives of your social media pages?

Whether it's Facebook, Snapchat, LinkedIn, Instagram, YouTube, WhatsApp, Tumblr or Twitter (or any other platform that emerges during the lifespan of this book), each one of your social media pages should have a specific objective that ties into your wider brand strategy and marketing plan. As a result, cross-promoting your content between social media platforms may not work. For example, hashtags used on one platform won't necessarily be the optimum hashtags to connect content on another.

First, the audiences are different. For example, LinkedIn has a more mature audience with a heavier proportion being men, whereas Instagram's current core audience are mostly under 40 years old and lean towards women. Second, the visual formatting might be different on each platform, meaning you could lose part of the graphics or distort the shape of your image, which in turn makes your brand look unprofessional. Third, the use of hashtags may differ from platform to platform, resulting in a lack of content optimization.

It's therefore advisable to think through each of your social media platforms based on how they fit into your wider brand strategy and marketing plan, and then create specific platform objectives for each. For example, you might say that the objective for LinkedIn is to connect with potential partners and suppliers, whereas your Instagram objective could be to create more of a consumer shopping experience with the integration of an IG Shop. Facebook, with the use of a private Facebook Group and Facebook Live, might be used for existing customer retention. Twitter's objective could be as your 'listening platform', to keep you updated on industry and consumer trends. Based on this, the content created for each would certainly be different. With each platform you're speaking to a particular audience, with very specific messages and CTAs (call-to-actions). When you have clear objectives for each social media platform, you can align these objectives to metrics that highlight the results, showing you the opportunities for growth.

To identify each platform objective, you need to think through the following:

- Who from Your Tribe is on that platform?

- Why are they online?

- How are they using that platform?

- What are their online expectations?

- What do they need from the platform?

- How can your brand use the platform to be a solution to their needs?

Understanding Your Tribe's social media behaviour will help you create effective content. There are some people who use social media purely for entertainment purposes; they go on YouTube and use it as a replacement for traditional television – for them it's entertainment. There are others who go on social media because they want to find information by looking for content that will assist them in their day-to-day lives, or they're searching for 'how to do X'. There are others using social media because they want to connect; they might be going on Facebook and Instagram because they want to connect with

Tribes. Some people use social media because they want to be seen as an influencer, or an expert in their own right, whereas others might be trying to get a job or trying to find love and genuine support. Why is *Your Tribe* using social media? What do they need? And how are they using each one of the platforms differently?

At SheBuildsBrands we realized that our 'BossSquad' (predominantly entrepreneurs and executives between the ages of 28 and 45 years old) use Instagram (IG) to find certain information, to be inspired or to be entertained on those 'down days'. IG for them is partly a mechanism to escape the stresses of their day, but also a vehicle to help them get through their day. Once we identified this, we made our IG objective two-fold: a) to be the branding go-to page for women in business between the ages of 28 and 45, and b) to educate and inspire our BossSquad in a non-conforming or sales-oriented way. These objectives permeate how we perform everything we do on this platform. From our Lives (which are always high energy and fun) to our behind-the-scenes videos (showcasing our day-to-day activities and how we get through our low moments) and the design of our posts (every other post is a branding tip). It determines what CTAs we use (never over-selling), our graphic style (always clean with bright colours that capture the attention) and the content direction (showcasing both my business and personal brand activities with a voice of authenticity and truth). Even if I'm having a bad day, I don't use our IG page to whine about life. Our job is to use branding as a tool to inspire and give hope to our BossSquad. So when things go wrong, we share the lessons, not just the pain. Combining branding tips and advice with a window to 'Kubi's world', with very little sales focus, has enabled us to grow our IG following from 1,250 to 11,890 in less than one year. What's more, in doing this, we have inadvertently been able to use IG to evidence our work, delivery style and industry knowledge. We have built trust, shown our personality and proven that we are who we say we are, which in turn has brought in 33 per cent of new business during the same time period. When we stopped trying to sell and focused on the needs of the end user, we actually grew our platform and increased our sales!

Facebook has a similar demographic (professional women either working in firms, seeking a way out of the 9–5, or having just left to build their own empires), though these women are slightly older, 45–60, and much more seasoned in their careers. However, they don't use our Facebook page to seek information; instead, they use it to be engaged. They want to join a conversation and be part of a debate. They use it as an escape and an avenue to stretch themselves. They enjoy connecting with like-minded people with different and often challenging opinions. They want dialogue, not motivation. It took us ages to work this out. This nuance between the needs of our Tribe – whilst they might be the same women – requires different usage on the different platforms. Prior to this knowledge we thought Facebook was no longer relevant to our brand – it was, just in a different way. To that end, we had to adapt our objectives and rethink our approach.

This degree of agility is necessary for your brand to grow on social media. Just because you have one objective today, doesn't mean it will be the same in two years' time. Audiences move, platforms change and your brand marketing approach needs to be flexible enough to move with the trends. However, a word of caution: whilst your brand marketing *approach* may change, your brand must always remain the same. Your Brand Promise, Brand Personality, Brand Vision, Brand ID, these things should remain, but the way you execute the brand may adapt as the platforms and the audience needs evolve.

## What is your social media mission statement?

Once you have identified your platform objectives, you then need to create a mission statement for each. For example at SheBuildsBrands our LinkedIn page is not used for the 'BossSquad' (as it is for IG or Facebook); on the contrary, our LinkedIn mission is 'to connect with potential B2B clients globally' and our objective is to focus on those in the HR, communications, sales and marketing industries, across sectors and within emerging markets around the world. As such, the content is not the same as that on IG because the audience and the mission is completely different. We are not trying to inspire, we are trying to show evidence that we are the right people for these global firms to connect with. We are not speaking to sole traders, junior executives, entrepreneurs or graduates; we are focused on high-level executives within medium to large international firms. Whilst the people for both groups are always women (as a brand our Tribe are 93 per cent women), the mission of how we serve those women is completely different. Normally the women on our LinkedIn page are seeking alliances to help them to perform better in their jobs. They want someone who can come in as a consultant and make them 'look good internally'. Whilst this woman might even be the same woman on Facebook, when she is on LinkedIn she isn't seeking debates; she needs partners. This knowledge highly impacts our approach on LinkedIn. The clarification between our platforms has enabled us to create blogs, case studies and articles that have increased our international corporate bookings by 10 per cent and our UK corporate bookings by 58 per cent all in the same year that we grew our IG page to 11,890 followers.

On the other hand, our Twitter is purely for listening. We follow all the trade publications, from *Marketing* to *Brand Republic*, *Marketing Week*, *PR Week*, *Campaign*, *CNN*, *Bloomberg* and the like. We only post when there is a specific win for our business, or we retweet when others have said nice things about us. But other than that, our mission statement for Twitter is 'listen, learn, be in the know'. I learnt a long time ago that as a consultant I can't just give and not pour something back into myself. I have to be reading around my subject constantly and then utilizing the information to benefit my clients. Twitter serves that purpose, so it is less about serving our Tribe, but rather using other people's platforms to stay relevant and informed.

This is critically important for your brand. How can you use digital to keep you up-to-date with what is happening in your sector? Are you subscribed to key newsletters, online portals or Twitter accounts? I personally dedicate one day a week to studying my industry. After all, I am promising information, so I need to stay informed!

## LET'S DO THE WORK

Fill in the table below.

| Platform | Objective | Mission statement |
|---|---|---|
| LinkedIn | | |
| Facebook | | |
| Twitter | | |
| Instagram | | |
| WhatsApp | | |
| YouTube | | |
| Snapchat | | |
| Tumblr | | |
| Google Plus | | |
| Other | | |

# Which platforms are generating the most value . . . and why?

'Kubi, which digital platforms should I use?' is a common question during my masterclasses. Attendees are always debating which ones are the best and whether or not they need to be on one, or all, of them. The answer, however, is very simple: you do not need to be on every platform, you need to be on the *right platform*. Wherever Your Tribe are, that is where you need to be. If they are on LinkedIn, get on LinkedIn; if they are on Snapchat, go there. The key is to align where Your Tribe are with what fits with your personal brand. If you hate taking pictures, even if Your Tribe is on IG, IG might not be for you, but Twitter (assuming Your Tribe is there) might be perfect. It's important to connect your brand with your audience, and use the platform that meets the two in the middle.

Beyoncé has 14.9 million followers on Twitter, but she only uses Twitter to promote her concerts, albums and send CTAs to her IG account. Beyoncé is a visual personality, which is why Twitter isn't a natural fit for her. This is evident as in the whole time of her career she has only posted 11 Tweets (as at the date of this book being written); whereas she has 126 million followers on Instagram, using rich and highly produced images and videos to show her talent, beauty and the power of her personality on this visual platform. She focuses on what works for her brand, and joins it with where her Tribe naturally go.

I once had a client who was adamant that she needed to be on Instagram; her children had told her it was the latest platform so she was fixated on being there. But she hated taking pictures, either of herself or anything else. She hated seeing herself on camera, so Lives and IGTV were out the question, but she absolutely loved writing. She was starting a physiotherapy clinic and wanted to help her clients maintain between treatments. After hours and hours of going over IG, and why it probably was not for her, I finally managed to convince her to focus on a blog site, Facebook and LinkedIn. Besides, her audience were men and women between the ages of 50 and 65, so despite what her children said, she didn't need to be on IG.

It's important to cultivate platforms that fit with your brand, and not focus on following trends. If you only end up on one or two platforms, that's fine, just make sure you are investing in them with consistent content, focused engagement, effective digital CRM (customer relationship management) and CTAs that lead your followers into your sales funnel.

# Which content style is generating the most value?

With so many different platforms there are a number of content style options that you can choose from: Promo Videos, Behind the Scenes Videos, Stories, Blog-Style Videos, Infographics, Editorial Images, Lifestyle Images, Live Streaming Videos, Boomerangs, Gifs and Animations. There are lots and lots of options, so how do you choose?

First, do not copy-cat your competitors. Just because a particular content style works for them, doesn't mean it will work for you. Even if it does work, why not try something different? After all, you want to jump out of the page, not look the same as everything else when Your Tribe are scrolling through their feeds.

Second, be authentic. Go with styles that feel natural to you. If you have never felt yourself to be particularly photogenic, don't start hiring photographers to create editorial 'model'-type images. Instead try lifestyle images that showcase you in your natural work setting or with clients doing what you do best. I once hired a photographer who was adamant that she knew my brand better than me, and she kept trying to put me in 'natural settings' with a big cheesy smile on my face. That's just not me – I am much more of a rock'n'roll entrepreneur! So it's important to partner with content producers who 'get' you, and don't want to change you. If you're struggling go back to your brand archetype, create a brand style guide and remember what your Brand ID stands for.

Third, delete is an option. If you try something and it doesn't resonate with Your Tribe, or you look back and it didn't work, press the delete button. There is no rule that everything you ever did has to be kept online. You have the choice to delete things that no longer work for you; trust me, as the years go by you might just want to press that button! The key is to monitor your content, try new things, review the analytics and then if it didn't work, change it. With each go, you will discover which style works for your brand and connects with Your Tribe.

The thing to remember when it comes to content creation is to do things that reinforce your brand and allow you to be social, on social media. Remember: you are not here to sell. Social media is about creating authentic connections and building trust, with a robust CTA and sales funnelling system behind it. Therefore your content needs to trigger emotive reactions.

If you're struggling to know where to start or how to find inspiration, look outside your industry. Whenever I work with clients I tell them not to focus on their competitors' pages (which will probably lead to you trying to copy and do the same thing) but rather to look to companies that are serving the same audience, but doing it from completely different industries. When you do this you will be surprised just how much inspiration comes your way. When I started doing my Lives (the content that generates the biggest return-on-investment for my brand), I looked to YouTube lifestyle vloggers for inspiration. How do they entertain? How do they structure their videos? How do they deliver CTAs that don't sound like a sales pitch? When I studied them I became inspired, adapted it to my natural flow and started my Lives. It took *three months* before I found my own groove. Yes, it takes time! But once it happened, the ROI (return on investment) became evident.

Once you start creating content, be consistent for a while. Give yourself at least a month (I always try four to eight weeks of testing something) before you try to change it. You need time to monitor the reaction. Just because you started doing something today doesn't mean Your Tribe are going to respond straight away. It takes time. Be consistent and monitor, monitor, monitor.

## LET'S DO THE WORK

List social media pages that inspire you that are outside of your industry. Not sure? Do some research and start becoming aware.

| Pages that inspire you | What do you like about them? | What don't you like about them? | How can you adapt them for your own social media pages? |
|---|---|---|---|
| | | | |
| | | | |
| | | | |
| | | | |
| | | | |
| | | | |
| | | | |
| | | | |
| | | | |
| | | | |

# Are you 'on-brand' throughout?

The term 'on-brand' means that you are consistently projecting your Brand Promise, Brand Values, Brand Mission, Brand Personality and Brand ID. When you fail to be 'on-brand' you are not keeping these things coherent across your social media platforms and overall marketing channels.

Remember the chap I mentioned earlier in the book who stated that 'Innovation Is Our Thing'? If, like him, you fail to allow your brand to come alive consistently across all of your brand touch-points, you lose trust. Therefore it is important, once you have identified which platforms and content style you want to use, to think through how your brand comes alive within all of this.

Before you start working with a content producer, or doing all the content yourself, remind yourself and your team of the following:

- What are my promises?

- What are my values?

- What are my differentiators?

- What is my voice?

- What are my points of view?

- What is my brand archetype?

- What are my brand colours?

Then ask – is the above evident across all my social media pages and marketing channels? Am I producing content and materials that reinforce who I say I am? If you are not, it might be worth revisiting the content and producing things that are 'on-brand'.

## LET'S DO THE WORK

Go through all of your brand touch-points and answer yes or no: are you on-brand throughout? (Use the facing table as a starting point but there might be other touch-points that you want to add.)

| Brand touch-point | Yes | No | What actions need to happen? |
|---|---|---|---|
| Website | | | |
| Facebook | | | |
| Instagram | | | |
| LinkedIn | | | |
| Twitter | | | |
| YouTube | | | |
| Business cards | | | |
| CV/Biography | | | |
| Media kit | | | |
| Presentation/Information packs | | | |
| Email signature | | | |
| Office décor | | | |
| Staff uniforms/Style | | | |
| Your personal style | | | |
| Printed materials such as flyers, posters, exhibition banners etc. | | | |
| Video content | | | |
| Advertising campaigns | | | |

# What does your audience need?

## Brand marketing theme

What is your brand's point of view? What do you want Your Tribe seeing as your brand talking point? What is the main theme across your marketing channels?

If we review David Beckham's profile, we can see that whilst he is a retired footballer he still keeps football as his main theme. This is because his current income is generated via his success as a footballer, and therefore to remain 'on-brand' he ties all his content back to his foundation and brand notoriety.

On his Facebook page he keeps his Tribe up to date with what he is doing, promoting, travel, family, charity work and endorsement deals; however, each area interconnects with his love for football. This theme is consistent across all of his platforms and marketing materials.

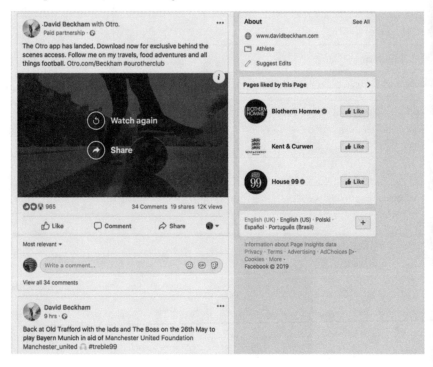

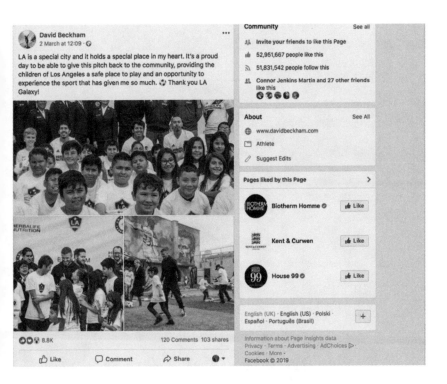

Meanwhile Jamie Oliver's brand is less about him, and more about how he can teach others how to cook. This theme is evident on his website, as he doesn't even have an 'About Jamie' page. Instead he focuses on recipes, step-by-step guides and videos in his top tabs. This theme of helping/teaching people is reinforced across all of his platforms, from his 4.2 million subscribers on YouTube to his 7.1 million followers on IG; in each post and video the focus is on teaching people how to cook.

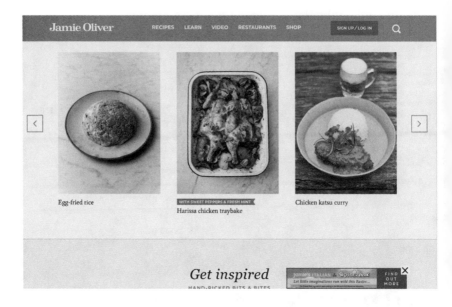

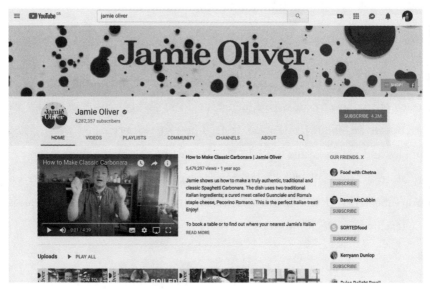

When thinking about your theme, also think about what you *will not* have attached to your brand marketing. What things do you not talk about?

As an example, a client of mine got into some hot water when she started having political debates on her Facebook and Twitter pages. She didn't recognize that her global audience of stakeholders ranged from suppliers to partners, and ended up alienating some of her Tribe. When I started working with her, we produced social media guidelines that outlined what to do, and what not to do, for both herself and her freelance team.

---

## LET'S DO THE WORK

*What is the theme that will resonate across your platforms?*

_____

*What will not be part of your brand theme?*

_____

_____

---

# Brand tone, look and feel

It is important to know the emotional state of Your Tribe because the words, the images and the tone that you use need to be designed to help them move from one emotional state to another. There is no point posting content that doesn't factor in the day, time and thus emotional state of Your Tribe because it probably won't resonate and convert.

For example, I have noticed that when I do my IG Lives on a Thursday evening, I get the best response when I factor in music. The fast-paced gospel and pop classics help push up the energy levels and get the viewers better engaged. After all, I know that it's coming to the end of the week and they might be feeling a bit tired, a bit down, or maybe work hasn't gone well for them that day. So, I don't focus on brand teaching, I focus on brand inspiration; my job is to lift them up. As a result, the content is more engaging. I tell my audience to dance and show me the dancing emoji. I encourage them to use my Live as a platform to network with each other and talk about what they are looking for in their businesses. I focus on the possible global connections they can make using my platform and get them to do business with one another. Whereas at the beginning of the week when you watch my Lives, on a Monday for example, I'm a lot more serious and I have a much more structured format; this is what we are talking about, have you got your pens, are you ready? Let's go! I start the week like this because I know my audience's emotional state is that they are ready to build their brands and they are fired up to make this new week a success. Combining both approaches at different times in the week results in more followers, DMs (direct messages) and sales leads.

When you know Your Tribe, you know what sort of atmosphere you are creating based on where they are. Whether you use industry-appropriate humour or more traditional posting styles, the key is not to post what you want, but to post based on what they need at that time, on that day, for your platform to convert leads into sales.

But how do you learn about Your Tribe?

You ask them questions. You use your platforms to find out what they like, what they don't like and how they want to engage with you. But don't ask questions that are too broad because a lot of people aren't going to tell you the truth. If I say 'How do you feel about my Lives?' they might not mention how they really feel. But if I said 'Did you enjoy the music on today's Live?' they might say 'Oh, it was really fun, it helped me feel welcome and less stressed' or they might say 'I hated it because I couldn't concentrate on your teaching and I want more tips from you.' This direct and specific questioning helps you get more focused answers.

There are a number of ways to find out information from Your Tribe using your digital platforms. You can:

- *Ask them!* Literally go on Live, or post a question and ask them. It sounds straightforward but the number of people who are afraid of asking questions of their Tribe is unreal. If they don't answer the first time, try again.

- *Competitions* – Tie the questions to a giveaway. People always like freebies so if you want answers and no-one is giving them to you, throw in an incentive.

- *Polls* – conduct online polls on your social media. Facebook, Twitter and IG are good for these, or on your website. Again you might want to incentivize answers.

- *Questionnaires* – I would do this with existing clients, not potential leads; get those who already trust your brand to complete a questionnaire that will help you learn more about them and their social media behaviour.

Once you understand their emotional state, be clear on what five key words you want Your Tribe to *feel* when they think about your brand.

The feeling you create across your brand marketing helps or hinders your connection. For example Yoga and Pilates specialist Boho Beautiful are a couple that describe themselves as 'yoga digital nomads'. They travel the world finding beautiful places to film their classes and give inspiration to those seeking wellness practices. Their page oozes emotion. If you are wanting to be relaxed, you are drawn into their images and if this is the feeling you desire, you are keen to learn more. This emotive connection creates the *pull* that you want your brand to have.

Whereas Oliver Rousteing, creative director of Paris Couture House, Balmain, uses his social media to conjure up a feeling of stardom and exclusivity with his platforms. From shoots with celebrities such as Rihanna and Beyoncé to advertising campaigns of him with supermodels, the emotion is strong, fierce and clear. Again, if his Tribe want this feeling, they are engaged and ready to get more. The use of colours, formatting and styling helps to harness the desired emotion, and none of it is done by accident.

## LET'S DO THE WORK

*What emotion are you trying to create?*

_____

_____

_____

_____

*How will you achieve this?* Create a Vision Board of images from other people's platforms to help you identify the feel for your own. Then work with freelancers, interns or professionals (depending on your budget) to get the desired outcome.

_____

_____

_____

_____

## How will you use social media as part of your wider marketing activities and feed it all into your sales funnel?

To effectively convert Posts and Likes to Engagement and Sales you need to revert back to the buying cycle, buying period, and your Friend Profile, as outlined in Chapters 3 and 4. You want to be crystal clear as to when Your Friend is ready to buy, and what their pain-points are at that moment.

For example, if you were trying to target someone like me, first you will need to be clear on my profile: female, entrepreneur, mother, middle class, religious, lives in the suburbs, travels for work, loves fitness, etc. Second, you will need to be aware of my habits and lifestyle: a) generally speaking, on the weekends I don't work because I'm in 'mummy mode'; Saturday afternoons tend to be spent chaperoning my daughter to yet another birthday party or waiting for her to finish her Saturday performing arts school; b) My work focus is Monday to Thursday, doing on average of 12 hours a day; on Fridays I finish by 3 p.m.; c) when I am on social media during the week I only go on to post or respond to comments, I never scroll, and then I am off again; d) on Sundays I go to church in the morning and have family time in the afternoon, so generally I am only really on social media (not using it for work and with the time to spend discovering your brand) on a Sunday evening.

When you review my consumer profile, my habits and lifestyle outline clearly when you should communicate to me. For example, if you are expecting me to be on Facebook at 7 p.m. during the week, trying to advertise to me, I'm not there; I am putting my daughter to bed or in my home office still working. Equally, if you want me to see your Lives on a Saturday afternoon, I am not there; I am out doing mummy duties. If you have a radio advert airing at 10 a.m. on a Monday, I am at work in meetings, not listening to the radio. Therefore knowing what I am doing, and when, determines not only how you post, but what time you post and what CTAs you should use to get me to buy!

Many of my clients, both large and small, are failing to really understand and study their Tribe, which means that their marketing is not hitting the target. You simply can't afford not to know, as you will literally be wasting your time, money and resources. As mentioned in previous chapters, you need to view Your Tribe like your friend, and it becomes detrimental when you start marketing without this knowledge.

So how do you do this? Start by using your social media analytics to gauge what Your Tribe are doing, and when.

Each platform has its own backend analytics. If you are not yet using them, you might need to turn your page from personal to business to access them, which is free. You can also attach your website to Google Analytics to monitor the flow from your marketing activities to your website sales funnel. Once you do this, you can monitor the trends over the course of two to three months to source the information you need. Using this data you should start to play with your marketing to see what lands. Design content and gauge the reaction; go Live and see what they respond to; try different CTAs to monitor which ones increase clicks to your website. Play with your website homepage to see how they respond to your new customer journey. Measure and review your conversion rate, which is when people click on your website and then go on to make a purchase. Be clear on whether or not this is increasing or decreasing. Measure your bounce rate; if you are posting constantly and people are clicking through to your website, but not staying, this is your bounce rate.

Monitor your landing pages; a lot of people put great content on social media but then they direct their Tribe to their website homepage rather than a landing page. A landing page has all the information for the direct thing you are promoting. If you fail to have a landing page, this can decrease your chances of conversions.

Analytics is everything; data drives decisions!

Monitoring doesn't stop at digital; you should also have a 'review and learn' approach to all your offline marketing activities. Go to networking events to identify if it can work for you, but take time to see which contacts you made do actually follow up, and use a CRM system to check on how long it took for the lead to turn into a sale. Secure partners and put in contractual review periods to identify the progress of the partnership. Pitch to journalists and see which story ideas they like; change the wording of story titles to ascertain if that grabs them better the next time.

The key with all of this is to test, review, monitor and go again! If you try one thing and it doesn't work, try something else. It is in the doing that you will see what lands! Too many of you are not doing this because you're afraid it won't work. But so what? If one marketing activity doesn't convert, try another. Learn from your mistakes and limit your spend as you undertake your test period. But don't be discouraged. We all are constantly testing because trends dictate change and so we have to consistently review, monitor, analyse and, where necessary, try a new approach.

## Metrics and ROI

Everything you do in marketing is about driving your ROI (return on investment), which is why you need campaign metrics in place to measure and calculate your ROI.

The most obvious is an increase in sales, i.e. you do a campaign and you expect X number of sales or X amount of repeat business, but there are so many more ways to measure campaign success:

- *Brand impressions* – When embarking on any ATL (Above-the-Line) activity, you need to think about the brand impression. Every time someone looks at the poster – that is one brand impression. How many people will see that poster? How many times will they see your brand? When you are doing media buying, the agency you are working with to secure your billboards or tube advertising should be able to indicate the level of traffic in any given area and thus the projected brand impression, e.g. how many people go up the escalators each day and see the tube advertising? That will give you the estimated brand impression. These brand impressions are all of your potential customers with whom you're creating a brand recognition.

- *Press coverage* – PR activities all generate press coverage, so you need to gather all of your press clippings, audio records and podcast records to use as evidence on your website that your brand is what you say it is. Each PR activity should include a call-to-action or a backend link to get people to go to your website, which you can then track via Google Analytics.

- *Web traffic* – This assumes that you have a website, which I think in today's market is an absolute must! As a personal brand working for a company, I would encourage you to have a résumé website; as a freelancer you should have a portfolio site; and as an entrepreneur you should have a business site. You can keep your budget low by using existing platforms such as WIX and WordPress to create them yourself, or pay a web designer to assist you. Once you have your site, you need to ensure that you are tracking activity on the backend. One of the most popular, and free, ways to do this is to use Google Analytics, along with Yahoo Web Analytics, Crazy Egg, Optimizely and Clicktale. These will tell you things like how many visits you have, either unique or returners, how long they stayed on each page, their profiles, where they are in the world, whether or not they came to you via your social media sites or general search, and what time of day they visited your site, etc. These metrics will help you to learn more about Your Friend and their digital behaviour as it relates to your brand, and subsequently will help to better shape your future campaigns.

- *Subscription* – When visitors come to your site, are they subscribing to your newsletter or blog? But here's a tip, you need a subscription box to get them to subscribe! Make sure you have one on your homepage and, if possible, on some of your site's subsidiary pages as well. You could have pop-up subscription boxes or a subscription banner on the side, bottom or across the page under the scroll line. The key with this is that when you're doing your social media activities, you want to drive people to your subscription list so that you have warm leads to convert to clients/customers later. This is extremely important as I've seen people with thousands of followers on Instagram but zero people on their own database. This is troublesome because, if for any reason your account was switched off, you could potentially lose all of those leads and would have to start all over again.

- *Social media engagement* – On your platforms are people liking, sharing or commenting on your posts? If not, why not? Is it the time of day, the quality of the images, the quality of the captions? Are you failing to use the right hashtags? Are you using your Story to let them know there is a new post on your page? Are you being inconsistent with the frequency of your posts and therefore they don't expect anything from you, so they are not jumping on your page? Have you failed to be clear on the objectives of your page? Are you adding any real value?

- *Social media reach* – How many people are following you? What is the total reach across all of your platforms? When you're trying to secure partners, you need to talk about your total reach as opposed to just your individual reach. You also need to have clear metrics, either via downloading key apps or via the existing social media platform metrics.

- *Lead volume* – When you run a campaign, how is this turning into leads? What call-to-action do you have to get people calling or emailing you, such as 'Join today and get X' or 'Register now and get Y'? When people do call, visit or email you, what do you do with those leads? What systems do you have in place to monitor the leads and note any increase or decrease in volume? This is where an effective CRM tool is needed. Your CRM tool should be used to enter the leads and then track the sales pipeline from lead to deal closed.

- *Quality of leads* – Lead Quality Score – how many of your leads compare to your brand's ICP (ideal customer profile or ideal client profile)? In other words, how many leads are actually Your Friends? I have worked with many influencers in the past who can't seem to make money from their platforms. They might have 500,000 followers on Instagram but they can't seem to convert; this is normally because their ICP is not following them. They have focused on content that attracts people, but not the right people! When your campaign creatives are on-brand and driving the right messages, you will start to increase the quality of your leads. This is why you shouldn't worry when people unfollow you. You only want your true ICP, so let those who don't fit the profile go!

- *Lead to sale conversion* – If you have 20 leads coming in each day, how many are converting into sales? If eight out of those 20 convert, is that high or low in your industry? What are normal conversions in your sector? It is important to know your industry conversion rates to be able to measure the effectiveness of your campaign.

- *Frequency of sale* – If you are selling a particular service, how often does the same customer come back and repeat buy? If you run a hair salon and a customer comes once a month and you are able to convince her to come twice a month, you have doubled the frequency of sale.

- *Referrals* – How many of your customers or clients are referring you on to new customers? What initiatives do you have in place to encourage clients to promote you? Who else in Your Tribe could you use as a mechanism to gain referrals? Most importantly, how are you tracking the increase or decrease of the referrals that are coming your way?

- *NPC (net-promoter-score)* – This is based on the theory that if someone in Your Tribe recommends people to your brand, then your NPC is high. One way to measure this is to ask your followers, colleagues, partners or customers if they would recommend your brand to a friend. If most of them say no, you have a low NPC and you need to think about why that might be the case and how you can harness your campaign to increase that score.

In summary, marketing can, and should, be measured, so make sure you include metrics in your personal brand marketing campaigns. Once you understand what is going on, you can tweak and amend for the second campaign, each time improving as you go along. I often tell clients to treat this like a game. Each time you get better at learning the rules and playing, one day you score higher, and eventually you'll win!

---

## LET'S DO THE WORK

*Which of the above metrics will you use for your next brand marketing campaign and why?*

_____

_____

_____

_____

_____

# Tie it together

The most successful brand marketing activities are the ones that have an integrated approach. When you tie in both online and offline efforts, within a specific time, with clear messages, metrics and targeted audiences, results do happen. This is perfectly illustrated by the success of Luiza Gibb, who is the Managing Director, Curator and Founder of Flat Space Art (FSA) in London. She built her platform to 28.7k IG followers by being extremely strategic about her brand marketing. She started with social media and then went onto a multi-channel approach to generate sales. Here is what she recently told me:

> The starting point for me was by doing a thorough analysis of the marketplace to see where the niche lay. This helped me come up with my most important strategic decision which was to have my gallery as purely an online business, and not in a bricks and mortar space. I then needed to create my niche, online and through core brand values which I define as: entrepreneurial, innovative, philanthropic and approachable. These four key values are at the heart of every key strategic decision.
>
> My next key strategic decision was to leverage social media to raise awareness, so I set up two social media accounts: Flat Space Art and Luiza Gibb to build a profile for both my business brand and my personal brand.

Inevitably, as I'm the founder of FSA my business account embodies the same values as my personal account.

But awareness isn't enough and creating strategic sales channels has been a core decision – getting this right is a make or break moment. So, as well as our own website – which took many hours of blood, sweat and tears – I knew creating collaborations with the world's leading art affiliates, specifically with 1st Dibs (who I persuaded to come over from New York to meet with me), was the answer. Once they signed us as their approved dealers for London; Artsy and The List shortly followed thereafter. And, hey bingo! Our artists' works were now being seen on a global platform.

On the back of our sales channel affiliates, we then focused on lifestyle collaborations with organizations and like-minded brands that have an interest in art culture; Soho House, Blacks Club, and London hotels such as The Langham and Claridge's (in my case) are now running regular masterclasses with their members.

Underpinning all the above is a high-level print media strategy using aspirational lifestyle titles to spread awareness for both FSA and individual artists – as well as building awareness. This strategy has helped to build our customer database and ultimately drive sales.

## LET'S DO THE WORK

Complete the table below and build on what you have been noting down earlier:

| Channel – what channel will you use? | Mission – what is the mission or objective of that channel? | Content style – what will be your content direction? | CTA – what call-to-actions will you put in place? | Metrics – what metrics will you use to measure the success? |
|---|---|---|---|---|
|  |  |  |  |  |
|  |  |  |  |  |
|  |  |  |  |  |

| Channel – what channel will you use? | Mission – what is the mission or objective of that channel? | Content style – what will be your content direction? | CTA – what call-to-actions will you put in place? | Metrics – what metrics will you use to measure the success? |
|---|---|---|---|---|
|  |  |  |  |  |
|  |  |  |  |  |
|  |  |  |  |  |
|  |  |  |  |  |
|  |  |  |  |  |

# 9

# Know Your Worth, Then Add Tax

*Opportunities do not float like clouds in the sky. They are attached to people.*
*Venture Capitalist,* RICHARD STROMBACK

I recently worked with a client who, in her early 40s, had lost her job. Having been with the same company for 13 years, she found herself without work. By the time she was fired, having given all those years of sweat and grind to one company, she realized she had not built her own personal brand for it to be able to thrive outside of her previous role. Whilst working, she had no interest in branding; as the COO (Chief Operating Officer) she wasn't on social media (for personal or business) as she didn't like the idea of giving away all of her data. She worked long hours and didn't see the need to be out there networking. She once told me, 'Kubi, I'm old school,' believing that as long as she worked hard, she would always be ok. As it turns out, simply working hard wasn't enough. She had a small number of contacts, zero digital footprint and hadn't networked to build up her power and influence. Six months later and still looking for work, she came back to me. The brief was simple: 'I need a new job, how do I position myself to get it?'

The sad truth is that my client is not alone. According to entrepreneur.com, one in four people don't network, and yet 85 per cent of jobs are filled through networking. This is a shocking statistic, particularly if you're not building your social capital. But what do you need to do if you want to expand your contacts?

First, identify what has previously been stopping you from networking. What has held you back? Is it fear, time, complacency, anxiety? Do you feel you don't have much to offer or you're not sure where to start? If this is the case, I would encourage you to write a list of the reasons as to why you've not been networking or haven't been consistent, and then go through them all to identify how you will combat each one and find a solution. My client started off by saying it was time that stopped her. So we identified what she needed to give up to free one evening a week for making connections. As it turns out, she was trying to be there to collect her daughter from after school club every day, when really she could skip one of them without feeling guilty, and ask her husband to collect instead. This time could then be used to attend meaningful networking events.

Once we found a solution, she then revealed that she just didn't know where to start when it came to effective networking, and like many of us didn't want to waste her time just 'going to events'. Together, we were able to identify appropriate events for her industry and seniority level. Then she revealed her truth: she hated the prospect of stepping into a crowded room full of complete strangers and having to make conversation. To date she had gotten away with simply knowing everyone in the company, starting from the bottom and working her way up into a senior position, so the idea of really putting herself out there was terrifying.

Erinn Collier, Co-Founder and Chief Revenue Officer for technology firm Just3Things, addresses this fear:

> I think even for extroverted people (like myself), networking can often feel
> disingenuous. It's incredibly uncomfortable, something I experienced a lot

in my career; when I moved to Europe I would literally be asked to attend industry events where I did not know a single person! You are always going to be nervous walking into a room where you are expected to network with new people, and it's best to simply accept that nervousness, take a breath, and just force yourself to walk up to a circle of people and introduce yourself. That right there is the worst moment, but it all gets better from then on.

To combat the fear, Emma Liddiard, Area Business Director at Global Media, who is an avid networker, views it as more than just networking:

Don't network to sell a product or to do business ... Network to make a contact and a friend. The goal I always give myself is to make new friends. If someone likes you as a person, other opportunities will come naturally – often they will even look for ways to work with you! If you start with pitching a product, your conversion rate will be pretty low. If your objective is to make a friend, your conversion rate is massive! Try and find a way to help them without them even asking – they will remember this and it will come back around. But to be able to help others, you need a wide network of contacts, which means you should 'never say no to anything'. You never know who this person knows, how you can connect them with others in your network or where their career is taking them.

The idea of networking for connections, not promotions, is one of the key things I teach my clients. Your job when networking is to see how you can serve others first. The principle of givers-gain applies here. The more you give, the more you naturally will gain. When you keep giving, people go out of their way to give back to you. It's really a natural part of life, which somehow gets forgotten when it comes to networking. If you enter an event with the intention of seeing how many connections you can make and support, it takes the scariness out of the way. After all, you are not there to try to sell yourself; you are there to connect and help others. People love that, and I have often found the very people I least expected to pay it back were the ones who opened the most important doors in my career.

Maria Purcell, Leading Commercial Partnerships EMEA at Workplace by Facebook, echoes this sentiment:

> When I meet someone who I feel connected to, the first thing I think is 'how can I help?'. Where do they want to get to? Is there any tool in my arsenal that will get them there? Sometimes it's directly from me or it's the company I work for or people I know. If you truly connect with someone and can provide the value, you will build a strong network; in doing so, they'll come good and return the favour. Usually when you need it the most.

Of course it is normal to feel nervous about networking – not knowing what to say or where to start. But, as outlined above, when your focus is less on the networking and more on the connecting, it changes everything.

## LET'S DO THE WORK

What is holding you back from networking and what could you do to combat the problem? It's time to get rid of the excuses.

Complete the grid below:

| Reason for not networking | What could you do to combat this? |
| --- | --- |
|  |  |
|  |  |
|  |  |
|  |  |

# Three Tiers of Networking

The power of building your network doesn't just happen at networking events or trade shows. Your ability to network is literally everywhere and with everyone. In brand marketing we call this the 'Three Tiers of Networking'.

## First tier

The first tier is your Professional Network, usually people you work with on a day-to-day basis: those who are in your company, or department, or part of your project teams. These are naturally easy networks to create as they are part of your ability to deliver on the day-to-day job at hand. However, even at this basic level, people tend to not explore these networks. They often think their colleagues are just people they work with. Instead, if you view every connection as part of your arsenal to help others, and thus yourself, you can explore these networks much more effectively. Since we will spend approximately 90,000 hours at work over the course of our lifetime, it's important to try to develop connections who can support your journey and day-to-day activities.

According to a recent *Harvard Business Review*, research reveals there has been a 300 per cent rise in loneliness in the workplace, and 50 per cent of CEOs report being lonely, which is partly due to a disconnection with our Professional Network. In her book *BELONG*, author Radha Agrawal (2018) states that loneliness in the workplace is because 'as humans, we're hardwired for social connectivity, but in the West we are taught to celebrate individualism'. Her solution for this is that every professional person has to increase their 'Social Connectivity Score'. This identifies people who are able to connect best with others. Those with a high social connectivity score are those who give out hugs, or smile, are friendly or support others. Your ability to increase your social connectivity score has a direct impact on your ability to do well at work. As outlined in *BELONG*, if you're in the top 25 per cent of people in your company in terms of social connectivity, you are 40 per cent more likely to get a raise or promotion. We think that promotions come from hard work alone, but they don't. We think that new client wins come from the people who give the best pitch, but they don't. It's the people who are able to connect best with others. People buy people. It all leads back to that emotional connection with your desired audience. Your brand requires you to network, so that your brand can connect. It really is that simple. As such it's important to become intentional with your connections and networking at the Professional Networks level. To start this process, why not try being the one to connect people for Friday night drinks, or the one who invites the projects team out for a group lunch. What's the worst that can happen? People say no – OK, so you try someone else in another department or working on a different project. The key is to not overlook those in your first tier of networking and to remember that you do not need to have everything in common with them, but you do need to be able to make a genuine connection.

## Second tier

The second tier includes our Personal Networks: those who are part of our life outside of work, such as the other parents at your children's school, or people who go to your fitness classes or attend your church. It's important to include these people in your network and to identify ways you can learn more about them to see how you can aid their careers and vice versa. Since 80 per cent of jobs are never advertised, it's imperative to expand your Personal Network, and build your influence amongst your peers.

Some ways to do this include volunteering: joining a charity that feeds into your passion or interests and building your networks from within their circles. Becoming part of a political party and helping with the campaigning will expose you to more of your Tribe. Going away with friends and extended family members will increase your circle as each person brings someone new to the fold. Starting a new fitness class, heading to a yoga retreat, finding a new hobby that includes others or joining a team. All of these will open new doors and broaden your Personal Network, which in turn widens your chance of success.

Luiza Gibb, Managing Director, Curator, and Founder of Flat Space Art, describes how, when she started her art gallery, she used her Personal Network:

> I made a concerted effort initially through my children's school and the network there, but I would have been mortified if anyone had ever felt pushed into buying a piece of art. My networking was more based on the love of art and being able to share this through a conversation with a fellow art enthusiast.

She found the connection and allowed that to be the driver to build her business.

## Third tier

The third tier is your Strategic Network. This is the ability to outline where you want to go and to identify key people to assist the process. Your Strategic Network can be built online through the power of social media and offline through membership clubs and key associations. The principle with Strategic Networking is to see each connection as a stepping stone taking you closer to your goals.

Narjice Basaran, Digital Marketing Consultant, eSecta and PureModus, understands this explicitly:

> Early in my career I used LinkedIn almost daily to increase my business reach and it worked well for me, even though nothing will replace good old face-to-face networking. That doesn't just have to be in a business sense; I do go on business courses and attend industry events, but these connections have also come from community networks, social events and charity work I have done. My advice would be to get out of your comfort zone; you won't learn anything from sitting in a room full of people who had the same experiences as you and agree with everything you say. Find associations, institutes and societies that have a thriving social network, and join them.

This type of networking is the one that tends to scare people the most. Again, if you view it as less of a self-promotion and more of an opportunity to make a friendship or genuine connection that you can help first, you will find it so much easier to join a members club and participate in their activities.

Lydia Slater, Deputy Editor of *Harper's Bazaar* and *Town & Country* magazines, summarizes it perfectly:

> The most effective networkers I know are quite upfront about their wish to connect, but at the same time, they start by offering to help you out first, rather than seeing what they can get out of you. I'm always impressed by the personal touch – people who send a note after an event, for instance. Something I admire enormously, though I find it very hard myself, is the ability to remember not only someone's name but incidental information about them, which shows a genuine interest. I think a strong network is hugely important – in my own career, I don't think I've ever applied for a job, I've always been approached via the contact and asked to put myself forward.

## LET'S DO THE WORK

*How can you use the Three Tier networking technique to increase your social capital?* Answer the questions below:

Professional Networking – who in your company could you network with better?

_____

What activities could you do to network with these people?

_____

Personal Networking – who is in your personal circle that you could harness a better connection with?

_____

If no-one, what personal activities or hobbies could you take up to increase your personal network?

---

Strategic Networking – what members' clubs, associations or trade institutions could you join to increase your strategic networking?

---

Who could you buddy with to keep you focused and unafraid of building your strategic network – who could be your accountability buddy during this process?

---

# Time to ask for more!

*61% of women would rather talk about their own death than about money!*

MERRILL LYNCH (2016)

This is probably one of the most shocking statistics I've read about women and money, but it's not the only one. Here are a few more to make the hairs on your neck stand up:

- American women are 80 per cent more likely to be in poverty after retirement than men!

- Part of what fuels the wealth gap is women's lower access to wealth escalators – those benefits that help to grow one's money faster than income alone, e.g. investing opportunities, 401(k)s, 529s, Health Savings Accounts, and more.

- Women's media is not helping: of 1,594 pages of editorial in March 2018 issues of the top 17 women's magazines, less than 1 per cent were about personal finances (Merrill Lynch, 2016).

When it comes to money, why are women so reluctant to talk about it? Why is it not more of a priority and why aren't we supporting each other on the journey to wealth creation?

I put this question to some of the featured women and here is their take on the issues, plus advice on when they became comfortable to ask for the appropriate remuneration for their services, salary or contractor fee.

Marisa Peer, Founder, Marisa Peer Method:

> The reason why [women do not ask for more money] is because they never feel 'enough' – not smart enough, not good enough, not deserving enough. They need to understand the link between 'not enoughness' and money blocks. Women have a harder time than men as they are judged in so many different areas where men aren't, and they have the perpetual guilt that they have to pay a price for working hard – their health, their family or personal life. None of which has to be true ... When I (personally) began to see the value I was offering people, I realised that giving people freedom and empowerment, and good emotional and physical health, is a very worthwhile investment.

Being unafraid to ask for more and knowing you are 'enough' is the technique that Marisa teaches to people all around the world.

Lydia Slater, Deputy Editor of *Harper's Bazaar* and *Town & Country* magazines:

> The reason why [women do not ask for more money] is because it is socially unacceptable. You are definitely judged as greedy or grasping, in a way that a man wouldn't be. I still find it hard to ask for a pay rise, but I tell myself I'm not doing it for me, but for the kids and the dog! ... When it comes to negotiating for more money I always say: pretend you're advocating on someone else's behalf. If you feel greedy asking for yourself, think about how it will help the people you love if you earn more ... This principle of seeing the benefits of money for those in your life is brilliant for women, as

77 per cent of women say they see money in terms of what it can do for their families. Who in your life could you think of when you're feeling afraid of asking for more?

Datuk Dr Hafsah Hashim, Chairman, Serunai Commerce Malaysia:

Women find it difficult to ask for a pay rise/more money because their maternal instincts will always picture the person who is asking for assistance as their own family. It's inbuilt into women's DNA that offering help and assistance to others is second to none. Getting a pay raise/more money is a bonus. The satisfaction of seeing one succeed because of the help/guidance that women offer to others is so self-satisfying and that will bring happiness to us ... The minute I became a government retiree, I was more comfortable to ask for an appropriate fee for the expertise that I impart on others. But to do this I would say rehearse, rehearse and rehearse! Rehearse the negotiation and strategies various scenarios – should option A not be acceptable, prepare Option B and C before entering a negotiation.

The art of effective negotiation is echoed by Maria Purcell, Leading Commercial Partnerships EMEA at Workplace by Facebook:

I don't think all women do [have a problem asking for more money], but I do think we ask too late. Usually, by the time we are ready to have that conversation, we are doing so from a position of weakness and frustration. Comparing yourself to your peers is often the driver, but if you can quantify the impact on the business it makes having those conversations that little bit easier ... My whole career, I've always been target driven. Working in a sales role later on in my career really helped to quantify the impact I could bring. Having numbers attached to your performance means you can drive the conversation from metrics and business outcomes, which is definitely a position of strength. One of the things I do in a negotiation is make sure to anticipate their arguments and develop a strong counter. What will be their 'no's? Then have answers for each one.

Using metrics and outcomes to drive the conversation is a message reinforced by Jaz Rabadia MBE, a Senior Manager of Energy & Sustainability at Starbucks:

> I had an awakening – one day it really dawned on me – I knew and understood things people didn't have the faintest idea about! Once that happened, I started to charge what I was worth, not what I guessed they could afford. As such I put a rule in my career as an employee: I had to get a promotion, pay rise or learn a whole new skill every year in a job or I would immediately start applying for new jobs. I was loyal to the companies that invested in me, but if they stopped investing in me, I had to walk away!

The art of that negotiation is therefore three-fold:

- Understand and know your subject matter like the back of your hand. Have evidence of your outcomes and your metrics of success.

- Find out the background and know the personality with whom you are going to negotiate, especially his/her weaknesses and strengths. What is driving them and their decisions? How do you and your skills fit into the wider business picture?

- Have you been likeable? It's hard to say no to someone you like and that's part of the oil in the mechanism for a good negotiation.

This idea of having a strategic approach to negotiating for more money was effectively outlined during my conversation with Erinn Collier, Co-Founder and Chief Revenue Officer for technology firm Just3Things. We talked about how to secure that promotion, using strategy not emotions. Here is what she had to say:

> **Erinn** *First of all, it's really important not to get personal or emotional, it's got to be a data-driven discussion. Negotiating cannot be about what you need or how you feel undervalued. Even if all those things might be true, get that feeling out ahead of time: talk to a friend, talk to your partner, whatever may help you get out all your frustrations. But when you go to have a meeting*

*about asking for a raise or change in responsibilities or to be taking a step up in terms of your agreement, you've got to come with a clear track record. Ask yourself what have I done? What are the outcomes? Where is the evidence that you have delivered?*

*You need to remember that it's not just a one-time discussion. You have got to be laying down the groundwork; if you think that you want a raise or a promotion, you have to be thinking six months or a year out; you need to be planting that seed. For example, you could bring it up by asking 'you know how I asked you as my boss for more responsibility? Here is what we agreed'. You could do this in writing, which is a bit more methodical or talk about it over email. You then need to show that you took on the task at hand and delivered. You could also have some colleagues to back up the evidence of your work – for example, you can suggest to your boss 'why don't we talk to x as they seem pleased with what I've done'.*

*By taking this first step, you've already built up that track record for them and then hopefully their response is either: one, they don't agree with your request (which is not the end of the world), two, there is no budget for it (which is disappointing and maybe you can challenge it but again it isn't personally about you); or three, maybe not now and maybe at some point in the future (which is fine you just need to keep doing what you were doing). But I think it's all about being prepared and not having a spur of the moment reaction, of finding out that you have a male colleague who is earning more than you do, and then asking out of frustration. You can never go to somebody on the inside and say, 'I know that these people are making more than me' and nothing else; you shouldn't make that the whole or only reason to demand a raise because it is just not strategic enough. What you could do is suggest that your manager includes you in some sort of performance review plan, because it is never about anyone else. It has got to be about you and your ability to deliver and thus earn more.*

**Kubi** *I like the methodical, strategic approach. Talk me through that. So if they have found out that their male colleague earns 20 per cent more than them, what is the six-month lead-in that you would say they should be doing?*

**Erinn** *So go talk to your girlfriend, have a cocktail, have a little shout to your husband or boyfriend/girlfriend or whoever it might be and then sit down and think. Ok, I obviously can't go to my boss and say 'Johnny makes 20 per cent more than me, this is b\*\*\*\*\*\*t, sort it out'. So what you've got to do is, in the six months to nine months before you go to them, sit down and do some thinking.*

*What is your day job? What are its core responsibilities? Whether that is selling something, marketing something, acquiring clients or whatever that is, how does that break down week by week? How would you document the primary work streams of your business – and now if you have to prove to someone that you are good at that (which is annoying – no one likes to feel like they're not good at their job but obviously you are good at your job otherwise you wouldn't be there!), how would you take the question of whether you are good at your day job off the table?*

*For example: what are the KPIs you use to measure the business and in your responsibilities for the business? How have you been tracking against those? Who in the business, if you ask them, would vocalize their approval of you? Do you work well cross-functionally? Do managers, other departments and other areas of the business validate your work? So you collect all that track record and you use it as preparation to go to your manager and say: 'Look, I am really happy, here is what I like and then here is what I have noticed might need some improvement.'*

*So at this point, you're are being proactive, right? How else could you get involved in the business? What is that thing that annoys you? You could use this as an opportunity to show that you can do the day job and go above and* beyond. Now you're breaking it down to tactical measures; you're ready to go and propose your idea, for example: 'we don't have good social media presence or we need to be entering this market segment, no one has done market research on it, would you be comfortable (now it becomes a proposal) with me taking half a day a week, two days a week or whatever it might be, and doing a sideways project to evaluate the risks for you?' After this, you can then follow up by scheduling recurring meetings and say: 'I'm going to come back and bring you my findings or run a test and show you what the results are. Then we know what improvements we can make to improve the business.'

Great! So here's a result: you know you're good at the day job, you've got a proposal to do something that is going to benefit the company, make your boss look good, show that you can be stretched (and hopefully it is something you enjoy, because you shouldn't choose something horrible – that would be stressful for you), and then you set the meetings and say that you would like to follow up with this on a monthly basis, etc.

You go into those sessions (but don't ever go to a one-on-one with any manager or your boss without an agenda, even if it is just three bullet points) and state 'here is what I would like to talk about, here is the report for the month, here is what is going well, here is what's not, here is what I need your help on', and then at the end of the of the lead time (whatever it may be) you can specifically ask for a longer one-on-one and say: 'I would like to talk about how my role is going to expand in the future'. At that point, talk about what that means, how you are going to take on more responsibilities, how it is going to allow you to help scale the business and then you ask for more money.

Does that make sense?

**Kubi** Yes, it is strategic, methodical, data-driven, and more importantly you are giving before you make a request. Which everybody knows it is the basic rule of business – you have got to give to get, right? And you are showing that, *over the six months, you yourself are giving to the organization, and, actually, you care and you are a valuable member of the jigsaw puzzle and now you need to be given a raise.*

*What you would you say to somebody who has followed this process, but is still not getting the value they think they deserve? At what point do they leave?*

**Erinn**  *Obviously, it depends on lots of things – for example, do you still like working for the company? Is your daily work life gratifying to you? To me that is the number one thing. I used to have a boss who was very straightforward and he said 'Look, unfortunately we spend more time with each other in this office building than we do with our families,' so life is too short to be unenjoyable.*

*If the work is enjoyable and you like the people, then that dynamic isn't always easy to find; I think you need to be honest with yourself about whether or not it's worth jumping ship just because you're not getting the promotion. Decide if it's worth waiting for one more cycle before asking: 'Do you think this is something we can revisit in six months?'*

*During those six months, you can start to put your feelers out – what other types of jobs are out there? Who can I connect with? In this way you can have a clearer understanding of what your options might be if you don't secure that promotion or raise.*

*I've lived a lot of my life terrified of being fired and failing. It took me nine years to realize that actually there's not going to be a point in time where I can't find a job doing something I'm skilled to do. So don't be afraid about that. Honestly, life is too short – there is a lot to do out there and the further you get into your career, the more unlikely it is that you're going to have to take a dramatic pay cut if you decide to leave. So make sure you're laying the necessary ground work and preparations to get the hell of out there if it's not making you happy!*

## LET'S DO THE WORK

*What salary/fee are you on at the moment?* _____

*What are the comparable salaries/fees in the market?*
(You will need to go back to your PESTLE research to answer this.)

_____

*What strategic steps could you take to get that promotion?*

a) Where is the evidence of your deliverables? _____

b) How are you tracking your day-to-day successes? _____

c) What project could you take on to show added value to your company or clients? __

d) What reasons could they give you to say 'no'? _____

e) What will be your counter agreements? _____

*If all else fails – what date will you put in your diary as your leaving date?*

_____

# Resources

Agrawal, Radha. (2018). *BELONG: Find your people, create community & live a more connected life*. New York: Workman Publishing. https://belongbook.com/

Harvard Business Review. 2017. Work and the loneliness epidemic. https://hbr.org/cover-story/2017/09/work-and-the-loneliness-epidemic

Merrill Lynch. Bank of America Corporation (2016) Women and Financial Wellness: Beyond the Bottom Line. http://agewave.com/what-we-do/landmark-research-and-consulting/research-studies/women-and-financial-wellness/

# 10

# I AM . . .

**Decision. Vision. Clarity. Strategy. Tactics. Metrics. Ownership. BE UNAPOLOGETIC**

Even if they don't see you.

Make sure you see yourself.

If they don't see your talents, your gifts or your skills.

If they don't see your beauty, your brilliance or your mind.

If they don't understand your funny side, your laughter or your effervescence.

If they don't see your warmth, your gentleness or your heart.

If they don't see how much you care or how much you love.

If they don't see your strength, your tenacity or your resilience.

If they don't see your growth or your future.

Even if they don't see it.

Make sure you see it, and then leave those who are blind behind.

I wrote that when I was at my lowest, when I wanted one of the most important people in my life to see me. I wanted them to not only see me, but to appreciate me, and be wowed by what they saw. I wanted them to hold the spotlight and shine it brightly over me, and be in awe of who stood in front of them. I wanted them to see the imperfections, and love them anyway. To adore the brand, praise it, smile when they engaged with it, be connected to it and take from it. But they never did. The very thing I had spent so long trying to get right, they disliked.

I remember one night sitting in my home office crying. It was late, maybe 2 a.m., I had jazz music playing softly in the background as tears of complete confusion and sadness ran down my face. 'Why?' was my only question – why don't they see me? I felt lonely; as if a sword of rejection had pierced my soul. I felt useless, incomplete, irrelevant! I wanted them to validate me. No, I *needed* them to validate me. I was desperate for it. I had put so much into my brand, constantly striving for perfection, which I wanted so badly to be amazing in their eyes. But in my pursuit of being seen by them, I had forgotten that the audience of validation starts with the audience of one.

I didn't need them to see me. I needed to see myself. I had to hold the spotlight and shine it brightly on myself.

I needed to see my brand's imperfection and love it anyway. I needed to shine my own light and smile at my own reflection. I needed to love – me. Appreciate – me. Validate my damn self! I couldn't expect anyone else to do it, until I had done it first. I had to learn that it's ok to want acceptance from others, but it's imperative to accept and love yourself first.

How do you do this?

Honestly, at first, I didn't know. I sat there for ages trying to figure it out but all I learnt was just how much my life had been a journey of external acceptance. As a child, I had looked to my parents for validation. Then school teachers, dance instructors, university professors, business clients, staff, then business partners. I had turned to social media and seen the 'Likes' as another form of validation. Another 'Share' proved that I had been seen – that I was good.

One day I got sick and tired of feeling sick and tired, and said *enough is enough* and started researching: 'How do you validate yourself?'

Writing in my journal, here's what I learnt:

1   Be the parent to the child in you! At first this sounded odd, but then I
    kept going with it. Unfortunately, there are many people who didn't
    experience parents who were kind, loving and supportive. Even if we
    did, as adults we forget and can still be overly harsh with ourselves;
    often buying into society's unrealistic expectations of who we're meant
    to be. By acting as a parent to yourself, you talk to the little child in
    you, and you should be kind to her. You love her, acknowledge her
    feelings, and give her what she needs. I've tried it and it made me smile.
    It gave me this warm fuzzy feeling, as I sat there and pictured myself as
    the little me, with two braids and a ribbon tied in my hair, pot belly and
    big brown eyes. I spoke to little Kubi and I told her that everything was
    going to be ok. Doing this made me feel relaxed and comforted. In
    some strange way it worked. You try it: *What do you need to tell the
    little child in you?*

2   Normalize your feelings. According to psychologist Marsha Linehan,
    there are six Levels of Validation, of which number five is Normalizing.
    When we feel a certain way, we need to think about the situation and
    ask ourselves how we would feel if we heard it had happened to
    someone else. Would we be surprised by how they felt? If the answer is
    no, it means the feeling is normal. For example, if someone at work has
    said something to upset you or make you feel worthless, it's important
    to know that it's ok to have feelings of sadness and rejection. After all, if
    you heard this had happened to someone else, the chances are you
    would sympathize with them and their feelings. When it happens to us,
    we need to see that how we feel is to be expected. We should forgive
    ourselves, knowing that it's perfectly normal to feel that way.

3   Don't simply increase your self-esteem, increase your self-compassion. I
    read an interesting article by Professor Rob Henderson who said that
    self-esteem means we rely on external validation and the desire to

constantly prove our competence. For example, when we do well at work and our boss is happy that we delivered the project on time, our self-esteem goes up. When someone says we look good, our self-esteem goes up. But self-compassion does not depend on the image we have of ourselves or the approval of others. Rather, it enables us to embrace all of our experiences from a place of non-judgement. According to Professor Henderson, when we have self-compassion we let go of the idea that every experience is a reflection of who we are as a person. So if the project at work goes well, it doesn't make you great; you were great to begin with! Equally, if the project bombs and no-one is buying into it, it's the project that isn't great and has zero reflection on your greatness.

> 'You have been criticising yourself for years, and it hasn't worked. Try approving of yourself and see what happens.' – Louise L. Hay

During the writing of this book, I found out what I was truly made of. To give you the best of me and create this book from a place of authenticity, I had to do the homework I was setting for you. I had to go on a journey of self re-discovery: Who is Kubi at age 40 and what does she choose to do with her 20-plus years of brand marketing experience? What exactly is my 'I AM'? I realized that if I wanted you to tell yourself the truth, I had to do the same. Just as I asked myself that question, life showed it to me in a big way, and my 'I AM' jumped out at me, but it came through in the form of pain.

Less than two months into writing this book, I found myself at a Harley Street clinic in London; a number of tests and £500 later, it was confirmed that I could no longer have children. My periods had stopped when I was 36 years old and now, at 40, there was literally nothing there. According to the doctor, the only way I could ever have children again would be if I used someone else's eggs. Two weeks after this bombshell, I discovered that my husband had been talking to other women. Not one woman, but multiple women. Only a few months away from celebrating our two-year wedding anniversary, we were facing the heartbreak of divorce.

Everything about me as a woman, I questioned. I felt like I'd been kicked in the stomach. My whole world had been crushed. My self-questioning started with: 'Am I good enough?' 'Worthy enough?', 'Pretty enough?', 'Womanly enough?'. Yet somehow, some way, I still had to deliver this book. Life is a bitch like that: it will throw everything at you – all at once – to test you. To give you a challenge, to see what you are made of. Your true 'I AM' shows up during life's darkest moments. It's in the pain that you rediscover You.

The night I realized my marriage was over, I cried and cried, all night. I was hurt, angry and disgusted. I felt betrayed and used. I felt ugly. My husband's head had been turned by other women. Other women who were beautiful. I mean, Instagram ready. Ten years younger than me, pre-children bodies that were banging; small waists and the largest bums that seem to be the desired body nowadays. I had a post-child body and my bum was never that big to begin with! So I cried tears of comparison and I felt old. All night I cried, and without any sleep, the very next day I woke up, put on my make-up (with extra under eye concealer) and made my way to a speaking engagement. I had to deliver a speech for the entire team of my publishing house, and to this day I am not sure how I got through it. I am not sure how I stood on that stage and performed, or stuck around afterwards and answered people's questions, smiling whilst my heart was aching. Weeks later when the video came out, I watched my speech in amazement. I could see that my eyes were still puffy from the lack of sleep and they were deep red from the river of tears the night before. I smiled to myself – wow Kubi, you did it. In that moment, with clarity, I saw my 'I AM'. I am that woman who can get up and deliver despite whatever else is going on in her life. Since the age of four, I have learnt through dancing on stage that, no matter what, the show must always go on. I live by that motto. My 'I AM' is that I will keep going and deliver, no matter what life throws at me. Nothing and no-one will stop this.

Facing divorce, there were many times I felt rage. Real rage! The kind where your blood is boiling, and you can feel every vein popping. One night, I was so mad I got out of my bed, went downstairs and ran up and down my garden. I am not sure how long I was out there, but I ran in my PJs up and down, in the dark, in the middle of the night. It must have been about 3 a.m. but I didn't care. I ran and ran, back and forth. All I knew was that if didn't run I might do something I would regret, so I just kept on running. The only light in the garden was the moon and the small garden lights that lit the pathway, so I used those to keep me going. Then, when I couldn't run any more, I fell to the ground and sobbed. Curled up in a ball on the floor I sobbed, tears flowing uncontrollably from my eyes, snot dripping from my nose. I sobbed until I was so exhausted, I had to go back to bed. In that moment, I discovered that my 'I AM' is smart. Smart enough to not allow my emotions to get too carried away. Smart enough to not wake my husband up, with our daughter in the house, and start a raging argument. I learnt that at the core of me, I am very, very smart. That I can take control of my emotions and I can deflect until I am back to 'me' again. 'I AM' not a victim of my circumstances.

As the weeks followed and it was time to start the negotiations with my soon to be ex-husband – of who would get what – I forced myself to approach the situation from a place of love. Yes honey, somehow, and in some way, I turned to love. Even though I felt completely unloved, I wanted to be loving. I didn't try to get everything from him. I didn't want to call the lawyers and milk him dry. Instead I wanted to be fair and keep the negotiations civil. I wanted this for me, for our daughter and, yes, for him too. I realized that hurt people hurt people. So I became empathetic and I took myself out of my own shoes and pain and tried to stand in his. Through that process I learnt that I am kind. I am a really kind person. I have a unique ability to see situations from both my own and the other person's point of view. It's the very reason why I am so good at deal negotiations in business. It's the reason why I can persuade sponsors to give me money and partners to say yes to my brand. My 'I AM' is so strong, that even in my deepest darkest pain, I can still see your pain. Compassion and empathy are powers that all women hold. I chose to use this power.

Once the reality of the situation started to sink in though, the sadness kicked in. Deep, deep sadness that I had never experienced before. How do I tell my daughter that mummy was not capable of giving her the little brother she longed for? How do I tell her that daddy will be living somewhere else? How do I face the Tribe, having spent the last two years bragging about how amazing my marriage is, standing on stages around the world saying 'look at what we have built together' – how do I face the crowds again? How do I convince myself that, actually, I didn't do anything wrong? That the marriage failure wasn't because I was a working woman, not home every night to cook at 5 p.m. Or was it? My sadness stayed with me like a dirty cloud that wouldn't go away and the questions, with no answers, consumed me. I didn't want to leave my house, I didn't want to get out of bed, I didn't want to talk to anyone. I didn't want to work. I just felt . . . sad.

In those moments, I didn't appear on social media, I put my phone on 'do not disturb'. I told my assistant to reschedule meetings and cancel my group coaching sessions until further notice. I had to give myself permission to stop. I had to give myself a moment to just do nothing. I often sat in silence staring out the window just listening to my own thoughts. As I sat there, I tried to convince little Kubi that it would be ok. I prayed to the God that lives in me and asked for healing. I remembered my granny and, through tears, I asked her, 'Grandma, what do I do next?' I told myself that no matter what, I would come out of this situation better, not bitter. So I forced myself to go to the gym. Hitting the boxing bags again and again, I released my anger. I went to fitness classes and pulled my baseball cap over my eyes and worked out at the back of the class with tears and sweat streaming down my face. Then, I'd come back home, make myself a coffee, and go right back to sitting in silence.

Eventually, I reached out to people and the love they showed me was overwhelming; my publishers gave me an extension, my agent sent me adorable 'checking on you' WhatsApp messages, my assistant handled absolutely everything, my girlfriends and family members called me every single day, my brothers advised me, and my parents helped me pick up the pieces of my broken heart. During the entire period I was reminded that whilst it might take a village to bring up a child, it also takes a village to support an adult. All of us need our own village. No woman is so super and so powerful that she can do it all on her own. My 'I AM' is that I am part of a Tribe. When you see me, you see an army of people that came before me, and an army of those who stand right next to me. I might be on my own, but I'm never really alone.

It's ironic that as my personal life was going through challenges, my professional life was taking on a new adventure. Despite how I felt personally, I couldn't stay away from the world forever; I had contractual obligations and bookings with deposits that had already been paid. I had international contracts and consultancy work to do. So, regardless, I had to keep going, I had to keep moving forward. In the process I got to see my 'I AM' play itself out and it reminded me that you can't build a personal brand until you have taken the time to discover, or rediscover, the person. You simply can't market what is not there! Of course you can try to manufacture it, but as I said right at the beginning of this book, you and I, we are not a Nike trainer, we are not a Coke bottle, we are humans with feelings and emotions. Since branding is an *emotional connection with your target audience*, you have to start by connecting with your own audience of one, before you can even think of connecting with an audience of one million. You have to face your truth, handle it and build your brand from a place of true authenticity. Once you have that, then you have the inner confidence to take your personal brand to new heights. Those who fail to do this find themselves losing in the end. But when you honour your truth, you discover the true power of your 'I AM'. You uncover your conviction, through the quiet dynamism that resides in you. Whilst I don't want everyone's 'I AM' to be revealed through pain, I have a feeling that, unfortunately, that's sometimes how life presents it to us. Like going to the gym, our muscles can't grow until they are put under strain. Our personal brand can't be built until we have first built the person. In my saddest moments, I discovered real strength. My 'I AM' jumped out at me with force and clarity.

I AM ...

- a child of God

- powerful

- smart

- intelligent

- talented

- funny

- nurturing

- dynamic

- caring

- giving

- loving

- kind

- prosperous

- well-travelled

- ambitious

- secure

- unapologetic

- a legacy

- oh and yes ... still fucking sexy!

Now over to you. What is your 'I AM'?

You have one chance in life, to fully be you. Stop denying who you really are. Bring all of you to the table. Acknowledge your weaknesses, but then master your strengths. Rediscover your brilliance, and share it with the world. Never hide from your uniqueness. Never be afraid of your gifts. Your talent and skills have been given to you, but they are not for you. The world is waiting for you to show up!

BossSquad, take charge of your personal brand, and create it with a force of intention, pride and purpose. It is time for you to build your brand, own your phenomenal self . . . and do it . . . without apology.

## LET'S DO THE WORK

Complete the sentence for yourself:

I AM _____.